DEVELOPING
Successful
Infill Housing

Diane R. Suchman

 ULI

**Urban Land
Institute**

About ULI–
the Urban Land Institute

ULI–the Urban Land Institute is a nonprofit education and research institute that is supported by its members. Its mission is to provide responsible leadership in the use of land in order to enhance the total environment.

ULI sponsors education programs and forums to encourage an open international exchange of ideas and sharing of experiences; initiates research that anticipates emerging land use trends and issues and proposes creative solutions based on that research; provides advisory services; and publishes a wide variety of materials to disseminate information on land use and development. Established in 1936, the Institute today has more than 16,500 members and associates from some 60 countries representing the entire spectrum of the land use and development disciplines.

Richard M. Rosan
President

Recommended bibliographic listing:
Suchman, Diane R. *Developing Successful Infill Housing.*
Washington, D.C.: ULI–the Urban Land Institute, 2002.

ULI Catalog Number: D105
International Standard Book Number: 0-87420-884-X
Library of Congress Control Number: 2002102990

Copyright 2002 by ULI–the Urban Land Institute
1025 Thomas Jefferson Street, N.W.
Suite 500 West
Washington, D.C. 20007-5201

Printed in the United States of America. All rights reserved. No part of this book may be reproduced in any form or by any means, electronic or mechanical, including photocopying and recording, or by any information storage and retrieval system, without written permission of the publisher.

Cover: South Bluffs, Memphis;
Troy Glascow @2002 TroyGlascow.com

ULI Project Staff

Rachelle L. Levitt
Senior Vice President, Policy and Practice
Publisher

Gayle Berens
Vice President, Real Estate Development Practice

Marta Goldsmith
Vice President, Land Use Policy

Richard M. Haughey
Director, Multifamily Development
Project Director

Nancy H. Stewart
Director, Book Program

Sandy Chizinsky
Manuscript Editor

Betsy VanBuskirk
Art Director

Helene Y. Redmond
HYR Graphics
Book Design/Layout

Meg Batdorff
Graphic Artist, Cover

Diann Stanley-Austin
Director, Publishing Operations

The work that provided the basis for this publication was supported by funding under a grant with the U.S. Department of Housing and Urban Development. The substance and findings of the work are dedicated to the public. The author and publisher are solely responsible for the accuracy of the statements and interpretations contained in this publication. Such interpretations do not necessarily reflect the views of the Government.

Acknowledgments

Writing a book is never a wholly individual effort, and this book is the product of many minds. The outstanding advisory committee members —Art Lomenick, David Mayhood, Anne Vernez Moudon, Ron Terwilliger, and Smedes York— gave generously of their time, guidance, and insights. Rick Haughey was an extremely helpful and able project manager. I am also indebted to ULI staff members Marta Goldsmith, Joan Campbell, Rick Davis, Jo Allen Gause, and Adrienne Schmitz for their substantive and personal assistance. Some of the case studies in the book were based on project reports that were originally written by current and former ULI staff members Sam Begner, Leslie Holst, Oliver Jerschow, David Mulvihill, and David Takesuye, and I appreciate their contributions.

I am grateful to the many practitioners who I interviewed for this book, most of whom are listed in Appendix B, and to the numerous authors whose work on this subject informed my research. In particular, the developers whose projects are featured as case studies, as well as their staff members, were generous in sharing their time, information, and insights. Among those who took the time to talk with me and provided useful information, but who were not directly quoted, I would like to recognize Truman Hartshorn, Maria Johnson, David Ley, Penny McNulty, Cy Paumier, Michael Pitchford, Mary Sorge, and Barbara Wells.

I would also like to thank the U.S. Department of Housing and Urban Development (HUD) for its role in sponsoring this research, and Edwin Stromberg, of HUD's Office of Policy Development and Research, for overseeing this work.

ULI's crackerjack publications team, including Nancy Stewart, Sandy Chizinsky, Betsy Van Buskirk, Meg Batdorff, Helene Redmond, and Diann Stanley-Austin, did its usual fine job of taking a raw manuscript and transforming it into an attractive and readable book.

And, finally, I would like to thank my husband, Peter Suchman, for his encouragement and support, and for his critical first reading of the entire book.

Diane Suchman

Advisory Committee

Arthur E. Lomenick
President
Workplace Urban Solutions
Dallas, Texas

David R. Mayhood
President
The Mayhood Company
McLean, Virginia

Anne Vernez Moudon
Professor of Architecture, Landscape
Architecture, and Urban Design
College of Architecture and Urban Planning
University of Washington
Seattle, Washington

J. Ronald Terwilliger
National Managing Partner
Trammell Crow Residential
Atlanta, Georgia

Smedes York
President
York Properties, Inc.
Raleigh, North Carolina

ULI Staff Reviewers

Hon. William H. Hudnut III
Senior Resident Fellow
ULI/Joseph C. Canizaro Chair for Public Policy

John McIlwain
Senior Resident Fellow
ULI/J. Ronald Terwilliger Chair for Housing

Maureen McAvey
Senior Resident Fellow
Urban Development

Marta Goldsmith
Vice President
Land Use Policy

Gayle Berens
Vice President
Real Estate Development Practice

Richard M. Haughey
Director
Multifamily Development

Adrienne Schmitz
Director
Residential Community Development

U.S. Department of Housing and Urban Development Reviewer

Edwin A. Stromberg
Program Manager
Office of Policy Development and Research

Contents

Foreword

For many years following World War II, residential development trends were dominated by "up and out"—that is to say, when incomes went up, families moved out of central cities and inner-ring suburbs: for those families that could afford it, the American dream meant moving to a larger house in the suburbs, where they could have more land, a two-car garage, and neighbors who looked the way they did.

Why Americans followed this path has many underlying explanations, including the increase in family size and household income that followed World War II; new highway construction, which connected outlying housing with job locations; and, during the 1960s and 1970s, a widespread perception of central cities as frightening places riddled with crime, drugs, and decay. Traditional local land use policies, especially zoning ordinances, also contributed significantly to the growth of low-density, single-use suburban development.

In recent years, a strong economy and increasing public investments in downtowns have made many urban areas more attractive places to live, work, and play—and public perceptions have changed as a result. Demographic changes, especially the trend toward smaller household size, are working in favor of urban living as well. At the same time, some people are beginning to find suburban life less attractive, particularly as traffic congestion and commuting times have increased. As a result of these and other changes, the popularity—and the price—of living in the city have increased significantly. It is too early to predict the effect of the recent economic slowdown or the September 11 attacks on demand for urban infill housing, but at the time of this writing, demand remains relatively strong, especially at affordable price points.

Renewed public and developer interest in urban infill housing has corresponded with ULI's interest in promoting "smart growth." Over the past five years, state and local governments, civic groups, and national organizations have focused on finding ways to accommodate metropolitan growth in "smart" ways that mitigate the negative effects of sprawl— low-density, unplanned development that isolates uses from one another, fails to protect open space, increases congestion and pollution, and places a strain on public infrastructure such as schools, sewers, and parks. Encouraging infill development in urban areas—particularly the redevelopment of blighted neighborhoods and brownfields (contaminated commercial and industrial sites)—is a key principle of smart growth.

In the early years, ULI's smart growth work focused on defining a vision and principles for smart growth and on building consensus among diverse national and local stakeholders. More recently, ULI's work has shifted toward implementation at the state and local levels: defining the barriers to smart growth, showcasing models of how such barriers have been successfully overcome, and working locally to help communities adopt and adapt those models.

Over the past two years, with funding from the U.S. Department of Housing and Urban Development, ULI has been exploring the barriers to infill residential development, devising strategies to overcome those barriers, and identifying examples in which those strategies were successfully applied. ULI has held forums in six cities around the country and published a booklet, *Urban Infill Housing: Myth and Fact,* that highlights the barriers and solutions. ULI is now working with three cities—Atlanta, Chicago, and Washington, D.C.—to help them adapt the best practices of other communities.

Developing Successful Infill Housing fills an important niche in ULI's smart growth work. It takes a detailed look at how some of the smart growth principles—especially those that recommend increasing development densities in existing urban areas, making optimum use of existing infrastructure, and redeveloping underused urban land—have been put into practice. In doing so, the book offers private developers, designers, and public officials some very important tools for accomplishing smart growth in their own communities.

Marta Goldsmith
Vice President, Land Use Policy, ULI

Developing Successful Infill Housing

1
Introduction

The dynamics of urban America are changing. Across the country, cities only recently written off as dying are now springing back to life. Riding the wave of high-tech economic expansion during the past decade, they have experienced rising incomes, vigorous growth in jobs and wages, and diminishing rates of poverty and crime.[1] As a result of visionary public and private investments, many of these resurgent cities boast new and creative retail and entertainment facilities; sports and convention facilities; cultural institutions and activities; and parks and public gathering spaces.

Rankled by the isolation, traffic congestion, and homogeneity of their living environments, many suburbanites, especially those without children, have found themselves eager to relocate to more lively and convenient urban settings. And, as cities have become more interesting, more exciting, and safer places to live, city living has become an appealing alternative. In recent years, the proportion of singles and childless couples in the population (the primary market for intown housing, because these groups are not troubled by the often-inferior city public schools) has increased dramatically. At the same time, the supply of desirable urban housing choices has expanded as public

The first phase of Post Roosevelt Square, located in downtown Phoenix's Roosevelt Historic District, has 403 apartments and street-level retail space. The project offers more than 50 floor plans, including lofts, one- and two-bedroom apartments, and townhouses.
©2000, Steve Hinds

3

Houston's down-
town population rose
69 percent in the
1990s. Even faster
growth is projected
for the period 2000
to 2010.

Houston Downtown Management District

officials have sought ways to encourage "smart growth," an approach to planning and development that emphasizes more compact development, the wise use of existing infrastructure and transportation systems, the redevelopment of brownfields and obsolete buildings, and the creation of infill housing.[2] In many cities, these and other forces have converged to create a growing demand for market-rate urban infill housing that developers are seeking to meet. As Doug Porter, president of the Growth Management Institute, in Chevy Chase, Maryland, observes, "The market is moving where public policy has been trying to go for some time."

Even in many neighborhoods once rife with abandonment and disinvestment, middle-class residents are reappearing. In a survey of conventional mortgage loans made to homebuyers who bought homes in "core" gentrifying neighborhoods of Boston, Detroit, Chicago, Milwaukee, Minneapolis–St. Paul, Philadelphia, Seattle, and Washington, D.C., "the growth rates confirm a dramatic rebound in parts of the inner city."[3] Though most people still prefer to live in the suburbs, the growing urban housing market represents a significant trend— "a harbinger of a return to the city."[4]

From a city's point of view, urban infill housing developments generate significant public benefits. People are the lifeblood of cities: it is concentrated human activity that gives cities their vitality, stimulates markets for goods and services, and creates the excitement and the diversity of opportunity for which cities are so valued. So perhaps the most important benefit is the addition of more city residents—who, according to one source, must number at least

20,000 within a mile of the city center to create a "24-hour city."[5] Infill also returns underused or derelict land and buildings to productive use. Left to deteriorate, idle properties can eventually weaken neighborhoods, cities, and entire metropolitan regions. Urban infill helps improve the city's image and living environment, provides homeownership opportunities within the city, helps attract and retain middle- and upper-middle-income residents, and creates new housing opportunities for downtown workers. In addition, such development can help strengthen and preserve the historic character of the city and its urban neighborhoods. Reuse of publicly owned land can help local governments privatize their inventories of publicly owned properties and put these lands and buildings back on the tax rolls. And new, intown housing development can fuel other kinds of investment in urban communities. Done wisely, infill development can "take advantage of existing infrastructure; provide higher densities in locations where mass transportation is already in place; and integrate new housing into the fabric of the community."[6]

Like all market-rate housing, urban infill development succeeds only when it can attract households who can choose where they want to live. Though market-rate urban developments are not directly subsidized for occupancy by households that meet specific income restrictions, cities often provide incentives to encourage infill projects—through, for example, writedown of land costs, public provision of infrastructure, or gap financing. Pioneering urban infill developers have tested the market and educated public agencies on the nature and benefits of these developments—and on the kinds of assistance that are needed to enable both public and private entities to succeed in meeting shared goals.

Fred Kober, president of the Christopher Companies, in McLean, Virginia, speaking in June 1998 at the ULI Infill Symposium in Atlanta, observed that the emerging group of housing consumers who are drawn to the character and cultural offerings of urban settings have created opportunities for locally oriented, small and medium-sized developers

—opportunities that do not require them to compete with national players. In addition, urban infill housing developments are socially valuable, create exciting challenges for land planners and architects, and are usually supported by local governments.

As illustrated by the project examples in this book, urban infill housing developments can take place in widely varying kinds of locations, are undertaken by diverse kinds of developers, and result in a huge array of distinctive—typically one-of-a-kind—developments. The projects can take many forms, depending on the dynamics of the market, the amount and configuration of the land (or structures) available, and the character and history of the immediate area. The range of product types is vast and diverse, including townhouses or rowhouses, "plexes," lofts, flats, and single-family homes on small lots; many projects offer a mix of products within a single development. Urban infill projects can be strictly residential, mixeduse, or multiuse developments. They can be targeted to a range of consumers, from moderate-

income to affluent, and can be produced for sale, rental, or condominium or cooperative ownership. Projects can include stick-built homes, manufactured or modular units, high-rise structures, and rehabilitated or adapted historic buildings or older properties. Often, infill housing developments combine various product, structure, and tenure types to yield a creative new urban product.

Though development of this product niche is fundamentally similar to the development of other types of housing, infill poses additional challenges. For example, infill housing developers must be prepared to encounter environmental issues; inadequacies in infrastructure; difficulties with land acquisition and assembly; outdated or more stringent regulatory requirements; neighborhood opposition; and, often, the need to piece together a financing strategy from public and private sources. Such problems can be especially vexing in the case of small projects that cannot benefit from economies of scale and receive little attention or assistance from the public sector.

Bridgecourt, in Emeryville, California, provides live/work opportunities in a mixed-use setting. The four-building complex echoes the industrial scale and architecture of adjacent buildings.

McLarand, Vasquez & Partners

Because infill projects are developed within established surroundings, the existing context affects the project concept and design, and the type, mode, and cost of construction; and current residents will often be well-organized and have strong opinions regarding what will be built. As a result, these kinds of projects can be more risky, costly, time-consuming, and difficult for developers to plan, finance, and entitle. Because every urban infill project is unique, the specific challenges confronting the developer will differ. (Appendix A lists the most typical categories of challenge confronted by infill developers.)

A project's location will also determine, in part, the development challenges it presents. For example, a city's age, history, physical configuration, political situation, regulatory framework, and economic climate will all affect the market potential and implementation requirements for infill housing development. Within any given city, project planning and development will also be affected by the immediate setting—for example, whether the project is to be developed in a pioneering housing location, in the downtown business district, or in an established neighborhood.

This book explores the rich opportunities offered by the development of urban infill housing, discusses some of the challenges involved, and highlights possible strategies for overcoming them. It is intended to assist developers, local governments, and others who would like to create or facilitate market-rate urban infill housing developments in their communities, or who are generally interested in infill housing development and the regeneration of America's cities. Building on ULI's earlier publications on infill housing development, the book will focus on how to address the issues that are specific to urban infill housing development and create successful projects.

For the purposes of this book, *urban infill housing* is defined as housing that is totally or primarily market rate; located in a developed "urban" environment within a city; and built on vacant or underused land or through the reuse of existing structures. Typically, creating infill housing means introducing more compact development patterns or increasing local development density—what Professor Anne Vernez Moudon, of the University of Washington in Seattle, describes as the "intensification" of land uses.

This book does not purport to be "the definitive work" on urban infill development; such an undertaking would need to be much more extensive and detailed, given the multitude of product types; changing economic environments; the diversity of regulatory frameworks, development entities, and metropolitan land and housing markets; and other variables. Instead, the book zeroes in on the key issues that most commonly affect market-rate urban infill housing developments. The information presented is intended to highlight the ways that urban infill housing differs from other types of

At 838 Fifth Avenue, in New York City, the Athena Group converted a landmark office building and an adjacent, mixed-use brownstone into residential condominiums.

development rather than to serve as a primer on infill housing development *per se.*

Focusing on challenges, opportunities, risks, and returns, chapter 2 describes some of the most significant ways in which the business of developing infill housing differs from that of other types of real estate development. Chapter 3 addresses the sources and nature of market demand. Chapter 4 explores how developers can find, select, and evaluate potential sites. Chapter 5 discusses some of the general considerations and principles that guide project and unit design. Chapter 6 covers the important ways in which cities can facilitate urban infill developments—through regulatory frameworks, tax policy, financial assistance, and other means. Chapter 7 describes likely community concerns and discusses how to address them. To illustrate the recommended strategies, the final chapter features 12 case studies that highlight a wide range of product types in different kinds of markets and locations throughout the country. While the case studies do not offer a comprehensive array of project types and market settings, these successful projects provide a sample of the rich and varied opportunities

for developers who are interested in creating urban infill housing developments.

The information in this book is based on the professional knowledge and experience of the author, supplemented by recently published information and interviews with urban infill developers and other industry participants.[7] Information in the case studies was derived from site visits, interviews with project developers, and printed materials provided by the developers. Though the author believes that the material in this book is timely and correct, no attempt was made to verify independently the accuracy of the information.

Traffic congestion and lengthening commutes have helped spur market interest in urban infill housing.

Notes

1. U.S. Department of Housing and Urban Development, *The State of the Cities 2000: Megaforces Shaping the Future of the Nation's Cities* (Washington, D.C.: HUD, 2000).

2. Brownfields are defined here as former industrial or commercial properties on which development at its highest and best use has been prevented because of actual or perceived contamination. See Robert A. Simons, *Turning Brownfields into Greenbacks* (Washington, D.C.: ULI, 1998), 3.

3. Elvin K. Wyly and Daniel J. Hammel, "Cities and the Reinvestment Wave: Underserved Markets and the Gentrification of Housing Policy," *Housing Facts & Findings* 2, no. 1 (spring 2000): 11.

4. Alex Krieger, "An Urban Revival for a Suburban Culture," in *ULI on the Future: Cities in the 21st Century* (Washington, D.C.: ULI, 2000), 42.

5. David C. Petersen, "Smart Growth for Central Cities," in *ULI on the Future: Smart Growth* (Washington, D.C.: ULI, 1998), 56.

6. Robert Mitchell, president of the National Association of Home Builders, quoted in *The Next Frontier: Building Homes in America's Cities 2000* (Washington, D.C.: National Association of Home Builders, 2000), 2.

7. Appendix B contains a list of people who were interviewed and whose presentations at various ULI forums were quoted in this book.

2

The Business of Infill Development

Despite the numerous challenges associated with developing residential urban infill projects, an increasing number of developers have become interested in this product niche. Urban infill differs from other types of housing development in important ways that create both advantages and disadvantages. This chapter explores the attractions of urban infill residential development from the private sector developer's point of view, notes some of the opportunities that may be available, and describes the types of skills and organizations that are most likely to be needed for this segment of the development business. The chapter also outlines some of the ways in which developers can mitigate the risks associated with urban infill housing development.

The Lure of Urban Infill Housing Development

According to Margaret Sowell, president of Real Estate Strategies, Inc., in Wayne, Pennsylvania, developers are building urban infill housing because (1) there is money available and money to be made by developers; (2) the returns are good, often because government agencies are cooperative; (3) infill developments are often popular, highly visible projects that replace unwanted

Alban Towers, a historic building in Washington, D.C., has been renovated to create 226 luxury apartments.

Old mill buildings along the river in downtown Minneapolis are being renovated to create loft-style housing.

—of significant importance in the economic slowdown of the early 2000s—less sensitive to fluctuations in the economy and in the real estate market.

One of the distinguishing characteristics of infill housing projects is that each is one of a kind. No two locations are quite alike. Sites differ in size, configuration, price, history, context, condition, and entitlement issues. The overall project concept and the design of individual units vary widely from project to project. While the "custom-built" nature of urban infill housing poses challenges for developers, it also gives such developments certain advantages over their suburban competition.

Compared with urban infill housing projects, suburban "production housing" developments are much more alike. Thus, suburban housing consumers select from a number of similar kinds of housing products that are differentiated largely by location and cost. As a result, notes Settle Dockery, vice president of York Properties, Inc., in Raleigh, North Carolina, "The suburban market is less forgiving. You have less flexibility *re* what you can and can't get away with. With infill, you have more room to maneuver. If you find a site and know there is demand, you will succeed if you don't screw it up and you don't overreach in terms of price. You don't have to be absolutely perfect."

Because the people who buy or rent homes in urban infill settings are looking for a particular lifestyle, the location and the character of the development are more important than specific features and finishes. People who like the lifestyle an infill development offers can obtain it only in *that* project, in *that* location. Because suburban subdivisions tend to offer similar kinds of products, suburban housing developers generally experience the downturn more quickly when the market gets tight. In contrast, urban infill developers report that demand for their projects remains strong in weak economic times. And, because urban infill rental units offer a lifestyle choice for which there may be few similar alternatives, developers of rental properties report that their urban infill developments experience less tenant turnover than their suburban counterparts.

land uses with something new and better—which is good for developers' portfolios and egos; and (4) there are market opportunities for infill housing development.

The most obvious reason for developers' interest is market demand, which is explored in depth in the next chapter. Though market depth for infill housing is highly local and may be difficult to gauge, some level of demand for a well-located urban product exists in most markets, fueled primarily by young singles and couples who prefer the excitement of urban life. In the words of Arn Bortz, a partner at Towne Properties, in Cincinnati, "The level of demand is not an issue." In fact, experience shows that the strength of demand is often underestimated, as the typically rapid absorption rates presented in the case studies demonstrate.

Compared with demand for suburban housing, the market for infill housing in urban locations is generally regarded as more lifestyle-driven than product-driven, subject to less competition from other developments, and

Because infill developments are, by their nature, idiosyncratic, developers generally do not compete for infill sites as they do for raw land. Instead, developers with entrepreneurial vision discover vacant sites in emerging residential areas or create new opportunities where marginal uses occupy prime locations.

Not only are urban infill developments themselves unique, but no two settings are exactly alike. The strategies developers pursue in developing urban infill housing will differ depending on the physical, economic, and demographic characteristics and the histories, policies, institutional frameworks, laws, and programs of the cities, metropolitan areas, and states in which they work. For example, in metropolitan areas where suburban jurisdictions are seeking to slow or limit growth, housing developers may find urban infill development an especially attractive market opportunity.

Without exception, every developer interviewed for this book mentioned another reason for choosing urban infill housing development: it's fun. People who choose this market niche do so in part because they find it interesting and intellectually challenging, and because it affords opportunities for creativity. And, for many developers, helping to recreate a vibrant city is part of the allure: transforming a blighted site or an abandoned historic property into a lively new community creates value beyond individual financial return. As Bortz explains, "We do infill because we love our city."

Managing Market Risk

Though they offer certain advantages, urban infill projects also typically cost more and are riskier to develop than similar suburban projects. Appendix A outlines the daunting array of challenges that infill housing developers might confront. Obviously, not all of these challenges will apply to every project, and some are more likely to apply than others. But in general, as Michael Loia, president and chief executive officer of Loia Budde & Associates, of Atlanta, Georgia, points out, the very fact that infill developments are unique makes them more risky. "You have a multitude of decisions to make that have no history behind them. There is nothing to compare them to." Because of the various risks involved, Doug Crocker, president and chief executive officer of Equity Residential Properties Trust, in Chicago, cautions that

Post Paseo Colorado is the residential portion of Paseo Colorado, a mixed-use joint venture of TrizecHahn Corporation and Post Properties in downtown Pasadena, California. The development will include more than 560,0000 square feet of retail space and approximately 400 apartments.

infill developers should "be sure to have an exit strategy."

Despite the fact that some level of demand for urban infill exists in most markets, market risk remains an issue. In pioneering developments (those undertaken in locations where the market has not been tested or that offer an innovative housing product), assessing the nature and level of demand can be difficult. Determining the depth of demand for large projects can also be especially problematic. No real comparables exist; there is no history of recent sales experience in the area (which also makes it difficult to obtain accurate appraisals). As a result, notes Joe Barry, president of Applied Development Company, in Hoboken, New Jersey, "These projects are not readily illuminated by market research."

One way to limit developer—and lender—exposure in untested markets, especially for large projects, is by phasing development. Building the project in small bites enables the developer to gauge the market before determining when and how to proceed and to make market-responsive design and price adjustments as subsequent phases are developed. This approach not only reduces risk for the developer's financial partners but may also allow land to be purchased in stages, thereby lowering upfront costs. And, in cases where several phases of development are planned, phasing enables the developer to reap returns in later phases for value created during the high-risk first phases. Because successful infill developments can trigger increases in land costs, developers who stage the purchase and development of infill land can lock in land prices that will make their developments especially cost-competitive as the market matures.

Finally, staging development can help the developer make a project more attractive from the city's point of view. Phasing makes possible projects that are large enough to create a "critical mass" of new development, which can help transform a transitional neighborhood. Such large-scale projects signal to investors, current residents, and other developers the project developer's—and the city's—commitment to rebuilding the area. In addition, phasing can

be a means of accommodating the existing community's tolerance for change.

However, as David Mayhood, president of the Mayhood Company, in McLean, Virginia, points out, phasing may not always be possible. "In the case of small projects, developers don't have the luxury of phasing takedowns of land." In other cases, especially with high-density or mixed-use developments, phasing can be precluded by the project design.

Particularly in weak or untested markets, creating mixed-use developments, mixed-product developments, or mixed-income developments can help balance market risk by targeting more than one market segment. However, as discussed later in this chapter, these approaches complicate project financing; and, because few developers know how to do mixed-use projects well, particularly on infill sites, they often create partnerships for this purpose, which further increases the project's complexity and adds other kinds of risk.

Combining multiple housing types in the same development broadens the range of potential consumers. For example, in developing Marston Point Place, Carter Reese & Associates, of San Diego, California, offered four product types within a single city block, both to expand the range of potential buyers and to make it possible to build the project in phases, thereby lessening market risk. When Eakin/Youngentob Associates, Inc. (EYA), of Arlington, Virginia, developed the 287-unit Old Town Village project in Alexandria, Virginia, it included homes of different sizes and prices. EYA built the project's townhouses and courtyard homes, but, to minimize risk, sold the condominium and duplex portion of the property to another developer after all the entitlements were in place. Nevertheless, Mayhood cautions developers to beware of a scattershot approach. "You should be able to identify a dominant market segment of sufficient depth to which you can design and market your project."

Some developers manage market risk by entering an untested market with a rental product first. As Bortz explains, "In a fragile, immature market, we do rental because it asks the customer for less of a commitment. We develop rental properties to create a sense of place—we 'seed' it with apartments—and then follow with a for-sale product." According to Barry, this is an especially good strategy for developers working in transitional areas. In his experience, a major segment of the market prefers to rent in older, disinvested cities like New Brunswick or Morristown, New Jersey. Once reinvestment is well underway, those consumers may become willing to buy in that location.

In hot markets, such as downtown Chicago, one risk factor that has developed recently comes from condominium speculators: some purchase units without intending to occupy them, then simply flip the contracts when the building is completed; others buy units early with the intention of renting them. Speculation "creates a hard-to-track condominium rental market that can add . . . shadow rental units to the market."[1] Mayhood observes, "Though speculative purchase is a fairly common phenomenon, it is dangerous because it gives developers a false reading of market depth." Moreover, because investors may walk if the economy sours, speculation adds to the developer's risk. "To control this risk, some developers limit the number of units investors can buy; lenders may limit their risk by strengthening their underwriting criteria to include speculation caps and high presale requirements.

Development Considerations

Project development can also be more risky in the case of infill housing development. In addition to being subject to the usual site development issues, urban infill sites are always vacant for a reason. There may be rubble or chemical contamination remaining from previous uses. Existing infrastructure may be insufficient or in need of repair. Utilities may be inadequate. Nearby uses may be troubling. Structures may contain lead or asbestos. Zoning may be inappropriate for the intended use. Building codes may be unreasonably restrictive, especially for projects that involve rehabilitation. Nearby residents may oppose any change in the built environment, adding political risk

for which the local government may have little tolerance.

Because infill housing developments are typically built at higher densities than their suburban counterparts, the type of construction required tends to be more difficult and to require different knowledge and skills. Ron Terwilliger, national managing partner of Trammell Crow Residential, in Atlanta, comments that many development companies, including Trammell Crow, have learned the hard way that because the construction of higher-density projects involves both wood and steel (and, in the case of high rises, concrete as well), construction executives may have trouble making the transition from managing wood-frame residential construction to managing higher-

Resurgent interest in urban living has created a market for the adaptive use of industrial buildings. Apartments in such buildings offer large open spaces and high ceilings.

In downtown Eugene, Oregon, Broadway Market occupies street-level retail space in Broadway Place Apartments.

density housing projects of three or four stories or more.

As a rule, infill construction costs more than suburban residential development, and construction costs increase with density. Terwilliger estimates that construction costs increase by $20 per square foot when steel rather than wood framing is involved. Hank Baker, vice president for marketing for Forest City Stapleton, Inc., notes that in Denver, where his firm is located, construction costs are approximately $75 per square foot for a three-story building, $100 per square foot for a four-story building, and $175 per square foot for a high rise.[2] In addition, city building and fire codes tend to be more stringent than those in suburbia—and developers in some cities need to meet additional standards for withstanding earthquakes, vibration, or both.

In addition, building in urban locations dictates tight construction-staging areas that must be carefully planned in advance. Developers must minimize the intrusion of construction traffic on neighborhood streets, and determine where and how to store and secure building materials.[3] Finally, Bortz notes that because some contractors may be reluctant to deal with the city's typically more restrictive

hiring, wage rate, and record-keeping requirements, or may be daunted by the idea of delivering and securing materials at a downtown site, developers may have a smaller pool of subcontractors from which to choose.

The design and construction of infill developments are also affected by a number of other issues that rarely arise in suburban developments. Often, infill sites are less than ideal for the intended development. For example, it would not be unusual for an urban infill site to be hilly or irregularly shaped, to contain buried foundations from previous developments or existing structures, or to pose other challenges that would be unusual in a suburban development. In addition, some urban infill developments must be designed to conserve views valued by neighbors.

Careful design can often overcome these challenges. Sometimes buffering is required between the project and an adjacent, potentially incompatible use, both to separate the project visually and to protect it from negative externalities. For example, part of the Old Town Square development featured in chapter 8 abuts the site of a Chicago Transit Authority elevated track (the "El"). The developer placed a solid brick wall between the project's condominiums and the El, which effectively blocks noise from the trains and prevents the projects' residents from being disturbed.

Projects involving the reuse of existing structures can be especially exciting but pose a number of additional challenges. To avoid costly surprises during construction, the developer will want to carefully evaluate the building's condition and determine the rehabilitation needs before purchasing the property. Older buildings may contain contaminants such as lead or asbestos, which can be expensive to mitigate or remove. If the property contains rental apartments with current tenants, legal requirements regarding tenants' rights must be met. The rehabilitation of historic properties or the development of projects located within designated historic districts must meet the standards for rehabilitation set by the U.S. secretary of the interior. When rehabilitation or historic preservation projects require custom work, it must meet building codes designed for new construction—and, because of the specialized skills required, the work will interest

A Sampling of Strategies Pursued by ULI's Infill Developers

- Speaking at ULI's fall 2000 meeting, in Chicago, Dick Michaux indicated that his firm looks for markets where barriers to entry are high because of high land costs, low vacancy rates, and difficult entitlement processes, and where less than half of the residents can afford a medium-priced house. His firm focuses on serving the "discretionary renter" and, in areas where the economy is slowing, producing mixed-use developments. "We look for favorable community and metropolitan-area demographics, positive public sector attitudes and incentives, and markets with high barriers to entry."

- Speaking at ULI's 2001 Spring Council Forum, in Minneapolis, Al Neely, group senior vice president, Charles E. Smith Residential Realty, Inc., in Arlington, Virginia, described his firm's development strategy as follows: "The company is a niche player, producing high-end rental products, predominately high rises, in Washington, D.C.; Boston; Chicago; and southeast Florida. It develops large projects, 300 to 400 units or larger, that make possible the inclusion of amenities, including on-site personnel and services. The firm does not use public money, so rents are high. We serve the 'renter by choice'— who is a choosy renter, who has a lot of choices and enough qualifying

income to do what he/she wants, so we have to differentiate ourselves."

- Joe Barry, president of Applied Development Company, in Hoboken, New Jersey, noted that his firm produces $50 to $70 million of market-rate rental and for-sale housing in urban—often environmentally contaminated—areas, sometimes on waterfronts. He observed that childless young professionals, aged 22 to 35, working in the service industries, and empty nesters are core markets for urban housing. In areas employing many young singles and couples who earn $40,000 to $50,000, projects with ambience, services, and a lively street scene command high prices. He has found that office development precedes housing and retail follows it.

- Speaking at ULI's Infill Symposium in Atlanta, in June 1998, Marty Jones, president of Corcoran Jennison Companies, of Dorchester, Massachusetts, described her firm's projects as primarily rental and of two types: (1) community-creation projects (at least 20 acres in size, often public housing transformations) and (2) individual building opportunities on infill sites that have been overlooked because of site conditions, a reluctant owner, or environmental considerations, where the firm can develop between 75 and 100 units. The community-creation projects have

high visibility and a major impact on the community, and attract larger policy debates. The individual buildings have local, rather than policy, issues. To succeed, both need a market grounded in reality, though in the case of the larger projects, there is also an opportunity to create a market.

- Speaking at the same meeting, Pres Kabacoff, president of Historic Restoration, Inc. (HRI), in New Orleans, described HRI as being driven by the mission to renew cities through (1) the adaptive use of historic buildings and (2) the development of new construction in historic neighborhoods. The second approach is made possible by public/private partnerships consisting of the city, the corporate community, the nonprofit community, the cultural and arts community, the chamber of commerce, downtown organizations, and a mayor who understands the dynamic of such partnerships. The firm's projects tend to be neighborhood hotels or apartments with ground-level commercial uses, for which the city must provide incentives. HRI does both market-rate and affordable housing, and often uses historic tax credits and low-income housing tax credits. Its preferred locations are those near important community monuments such as schools, churches, and hospitals. ∎

a smaller pool of qualified contractors (which means less price competition). On the other hand, such projects may be eligible for public incentives and subsidies.

For a developer to acquire and prepare an infill site and obtain the necessary entitlements requires significant upfront investment, and the chances of the project unraveling are greater than for other types of housing development. One infill housing development firm reports that it typically invests $500,000 and one year's time in a project before knowing whether or not it will gain approvals. Knowing how far to go in pursuing a project of this type is problematic. Natalie Bock, development manager for the Alexander Company, in Madison, Wisconsin, cautions, "Some projects we pursued for too long; we should have cut our losses sooner. We almost never cut our losses soon enough, and upfront work is expensive and time-consuming."

One way infill development firms mitigate development risk is by controlling the process: maintaining and coordinating an array of capabilities in house. For example:

- Robert Youngentob, president of EYA, explains, "We built an organization that believes in this mission, and the whole company is focused on infill, for-sale development. We do everything in house. The sites are so complicated, it's difficult to hire out."

- Bob Silverman, chairman and chief executive officer of the Winter Companies, in Atlanta, notes that the biggest pitfall is the construction cost in adaptive use projects, especially if the firm works with people who lack adequate experience. "Architects tend to go wild because they see tremendous potential—and a big spread in architectural magazines," he explains. "We have to hold the reins tightly. Our integrated group of companies gives us a big competitive advantage because we can control the architects and the entire process."

- Hyde Park Builders, Inc., in Tampa, Florida, does all its own purchasing, rezoning, design work, construction management, and sales in house or through affiliated companies.

- Michael Loia credits the success of the Buckhead Village Lofts development, in Atlanta, to the fact that all architecture, development, and construction work was handled entirely by the development entity itself and so could be closely coordinated.

Even when a firm's staff does not encompass a range of disciplines, advises Terwilliger, "You can cut risk in urban infill by establishing an ongoing working relationship with a familiar architect, engineer, building inspector, and so forth, because these people have a strong effect on project outcomes."

Pricing

Pricing infill products can be challenging. Comparables are rarely available, and the market is often stronger than the developer perceives. In a number of the case studies prepared for this book, the projects sold out so quickly that the developers felt they had underpriced the units. Of course, rapid sales yield rapid returns, and erring on the side of conservative pricing lowers risk. In addition, as Smedes York, president of York Properties, Inc., in Raleigh, North Carolina, points out, "It's nice to leave something on the table for the buyers. If they can resell their units and make a profit on the appreciation,

The 163-unit Old Town Square development, in Chicago, offers a mix of product types, including townhouses (shown here), single-family homes, rental apartments, and condominiums.

they will be more likely to purchase again at one of your projects and to refer their friends." And, as he advises, "In pricing, you want to make a profit, but you want to win the war, not the battle." Quoting his father, he adds, "In this business, there's plenty of room for bulls and plenty of room for bears, but no room for hogs."

Partnerships

Typically, developing urban infill housing requires that developers and city government forge a partnership, with some financial support forthcoming from the city. In high-cost areas, land prices may prohibit the development of housing that is affordable to all but the very rich. In lower-cost areas, even with reasonably priced land, low rents and sales prices often create a "feasibility gap" between what it costs to produce an urban infill development and the expected returns. As described in chapter 6, in addition to financial support, cities must typically provide other types of assistance to enable an infill housing development to succeed. Where city leadership is not committed to facilitating urban infill, or where the city lacks the human, financial, legal, or organizational resources to do so, many developers will opt out.

Developers may also form partnerships with large landholders, such as public agencies (the city, a redevelopment authority, a school district) or institutions (churches, universities, hospitals). Forming partnerships can offer the developer greater access to land or to public and private funding mechanisms, and add value to the project by making it possible to incorporate a variety of uses. Such partnerships may make the city more comfortable with the project, especially if the partnership results in a mix of uses that help the jurisdiction better achieve its revitalization goals. For example, the Parks at the Cathedral, in Jacksonville, Florida, the first phase of a pioneering, for-sale townhouse development in downtown Jacksonville, is the result of a partnership between St. John's Cathedral, Bank of America Community Development Corporation (the developer), and the city. The project was made possible

In the Denver Dry Goods Building, the terraces of loft apartments occupy what was once the patio of the Tea Room Restaurant.

Sage Strever, Perry/AHDC

through generous financial subsidies from the city and St. John's Cathedral, which helped underwrite project costs and lower the mortgage costs for consumers.

Financing

Many urban infill developers find that obtaining private sector financing can be challenging. The key financing issues include the comparatively high development costs (especially upfront costs); lenders' lack of familiarity and experience with the products; a dearth of good market research; environmental problems; and the absence of comparables on which to base appraisals. As a rule, lenders are reluctant to invest in unique types of projects or pioneering locations for which developers cannot demonstrate a proven record of acceptable risk. (However, once pioneering developments have demonstrated a market for an innovative infill housing product or for a nontraditional location for housing within the city, lenders generally become more willing to finance similar projects.) As Silverman explains, "Banks still have difficulty understanding the pioneering we are doing, and especially the neighborhoods where we are doing it." Art Lomenick, president of Workplace Urban Solutions and former executive vice president of Post Properties, in Dallas, agrees. "You pay a premium for capital. How much depends on how rough the area is." Furthermore, the idiosyncratic nature of infill projects means that financing must be customized for each project, which runs counter to the lending industry's preference for standardization. In summary, Bock believes that for many lenders, "It's just not worth the brain damage for the size of the loan."

A development firm that has a long history of successful projects in a particular city can often obtain financing from lenders with whom it has established a relationship and who have become comfortable with the developer's judgment. For example, Smedes York, a longtime developer whose family has deep roots in Raleigh, reports "no problem getting financing" for infill housing developments there. Similarly, the Bank of Tampa provided a loan for the Huntington, in St. Petersburg, Florida, based on its knowledge of Hyde Park Builders's track record with other kinds of residential developments. Lenders' comfort levels also increase when developers put their own equity into their projects.

One way to balance financial risks when developing infill housing, suggests Mike Curzan, chief executive officer of UniDev LLC, in Bethesda, Maryland,[4] is by creating a mixed-use project and allocating the costs asymmetrically, so that one use subsidizes another. A note of caution, however: a mixed-use development does not lend itself to the kind of product standardization that banks typically prefer. "The financial instruments and institutions underlying American development isolate components of the built environment to better securitize their risk."[5] Because most lenders tend to specialize in one type of real estate development, they shy away from mixed-use projects, which do not fit their experience with individual prod-

uct types and for which they cannot determine an appropriate risk premium.[6]

Mixed-use projects are also difficult to finance, in part because lenders cannot define the exit strategy. "Our investors need to have parcels that you can sell off individually," Silverman explains. Terwilliger notes that for that reason, "When building mixed use in a vertical platform, you may have to separate the retail and residential units into two separate condominiums."

Retail is often included to enhance the design and marketability of a residential development rather than because of demonstrable retail market demand. And local governments often require infill housing developments to include some first-floor retail space. However, the retail portion of a mixed-use project can be difficult to finance. For one thing, although shops and services can be important project amenities, this space can be difficult to lease—and, as Terwilliger points out, "Few residential developers have expertise in retail development and leasing." As a result, some developers do not even factor lease income from retail space into their pro formas; if it materializes, then it's an added benefit. "If the retail is intended to be a meaningful part of the revenues," Terwilliger adds, "financing becomes significantly more difficult."

Financing mixed-income housing developments is also challenging. As a rule, mixed-income housing cannot be financed successfully through conventional financing models and funding sources. Instead, the financing typically involves a complicated and time-consuming process of piecing together funds from a number of different public and private entities, each of which has its own goals, requirements, and schedules.

Financing rehabilitation projects can also be especially difficult. Many lenders view rehab as more risky because (1) developers are often unable to reliably predict all construction requirements; (2) costly environmental problems may emerge during construction (raising liability issues); (3) finding comparables on which to base appraisals is even more difficult than for new construction; and (4) lenders may lack

experience with the complexities of this type of development.[7] Furthermore, many rehabilitation projects, especially those involving historic preservation, require complex public/private financing.

As a rule, it is easiest to finance luxury infill housing, which is typically built in a city's premium locations. And it is relatively easy to finance low-income housing (targeted to households with incomes below 60 percent of the area median), for which there are federal and state financial incentives. Developing middle-income "workforce" housing, however, is gen-

erally more difficult, and almost always requires public sector financial participation. Financial institutions perceive middle-income infill housing as especially risky because developers can find appropriately priced land or buildings only in "transitional" areas; as a result, opportunities for developing this type of housing without subsidies are limited.[8]

In the view of some lenders, the many infill housing projects that include public money are more complicated and risky—and sometimes too complicated for the size of the loan. Bock explains, "It's harder to find a lender. Most of our developments have 15 to 20 percent 'soft money'—that is, money from tax abatements, tax increment financing, Community Development Block Grant funds, and/or federal transportation money. Getting that money into a transaction is a lot more complicated than financing new development on a greenfield site, where there are fewer risks that things will go wrong. We tend to work with local lenders who have an interest in the community and may be more motivated because of a desire to get Community Reinvestment Act credits or because of local pride."

According to a survey of lenders by the University of Colorado Real Estate Center, some lenders who finance infill housing projects have confidence in projects that offer the following characteristics:[9]

- A desirable location in a safe neighborhood;
- Pent-up market demand;
- Demonstrable leasing potential;
- A project team that includes an experienced developer as a principal participant;
- Location in a city that has a reputation for supporting infill development and that has adopted policies that will assist the proposed project;
- Tax incentives that will benefit the project.

In unproven markets, lenders may require that for-sale projects demonstrate a certain percentage of presales before funds are released. But because presale prices are typically lower (often much lower), high presale requirements can undermine a project's feasibility. Furthermore, because of the perceived risks involved, banks that make loans for urban infill develop-

Developed by Columbus Realty Trust, a real estate investment trust, Columbus Square is a mixed-used, luxury multifamily development in uptown Dallas featuring live/work lofts and living spaces above ground-floor retail.

Located in a former industrial neighborhood occupied by older brick warehouses, Johnson Street Townhomes, in Portland, Oregon, blends in with its surroundings and offers street-level live/work space with a separate entryway for each unit.

ments often require personal and corporate guarantees on the debt.

Bruce Levin, senior vice president of CIG International LLC, in Washington, D.C., whose firm provides debt financing for for-sale urban infill housing developments in Atlanta; Chicago; Houston; New York; Raleigh; Washington, D.C.; and Florida, notes that CIG is more likely to fund single-family or townhouse projects that

- Can "deliver out" (meaning that the homes can be built and sold quickly enough so that CIG can be repaid) within 24 to 36 months;

- Will yield a net profit margin of at least 10 percent before costs (after costs, at least 7 percent);
- Are fully entitled, so there is no entitlement risk involved.

Levin also notes that CIG does not require presales of single-family or townhouse units.

For mid-rise or high-rise condominium products—"anything vertical"—Levin explains that the criteria are somewhat more stringent: CIG looks for a net profit margin of 15 percent before costs and 10 percent after costs and requires that between 35 and 50 percent of the units be presold with binding contracts.

CIG charges an interest rate of 25 to 30 percent on an annual basis, and bases loans on a loan-to-value ratio of between 90 and 93 percent for single-family or townhouse projects and between 85 and 90 percent for condominium projects. Most of the developments CIG funds include a commercial/retail component (typically 10 to 15 percent of the project), but "the project must pay off from the for-sale housing component."

Depending on the project, financing for innovative products can sometimes be obtained from real estate investment trusts (REITs), pension funds, and insurance companies. However, sometimes they, too, are daunted by the pioneering nature of urban infill housing. Foreign investors, who tend to be more familiar with urban housing, are another potential source of funds. Jason Runnels, executive vice president and principal of Phoenix Property Company (PPC), in Dallas, reports that in the past, PPC's investors for suburban garden apartments were insurance companies and pension funds; but when he approached them to finance an urban project, the lenders were not comfortable with the expensive and pioneering nature of urban housing development. So PPC obtained equity for the Firestone Upper West Side project, featured in chapter 8, from a German bank instead. EYA's initial investors were Japanese. Rochelle Grubb, chairman of Grubb Properties, in Charlotte, North Carolina, reports that her firm routinely uses personal equity and personal guarantees to finance projects; in the case of the Latta Pavilion, a mixed-use infill

Eckert & Eckert Photography

project in Dilworth (a few blocks from downtown Charlotte), where the firm is working with two equity partners and two lenders, the two equity partners are Dutch.

According to Loia, he and his development partner, Roddy White, obtained financing for the Buckhead Village Lofts condominium project by describing it initially as a rental property, because Atlanta had a history of rental lofts but not of for-sale lofts. To mitigate risk, the units were constructed in two phases. The principals provided personal equity, and a conventional lender underwrote the first phase of the project as apartments, knowing that the units would be sold. According to Loia, "We figured that at worst case, we could always rent them." The first phase sold out in three weeks, at which time the bank released funds for the second phase.

For the Winter Company's urban rental housing developments, Silverman raises equity from friends. "It's become more difficult to raise 'country club capital'," he explains. "As a result, I'm spending more time raising equity. We looked at institutional capital but that's difficult because they want to exit so quickly. These projects get better over time; I don't want to pay taxes on the gains and have to find other projects; I want to stay in." According to Silverman, determining the exit strategy is a necessary challenge. Because these projects are not institutional grade, the exit is often to sell the units as condominiums. "We're always evaluating this as an option," he says. In the Bass Lofts project, in Atlanta, for example, "There is a huge potential profit as a condo sellout, but we decided to refinance because it just keeps generating cash flow."

John Leith-Tetrault, director of Community Partners,[10] the consulting arm of the National Trust for Historic Preservation (NTHP), reports that in August of 2000, NTHP established the Banc of America Historic Tax Credit Fund, LP, a for-profit subsidiary, to syndicate historic tax credits for downtown housing development projects involving historic preservation. Before the creation of the tax credit fund, Banc of America had been doing private placements—brokering arrangements between property owners and investors for historic tax credits. Even though small projects incur the same transaction costs, however, the existing syndication was not funding projects with under $2 million in equity investment. "Most historic rehab projects are actually smaller than $477,000 (midpoint value)," Leith-Tetrault explains, "And the fund will purchase interest in projects for as little as $500,000." The fund will have $25 million to start, and will primarily target developments that involve the conversion of low-rise buildings to housing in commercial areas of cities.

Financial Returns

Though developers are quick to agree that it is easier to build in greenfields and that infill housing typically costs more to develop—at least 20 percent more than a garden-apartment product in the suburbs—they also agree that when infill housing succeeds, the financial returns for lenders and equity investors are greater over time. According to Dan McLean, president of MCL Companies, in Chicago, "Infill developments typically sell faster, at higher prices and greater profits, than projects out on the suburban fringe."[11] Levin concurs, noting that in CIG's experience, "Profit margins for for-sale urban infill housing tend to be much greater than for suburban for-sale housing." Similarly, Lomenick reports that it is the greater long-term investment value that drives Post Properties's interest in infill development.

Depending on the project, returns may be received in the form of sales profits, or as cash flow from rents or various fees. As Bock points out, "The financing determines in part how we structure our returns. For a market-rate development with no historic tax credits, we will raise equity in one way. For a project using historic tax credits, we will seek different investors and change the way the company's incentives are structured."

Developers interviewed for this book provided the following descriptions of their typical returns on urban infill housing developments:

- According to one small development company that builds for-sale projects in a growing metropolitan area, the bottom line after all fees are paid—"what we and our investors pay tax on"—is "double or triple the typical production builder margins, with the returns averaging between 17 and 21 percent."

- "Projected profits [a combination of developer's profit and builder's profit] for a recent development were 17.2 percent," notes a local for-sale infill housing developer. "The actual profit was 21 percent. This level of return is justified by the skills required and the risks involved. In addition, there were psychic returns in the form of social satisfaction, the opportunity to have a real impact."

- "We look for returns of about 17 percent in the pro forma before going forward," comments another local developer of for-sale urban infill projects. "That's 17 percent after all costs, including development fees (3 percent). Actually, we are happy to see 17 percent, though we'd like to beat that."

- A developer who builds a variety of residential products in a single strong urban market reports that his firm looks "for a site that will yield a return [net profit] of 7 to 16 percent, based on 'gut judgment'."

- A local developer of for-sale urban infill housing developments notes, "We look for percentage returns in the 20 to 25 percent range. That's money in versus money out— the gross margin. Net would be 10 to 12 percent. We know the sales price and what it costs to build. The variable is the cost to buy and prepare the site."

- "We get 40 to 70 percent returns on an internal rate of return basis," reports a local developer of small rental projects. "Cash flows become infinite, because we get all our equity back in the first few years."

- A developer of rental housing who works in partnership with numerous cities reports, "Generally, we structure our returns as fee-based rather than through long-term cash flow. We price our development work at 6 percent of construction cost. The development fee is 5 to 6 percent of the total development cost. If we can get a fee for construction management, we do. It's usually

structured as a bonus for coming in under costs—and is usually one of the first things that evaporates. We charge traditional management fees. The cash flow is not of much value; we are happy if we get 50 percent of the cash flow after real debt service. The investors get 20 to 30 percent, and the city gets 10 to 20 percent in return for soft financing."

Not all projects yield high profits from the outset; and, because of the high upfront investment required, those that do generally take longer to become profitable than their suburban counterparts. For example, one national developer of multifamily projects, speaking of a multiphase rental housing development, confided, "This project cost too much for its initial returns, but we expect it to be very profitable over the long term. We expected the project to yield 10 percent return on costs. In the first year, on a stabilized basis, it will be $7\frac{1}{4}$ to $7\frac{1}{2}$ percent. That's a function of the market; there was a lot of apartment construction in the suburbs. But we are in the process of creating a market for downtown housing and we expect it to take off."

Organizational Factors Affecting Success

All types of development firms develop urban infill housing successfully: large and small; publicly traded and privately owned; specialized and diversified; local, regional, and national; for-profit and not-for-profit. However, because of infill's unique opportunities and risks, some observers feel that the best infill practitioners are specialists.[12] On the other hand, Dockery cautions, "It's hard to do infill as the only thing you do. The work is sporadic and inconsistent; you can only do so many at a time, because it involves a lot of hand-holding." Others agree: MCL Companies, another firm that develops infill housing as one of its product niches, maintains a diverse portfolio to ensure that if one market weakens, the company will have investments in other markets that remain strong.

Many in the real estate development field strongly believe that infill housing is best under-

Renaissance on the River offers single-family suburban-style garage townhouses in a downtown Minneapolis setting.

taken by local developers who understand the nuances of their home markets and have an established relationship with the city officials and departments whose cooperation will be needed to implement the project. Firms that do not have local knowledge can sometimes compensate by working with local partners. On the other hand, Mayhood feels that "Sometimes it takes an outsider to envision a creative new use for a longtime vacant or underused property."

York explains, "Part of our business strategy is to find niches where we have a competitive advantage. Our local knowledge enables us to find—and recognize—good sites for infill housing. We know the local politics and can walk it through for the two years it takes. It's harder for us to compete with national developers for large (400-unit), more standardized products."

Large national companies generally like to develop signature prototype projects that can be repeated in various locations, because efficiencies can be derived from following the same process. The unique nature of infill sites and projects means that they are usually not replicable. However, as the 932-unit Post Uptown Square case study in chapter 8 demonstrates, large infill sites may offer opportunities for

large regional or national developers. At the same time, for the reasons given earlier, it is hard for these companies to compete with small local developers in doing more typical, one-of-a-kind infill housing projects.

The challenges associated with developing urban infill housing create high barriers to entry and limit competition. The work is complicated and requires significant time, patience, and the personal judgment and participation of the development principals. Lomenick terms the work "both an art and a science." As Bortz explains, "Because this work is so difficult to do and requires so much patience and risk, if we can do it, we'll have less competition. Demand appears to be strong. If we can figure out how to do it, we'll have a limited franchise."

Infill housing development requires different skills than suburban production housing. York observes, "Because of the product competition, there's more of a science to suburban housing development; you have to be a better manager. The creative process is not as important as your production skills. For infill, the opposite is true."

Development firms need the following skills to succeed in developing urban infill housing.

Landscaped gathering places, which are typically designed as interior courtyards or rooftop gardens, offer residents of urban infill developments a respite from the cacophony of city streets.

Firms that lack staff capabilities in specific skill areas can often obtain them through partnerships or hired assistance.

- The ability to identify and analyze relevant market demographics and characteristics;
- Knowledge of the local market and the local government, and familiarity with people—such as architects and subcontractors—who have expertise in this aspect of the development business;
- A reputation that inspires the confidence of local government officials and lenders;
- Experience in a number of relevant areas—such as land assembly, renovation or adaptive use, developing in urban settings, planning to fit an existing context, and developing specific product types (e.g., high-rise developments, mixed-use developments, or developments that include structured parking);
- A decision-making structure and the financial resources that make it possible to move quickly;
- An entrepreneurial approach: the ability, tenacity, and patience to resolve the problems that will inevitably arise in developing infill projects.

Terry Eakin, chairman of EYA, emphasizes the need for "entrepreneurial courage"—the courage to see beyond the apparent comparables, to see opportunity where others see only risk, to focus on the development goals, and to resolve unforeseen problems in a creative way. "There is a reason why sites in urban areas are available; inherent problems exist. If you are going to be a pioneer, you will incur risk, but you will also have an advantage." Thus, urban infill developers must be well-capitalized and have a high tolerance for risk. Ongoing relationships with financial partners are, as always, highly desirable.

Opportunities

The infill development strategy pursued by a given firm will depend on a number of factors, including the interests and inclinations of the principals; the demographic, political, economic, historic, and physical conditions and characteristics of the chosen market; and the firm's experience and capabilities. Barry sees "tremendous opportunities for small, well-capitalized developers." He advises that "when contemplating a pioneering project, first study the area, looking for a location where people go to restaurants at night. Put up your own money for plans and architectural studies, to show the city your commitment. Then convince the city. If the city is opposed, it is probably wise to abandon the effort."

Notes

1. William H. Miller, John R. Jaeger, Gail Lissner, and Eugene W. Sunard, "Residential Resurgence," *Urban Land,* September 2000, 92–94.

2. According to Baker, these figures are on a "net rentable" basis, and apply to both rental and for-sale housing. High-rise development costs more because it requires more square footage for elevators, stairs, and halls.

3. Chapter 7 includes additional information on neighborhood concerns that may develop during the construction process.

4. Speaking at ULI's Spring Council Forum, Minneapolis, May 2001.

5. Karen A. Danielsen, Robert E. Lang, and William Fulton, "What Does Smart Growth Mean for Housing?" *Housing Facts & Findings* 1, no. 3 (fall 1999); available at http://www.fanniemaefoundation.org/research/facts/fa99s1.html.

6. Robert W. Burchell and David Listokin, *Linking Vision with Capital: Challenges and Opportunities in Financing Smart Growth,* Report No. 01-01 (Arlington, Virginia: Research Institute for Housing America, September 2001), 23.

7. David Listokin, "Barriers to the Rehabilitation of Affordable Housing" (vol. 1 of a paper prepared for the Office of Policy Development and Research, U.S. Department of Housing and Urban Development, May 2001), 65–66.

8. Bob Silverman, quoted in Gregg T. Logan, Todd M. Noell, and Lawrence Frank; Robert Charles Lesser & Co.; and Georgia Tech, "Mobility, Air Quality, and Development: Overcoming Barriers to Smart Growth" (draft paper written for SMARTRAQ—Strategies for Metropolitan Atlanta's Regional Transportation and Air Quality, n.d.), 17.

9. As reported in Northeast-Midwest Institute and the Congress for the New Urbanism, *Strategies for Successful Infill Development* (Washington, D.C., and San Francisco: Northeast-Midwest Institute and the Congress for the New Urbanism, 2001), 86.

10. Community Partners is a real estate and financing group within the National Trust that provides resources for historic preservation in culturally diverse historic districts.

11. Quoted in Susan Bradford, "Neighborhood Renewal," *Builder,* March 1997, 130.

12. Bill Lurz, "Interesting Infill," *Professional Builder,* July 1999, 52.

3
Market Considerations

As the new housing developments sprouting up in America's cities attest, there has been a marked increase in demand for market-rate urban infill housing for a range of income groups. Generally, industry observers believe that three factors have fueled the rising demand: demographic trends, the resulting lifestyle choices, and the increasing attractiveness of cities as a place to live.

Although most parts of the country have witnessed an increase in demand for urban infill housing, the level and nature of demand vary from city to city and among locations within cities. Regional and local demographics, local culture, the character of the built environment, economic conditions, and public policies influence the market for infill housing in any given city. And, demand for a particular project within a given city will be highly specific, depending first on the project's location and then on its unique characteristics and amenities.

Regardless of the city or the development, however, demand for urban infill housing will, as a rule, be shaped by two key concerns: security and schools. Infill housing succeeds only in environments where people feel reasonably safe. And middle-class families with children, regardless of racial, ethnic, or socioeconomic background, use the quality of the schools as a

The industrial theme of the Oriental Warehouse project, in San Francisco, is carried into the residential units, but with plenty of polish. Riveted wood beams, corrugated metal ceilings, and exposed ductwork meld with glossy wood floors and smooth-finished drywall.

Fisher-Friedman Associates

In Memphis, the various residential developments of the Henry Turley Company have attracted people to the pleasures of living on the river and in the city.

primary criterion in evaluating housing choices. Because middle-class parents will generally not send their children to urban public schools and cannot afford private schools, most urban housing appeals to people who are childless and to families that are either rich or poor, rather than in between. Other key market issues are the availability and proximity of services (especially grocery stores) and mass transit.

National Trends

Though most new housing is still being built in the suburbs of America's metropolitan areas, recent evidence shows a resurgence of interest in living in the city, especially downtown. This resurgence is occurring throughout the country, and is being driven largely by white, childless, middle-class households.[1]

After decades of losing residents, many U.S. cities are now experiencing population gains.[2] Of the nation's 20 largest cities (including only census tracts within city limits), 16 grew in population between 1990 and 2000. In New York City, which led the pack in sheer numbers, almost 700,000 people were added during the decade, bringing the city's population to over 8 million for the first time.

Austin, with a 41 percent increase in population between 1990 and 2000, led in terms of percentage growth. Columbus, Dallas, Houston, Jacksonville, Phoenix, San Antonio, San Diego, and San Jose all posted double-digit population gains for the period. Smaller cities have also participated in this back-to-the-city trend. In the 1990s, Charlotte grew by more than 36 percent and Denver by more than 18 percent; El Paso, Nashville, and Seattle also posted impressive growth rates.

According to Donald Carter, managing principal at Urban Design Associates, in Pittsburgh, Pennsylvania, recent housing market studies for Charlotte, Cincinnati, Detroit, Indianapolis, Minneapolis, Orlando, Pittsburgh, and St. Louis all revealed pent-up demand for downtown housing in all categories—rental, condominium, low-income, middle-income, upper-income, live/work, subsidized, market-rate, high-rise, low-rise, loft, new, and historic rehabs.

Nationally, for central cities with regional populations between 1.5 million and 4 million, the annual absorption rate for downtown housing is estimated to be between 300 and 700 units per year, though in high-demand cities the number is much greater. Smaller cities have proportionately smaller demand, but the demand is still there. In most cities, anecdotal evidence indicates that new or renovated housing developments are absorbed quickly, suggesting that demand may well be higher than the market studies show. In fact, many new projects are preselling and prerenting before construction is complete.

The trend toward urban housing, however, represents a relatively small change in numbers, "more of a trickle than a rush."[3] Most of the cities that grew in the 1990s still have not regained the population they lost in the 1970s and 1980s, and four of the largest 20 cities —Philadelphia, Detroit, Baltimore, and Milwaukee—actually lost population between 1990 and 2000. In most metropolitan areas, moreover, the suburban growth rate far exceeds that of the central city. Finally, a portion of the population gain in some fast-growing cities can be attributed to annexation.

Nevertheless, after years of decline, the news of population growth in U.S. cities is remarkable. The back-to-the-city movement is now a clear trend that appears poised to continue well into the 21st century, as evidenced by increases in housing permit activity in cities at the end of the 1990s. Nationally, in the last year of the decade (1999 to 2000), the increase in city housing permit activity exceeded by 35 percent the average annual increase recorded between 1990 and 1998. In contrast, national suburban housing permit activity was only 21 percent ahead of the average level for the same period.

Table 3-1. Population Change in the 20 Largest U.S. Cities, 1990–2000

	2000	1990	Absolute Change	Percent Change	Rank in 1990
New York	8,008,278	7,322,564	+685,714	+9.4	1
Los Angeles	3,694,820	3,485,398	+209,422	+6.0	2
Chicago	2,896,016	2,783,726	+112,290	+4.0	3
Houston	1,953,631	1,630,553	+323,078	+19.8	4
Philadelphia	1,517,550	1,585,577	−68,027	−4.3	5
Phoenix	1,321,045	983,403	+337,642	+34.3	9
San Diego	1,223,400	1,110,549	+112,851	+10.2	6
Dallas	1,188,580	1,006,877	+181,703	+18.0	8
San Antonio	1,144,646	935,933	+208,713	+22.3	10
Detroit	951,270	1,027,974	−76,704	−7.5	7
San Jose	894,943	782,248	+112,695	+14.4	11
Indianapolis	791,926	741,952	+49,974	+6.7	12
San Francisco	776,733	723,959	+52,774	+7.3	14
Jacksonville	735,617	635,230	+100,387	+15.8	15
Columbus	711,470	632,910	+78,560	+12.4	16
Austin	656,562	465,622	+190,940	+41.0	27
Baltimore	651,154	736,014	-84,860	−11.5	13
Memphis	650,100	610,337	+39,763	+6.5	18
Milwaukee	596,974	628,088	−31,114	−5.0	17
Boston	589,141	574,283	+14,858	+2.6	20

Source: U.S. Bureau of the Census.

In a study of housing permit activity in cities, Alexander von Hoffman found that population size and land area correlate with the level of infill housing construction: during the past decade, large cities and lower-density cities generally experienced the most infill housing construction activity, though there were exceptions caused by specific local factors. Based on housing permit data, "hot" cities for infill housing development in the past decade included Boston, Dallas, Houston, Orlando, Phoenix, San Antonio, and Seattle. On the "cold" cities list were Baltimore, Detroit, Kansas City, Los Angeles, New Orleans, Philadelphia, Providence, Sacramento, and St. Louis.[4]

The extent to which the expansion of the market for urban infill housing was brought about by the high-tech boom of the 1990s (and may be affected by the slowdown experienced by that sector in the early 2000s) remains to be seen. However, ULI's members predict in a 2001 survey that infill housing is "expected to offer special areas of opportunity"; the balance of supply and demand will be "good," and prospects for profitable development will be "modestly good" for this product type in the near future.

Demand Drivers

Though reasons for housing location choices have not been systematically documented, analysts speculate that the factors driving the market for urban market-rate housing include demographic trends and lifestyle choices; the media's glamorization of urban lifestyles; disenchantment with suburbia; the renaissance of downtowns as places to live and work; and public policies that encourage urban housing development.

Demographic Trends and Lifestyle Choices

Because, as noted earlier, families with children tend to view urban public schools with skepticism, most middle-class urban dwellers are single people or childless couples. Nationwide, the average household size has been shrinking, reaching a record low of 2.6 in 2000. Married couples without children and single-person households make up the nation's two most numerous household types. In 1940, less than 8 percent of all households consisted of people living alone; today, singles make up 25 percent of American households. Between 1940 and 2000, the number of unmarried people living together as couples increased by 72 percent, to 5.47 million.[5] By 2020, married couples with children are projected to account for only one in five households.[6]

In addition, the oldest members of the baby boom generation, an age cohort whose members have had tremendous impact on all kinds of markets throughout their lives, are now well into middle age, and many are now empty nesters. David Mayhood, president of the Mayhood Company, in McLean, Virginia, observes that because they are so numerous, have had a small number of offspring compared with previous generations, and have longer life expectancies, "Baby boomers represent the first generation of Americans who will experience a new life stage: postchildren and preretirement." Thus, the aging boomers could potentially generate years of sustained high demand for certain types of city housing.

Finally, lifestyle choices, such as marrying later, have increased the number of single households, and various factors—divorce, delayed parenthood, alternative lifestyles, and choosing to remain childless—have increased the pool of couples without children.

With their exposed structural elements and high ceilings, converted industrial spaces that once appealed primarily to artists are now attracting a much broader range of prospective tenants.

Aderhold Properties, Inc.

Roy H. Kruse & Associates/Robert J. Heidrich

The Renaissance of Downtowns and the Lure of an Urban Lifestyle

As Bill Hudnut, senior resident fellow at ULI, points out, "Quality of place has become a paramount concern when employers and people shop for a place to be." In addition to their inherent appeal as the symbolic, physical, economic, and cultural centers of metropolitan areas, cities offer theaters, museums, sports facilities, restaurants, bars, parks and civic spaces, and areas of historic or architectural interest. In recent years, cities across the country have invested in building or attracting these kinds of places and activities. Among the case studies in this book, cities as diverse as Chicago, Fort Worth, St. Petersburg, and San Jose have all invested in creating downtown environments that are great places to visit, work, and live.

William A. Johnson, mayor of Rochester, New York, speaking at ULI's 2000 Fall Meeting, in Chicago, described what his city has done to recreate a vital downtown. "The primary catalysts for downtown revitalization were the creation of three downtown entertainment districts and a focus on our waterfronts. Six years ago, over $26 million in public funds were spent to improve infrastructure and renovate three vacant historic buildings as entertainment venues. Additional public funds were used to clear old industrial land bordering the Erie Canal and Genesee River, which flow through downtown Rochester, in order to create clean, attractive sites for development. Significant private investment followed, and these areas now attract many thousands of vis-

itors each week to entertainment, dining, and cultural activities."

In some cities, major events have triggered large-scale improvements that have had the side benefit of invigorating the market for downtown housing. In Atlanta, the 1996 Olympic Games created an opportunity for public and private investment in the city and its urban neighborhoods. In Los Angeles, public improvements, beautification efforts, and enhanced security in preparation for the 1996 Democratic National Convention created an environment that drew institutions, commercial activity, and residents back to the city.

Although it is a city's myriad attractions that most often draw residents downtown, housing development in some places has actually preceded the creation (or re-creation) of the places and activities associated with a lively, 24-hour city. For example, Jeff Sanford, president of the Memphis Center City Commission, explains that, spurred by "the magnetism of the river and a few visionaries," development of and demand for downtown housing preceded the revitalization of downtown Memphis.

Disenchantment with Suburbia

As the low-density housing developments and shopping centers of America's burgeoning suburbs stretch farther into the countryside, some people have begun to balk at the resulting traffic, monotony, and isolation of these environments. Some suburbanites who are weary of lengthening commutes and increasing dependence on the automobile regard city living as an alternative that will give them more time, more choices, and more freedom of movement.

For many, preference for city living is motivated by a desire for a better quality of life. According to Lawrence Houstoun, principal at the Atlantic Group, in Cranbury, New Jersey, a key aspect of quality of life is access to a rich variety of choices and opportunities, both of which tend to increase with density of population and development. "Why live in settings with little stimulation," he asks, "when more attractive opportunities are available?"[7] William Lucy, professor of urban and regional planning at the University of Virginia's School of Archi-

Demand was so strong for townhouses at the Pointe at Lincoln Park, developed in Chicago by MCL Companies, that signed contracts were taken for all units in Phase I in just one week.

Natural light from large windows fills the spacious "great room" of a corner unit in Victoria Townhomes, in Seattle.

Robert Pisano; Courtesy of Mithun

tecture, notes, "The popular impression of what constitutes 'quality of life' is changing. The suburban ideal after World War II is eroding. The notion of a pedestrian-oriented community with a mix of uses, where people can be out in public, is returning to America, just as it has always existed in other parts of the world—and, at one time, here. The desire for this kind of quality of life translates to potential demand for infill housing."

Public Policies and Incentives

Urban housing has also been stimulated by city governments' encouragement of infill housing development. The availability of both public and private funding has sparked interest in infill housing development; and, as described in chapter 2, successful urban housing developers can generate impressive returns.

Some of the targeted public sector policies and activities that have stimulated urban housing development include tax abatements; credits for historic preservation; below-market land sales; land-bank purchases; tax credits for first-time homebuyers; the revitalization of public housing; federal changes in mortgage finance (which eliminated many of the practices respon-

sible for redlining); Freddie Mac's and Fannie Mae's redirection of mortgage capital to underserved areas; economic development incentives and initiatives; and changes in local zoning and code enforcement.[8]

At the same time, in some metropolitan areas, growth management policies have made suburban housing development increasingly difficult, expensive, or both. The extreme examples of this phenomenon are in Seattle and Portland, where the cities' urban growth boundaries have effectively forced housing development back to the city.

Economic Considerations

Demand for urban housing is influenced by urban economic conditions, including business trends and job markets. In addition to creating jobs and contributing to regional population growth, the recent general economic prosperity has also helped fuel the back-to-the-city housing trend. At the same time, low interest rates have made both development financing and consumer home purchases more attractive. Along with job growth, factors that contribute to the influx of higher-income people include tight housing markets with a constrained housing supply, relative affordability, and good investment potential.

Jack Goodman, writing for the National Multi Housing Council (NMHC), suggests that when metropolitan areas boom, a disproportionate amount of construction occurs in central cities. One reason is that when housing demand is strong, suburban land becomes scarce and expensive, and some developers begin to consider new construction and redevelopment opportunities in the central city. Goodman also notes that certain kinds of jobs are returning to the city; for example, the industries that were most successful during the 1990s—technology and services—were more oriented to the central city; they also require less space than uses such as manufacturing.[9]

During the economic boom of the late 1990s, high-tech companies "led the charge downtown" in order to accommodate "new economy workers" who appreciate the aesthetics of downtown work and life. The move downtown is a response to the new economy's insistence that ideas—and the people that generate them—are a company's most valuable commodity. Cities like Austin have attracted companies like Intel and Computer Sciences Corporation, which have located campuses downtown. In the SoMa (South of Market) district of San Francisco is Multimedia Gulch, where old warehouses are bristling with new Internet companies and with workers who want to be close to nightlife and the seaside. New York has its Silicon Alley. Similar dynamics are at play in Atlanta, Chicago, Dallas, Philadelphia, Pittsburgh, Seattle, and Washington, D.C.[10] Whether (or to what extent) the economic slowdown of the early 2000s will have a long-term impact on the return-to-the-city momentum is not yet clear.

Other Factors

According to Edwin Stromberg, program manager at the U.S. Department of Housing and Urban Development, an array of environmental, physical, and community conditions affect the demand for urban infill housing in any given city. In addition to the type, amount, and quality of housing, important determinants include the quality of neighborhoods; essential public services, particularly schools; public infrastructure; and supporting facilities, such as shopping facilities. Older cities can face serious market disadvantages because of declining populations; deteriorating housing and public infrastructure; serious social problems, notably crime; and the lack of supporting commercial services.

Who Is the Market?

The question "Who is the market?" will have a different answer for different projects. However, in general, Hudnut describes the market for urban market-rate housing as made up primarily of "singles, mingles, and jingles"—in other words, affluent singles and couples, both married and unmarried. Bob Silverman, chairman of the Winter Companies, in Atlanta, concurs, adding that these households may be "young, old, singles, DINKs [double-income, no kids], or gays."

Young Singles and Couples

Young professionals like to live in cities because cities are fun: they offer a wide variety of recreational, cultural, intellectual, and social opportunities and experiences. In addition, cities are dense urban labor markets, where

To fill strong market demand for loft residences in Atlanta, Michael Loia and Roddy White constructed Buckhead Village Lofts, a new ten-story building that contains more than 100 custom loft-style units, each with a floor plan that features openness, height, light, and flexible use of space.

© Alan McGee

young people can "switch from job to job as they figure out what to do with their lives."[11]

Al Neely, group senior vice president, Charles E. Smith Residential Realty, Inc., in Arlington, Virginia, which builds high-end luxury housing in Boston, Chicago, Washington, D.C., and southeast Florida, says that the renters in the four markets share surprisingly similar demographics. "Most are 23 to 33 years old, in their second job, making $60,000 to $70,000 a year, but they have no money in the bank." Joe Barry, president of Applied Development Company, in Hoboken, New Jersey, concurs, reporting that two-thirds of his renters are young people (22 to 35) "who don't want to be tucked away in a garden apartment on some highway." However, Silverman points out that because young people tend to live with their parents for a longer time, opting for "zero rent and great services," the market for "young singles" includes people who are in their early forties.

Scott Shimberg, executive vice president and co-owner of Hyde Park Builders, Inc., in St. Petersburg, Florida, is among the many developers who have discovered that single women, in particular, love city life and constitute a large segment of the market.

One of the advantages of downtown is the stock of historic buildings and neighborhoods, which can yield a more unique and livable community than suburban alternatives, and which offer developers the opportunity to create cutting-edge products like lofts, which appeal to younger buyers. Silverman, for example, finds that young "techies" favor "cool loft spaces that are similar to the environments where they work." Members of the gay community "will pioneer and are able and willing to pay for 'cool' space." In fact, Silverman finds that "the gay community is our best market, especially if there is an arts component in the project." In his experience, the urban infill product "cuts across gender and racial divides. It attracts a community of shared values, where the arts are important and income levels are higher."

Many young singles and couples grew up watching movies and television programs that celebrated the delights of city life. Television shows have had such an influence that some developers report prospective residents requesting units with "a *Seinfeld* kitchen."

According to Margaret Sowell, president of Real Estate Strategies, Inc., in Wayne, Pennsylvania, singles of all ages seek lifestyle choices that enable them to socialize with other singles and live in a unique setting, such as a historic renovation or a neighborhood with a distinct identity. They look for amenities such as parking, concierge and business services, and recreational facilities, all within a safe neighborhood.

Aging Baby Boomers

As their children grow up and leave home, many baby boomers want to sell the family home and rid themselves of the responsibility and expense of its upkeep. William Frey, a demographer and research scientist at the University of Michigan, Ann Arbor, explains that boomers in the empty nester stage, aged 45 to 55, tend to be suburbanites who may move into the city one time before they retire. According to Sowell, wealthier empty nesters have a higher propensity to rent, and many "are actively looking for housing opportunities in or near downtowns—and, especially, in 24-hour cities." The safety of the living environment is especially important to this age group.

Silverman finds that, as in their youth, baby boomers in middle age are reaching out to learn,

The sales office at Block Y, in Chicago, echoes the architectural style and industrial finishes of the development's loft apartments.

want to have new experiences, and like to live near universities and cultural facilities. To meet this kind of demand, Silverman notes, "We are no longer developing buildings; we are developing *places*."

Other Potential Customers

In addition to young professionals and empty nesters, potential sources of demand for urban infill housing include

- Downtown office and service industry workers.
- Students, faculty, and staff of downtown universities and educational institutions.
- Employees of other institutions—such as hospitals—located in the city.
- Current and former residents of downtown neighborhoods.
- "Urban pioneers"—people who, regardless of their demographic profile, simply like city life and are willing to be among the first new residents in an emerging area of the city.
- Municipal employees, especially in cities that require everyone who works for the city to live within the city limits.
- Immigrants, a group that is expected to account for approximately 40 percent of future population growth. Immigration will be an especially important factor in the urban markets of California, Florida, New Jersey, New York, and Texas, where immigrants already make up a significant portion of the population.

In some cities, passive investors also constitute an important market segment. According to Tracy Cross, of Tracy Cross & Associates, Inc., in Schaumburg, Illinois,[12] in some locations, parents are purchasing downtown condominiums for their adult children with the intention of occupying the condos themselves after "the children" move on and the parents retire.

Qualitative Considerations

Market preferences will vary among projects, locations, and target markets. However, as a rule, people who choose an urban lifestyle are in search of a location that offers something special—whether it be interesting architecture, historic or cultural ambience, trendy

The brick, stone, and rock-face concrete-block details of the Renaissance on the River townhouses, in Minneapolis, reflect the architectural heritage of the nearby historic warehouse district.

or unique living space, or pedestrian access to urban amenities. And they are looking for convenience and a low-maintenance lifestyle. According to Bruce Ross, principal *emeritus* of Backen Arrigoni & Ross, Inc., in San Francisco, the expectations of urban dwellers differ from those of suburbanites because people who live in the city tend to shop daily and eat out more often. As a result, they generally require smaller units and less storage space than their suburban counterparts. Kitchens can be smaller, and there is less need for recreation space inside and outside the unit. Many developers have found, however, that people coming from the suburbs want suburban-style amenities such as garage parking, private open space, and well-appointed kitchens and baths. Kevin Augustyn, vice president of MCL Companies, Inc., in Chicago, has found that today's housing consumers value the ability to customize their homes and look for a safe living environment —which "is typically achieved by building at sufficient scale to create a new environment."

Rental versus For-Sale Housing

The urban infill housing built today encompasses both rental and for-sale projects. Developers choose a project's tenure type according to a number of criteria, including their own

Urban infill projects, especially those that target a market of single women, often incorporate security features such as gated parking courtyards.

interests, experience, and capabilities; the requirements of the project's financing sources; the project's characteristics; and the nature of demand in the project's specific location. In addition, local preferences may be a factor in the tenure-type decision. In Chicago, for example, where more than half the households are renters, "the city vigorously promotes home-ownership and the residents of many neighborhoods oppose new rental developments."[13] However, especially in pioneering or weak markets, developers may want to test demand and limit their exposure by renting out units in a first project or in the first phases of a large project.

Young householders tend to rent rather than own, which "may be the key to a larger number of young householders living in the city." Nationally, over 43 percent of householders aged 25 to 44 rent, compared with 22 percent of householders aged 45 to 64.[14]

Young people in their first or second jobs often choose to rent because they have not yet made a commitment to that work and that location, and want to be able to move easily if and when they change jobs. In addition to young professionals and aging baby boomers, the growing number of immigrants—who are more likely to rent than to own when they first arrive—will likely expand the pool of rental households in the near future.

Many urban infill developers who build rental housing target the so-called lifestyle

renters—those who can afford single-family housing but choose to rent. These upper-income customers make more than $50,000 per year and account for 17 percent of all apartment renters. According to NMHC, this segment grew by 13.5 percent in 1998, making it the fastest-growing segment of renters.[15]

Demand Analysis for a Specific Project

Market analysis for urban infill housing developments follows the same steps as for other types of housing: analysis of the site (discussed in chapter 4), the level and nature of demand for the intended development, and the supply of housing with which it must compete. The core issue is whether a market exists or can be created for a development that will yield a competitive return on investment. In identifying the market for housing in an infill location, developers need to ask themselves the following questions:

- Who are the potential buyers or renters?
- What do they want?
- What can they afford to pay?
- What can be built on the property that will satisfy their demands?
- Are there enough potential customers to justify the planned development?

Obtaining this information requires

- An analysis of area economic and demographic trends;
- Quantitative information on housing availability, condition, location, sales prices, and replacement needs (or rental unit numbers, types, locations, condition, vacancy rates, and rent levels);
- Qualitative information obtained through focus groups and interviews with nearby employers and institutions, real estate agents, and developers of successful similar properties.

Sowell cautions that because the analysis seeks to uncover untapped demand, accurately assessing demand for infill housing is often difficult. For this reason, local developers who have a longtime understanding of their city's market dynamics have an advantage. For example, Arn Bortz, a partner in Towne Properties, in Cincinnati, knew that the city's desire for high-rise luxury housing on the Gramercy on Garfield site was unrealistic. "We had been developing housing in Cincinnati for 29 years, and knew what the market wanted," he explains. "The Garfield site was not a location that would command sufficient rents to justify a luxury high rise."

Because every urban infill project is unique, typically there are no real comparables—or competition—to evaluate. In the absence of true comparables, it can be difficult for a developer to demonstrate that there is a market in a particular location. In such cases, developers will need to look at other types of projects, or at similar projects in a comparable submarket elsewhere in the city—or even in the suburbs. In some cases, the market analyst will need to draw on the experience of similar projects in other cities. Analysts need to consider carefully the characteristics of these surrogate comparables to determine what products, locations, amenities, or other features will likely yield rent or sale price premiums, then extrapolate to apply that information to their own project.

In many cities, experience has diminished concerns about the market for urban infill housing. Terry Eakin, chairman of Eakin/ Youngentob Associates, in Arlington, Virginia, notes that since the mid-1990s, his firm's perception of the market for urban infill housing in the Washington, D.C., area has changed. "Then, we were much more concerned about market risk. Since then, we have experienced the strength of the market and today feel more confident that an infill development in a good location will sell."

Notes

1. Haya El Nasser, "U.S. Cities Buck Trend with Boom Downtown," *U.S.A Today,* available at http://www.usatoday.com/news/nation/2001-05-07-down town.htm. Similar research is being undertaken by William Frey, a demographer and research scientist at the University of Michigan, Ann Arbor, who is attempting to determine to what extent changes in the population of cities' white residents with few or no children are related to the resurgence of urban populations.

2. The discussion of national trends in urban population originally appeared in Richard Haughey, *Urban Infill Housing: Myth and Fact* (Washington, D.C.: ULI, 2001), 3.

3. Rebecca R. Sohmer and Robert E. Lang, "Downtown Rebound," *Census Note* (May 2001): 1.

4. Alexander von Hoffman, *Housing Heats Up: Home Building Patterns in Metropolitan Areas,* Survey Series (Washington, D.C. and Cambridge, Mass.: Center on Urban and Metropolitan Policy, Brookings Institution, in collaboration with the Joint Center on Housing Studies, Harvard University, December 1999), 1, 7–8.

5. D'Vera Cohn, "Married-with-Children Still Fading," *Washington Post,* May 15, 2001.

6. Martha Farnsworth Riche, "The Implications of Changing U.S. Demographics for Housing Choice and Location in U.S. Cities" (discussion paper prepared for the Center on Urban and Metropolitan Policy, Brookings Institution, March 2001), 1.

7. Lawrence O. Houstoun Jr., "Urban Awakening," *Urban Land,* October 1998, 41.

8. Maureen Kennedy and Paul Leonard, "Dealing with Neighborhood Change: A Primer on Gentrification and Policy Choices" (discussion paper prepared for the Center on Urban and Metropolitan Policy, Brookings Institution, and PolicyLink, April 2001), 10–14.

9. Jack Goodman, "Measuring and Interpreting the Recent Increase in Central City Housing Construction" (white paper, National Multi Housing Council, June 8, 2000), 8.

10. Dylan Rivera and Bill Bishop, "High-Tech Companies Leading the Charge Downtown," *Austin American-Statesman,* March 3, 2000.

11. Edward L. Glaeser, "Demand for Density? The Functions of the City in the 21st Century," *Brookings Review* 18, no. 3 (summer 2000): 10–13.

12. Speaking at the fall 2000 meeting of ULI, Chicago, Illinois.

13. Maxine V. Mitchell and Robert E. Miller, "Chicagoland's Affordable Housing Deficit," *Urban Land,* September 2000, 96.

14. Riche, "Changing U.S. Demographics," 2.

15. Moody's Investors Service, *Urban In-fill Apartments: A Growing Opportunity for Multifamily REITs* (New York: Moody's Investors Service, May 1999), 4.

4
Land Acquisition and Assembly

Choosing, obtaining, and developing land for urban infill housing developments is perhaps the most crucial—and difficult—aspect of the business. On the one hand, as discussed in chapter 2, the attraction of urban infill housing is rooted primarily in location. On the other hand, the fact that infill housing is developed within an established context makes the process more complicated and more challenging.

To begin with, the surrounding environment may or may not be beneficial to the planned project. Other key considerations in site selection include business criteria, such as land costs; risk versus potential return; and the likelihood of getting approvals. This chapter describes these and other factors that developers need to consider in selecting property for infill housing development.

Criteria for Site Selection

In addition to location, considerations in selecting a site for urban infill housing development include its physical characteristics and condition, the acquisition and development costs, public sector attitudes and participation, and regulatory concerns. Terry Eakin, chairman of Eakin/Youngentob Associates (EYA), Inc., of Alexandria, Virginia, advises taking considerable care in selecting a site: "We spend a lot of time nailing down good properties."

To meet the demand for upscale urban housing, a deteriorating former office building at the corner of Park Avenue and East 60th Street, in New York City, was topped with additional stories to create 515 Park Avenue, a 43-story luxury condominium tower.

Frank Williams & Associates

Location

According to Natalie Bock, development manager for the Alexander Company, in Madison, Wisconsin, the single most important consideration for developers in selecting a site is, "Is this a place where people would want to live? Can we make it a place where anyone would want to live?"

Because of the importance of location, potential sites for successful urban infill housing development tend to fall into two categories: (1) sites within established housing markets that will draw prospective residents if properly developed; and (2) sites that are adjacent to undesirable uses or located in marginal neighborhoods but that are readily accessible to the delights of city life. The most promising sites in either category tend to be those that are located along transit corridors or near places of employment, or that are convenient to shopping, recreation, or cultural amenities.

The general appearance and character of the neighborhood and the nature of nearby uses are important considerations. Settle Dockery, vice president of York Properties, in Raleigh, North Carolina, explains, "We look for a neigh-

borhood environment that is decent, has a residential feel, is close to certain other activities, maybe has something special like a view opportunity." Scott Shimberg and Craig Ross, principals of Hyde Park Builders, Inc., in Tampa, Florida, look for neighborhoods "where you can walk the dog." Arn Bortz, a partner in Towne Properties, in Cincinnati, selects infill sites "in territory we know and understand," and looks for "soft edges" of green space and developments in the area "that reinforce the sense of place and neighborhood context."

Because people who choose urban living are also seeking convenience, proximity to neighborhood-serving stores and services is a real plus. As Henry Turley, president of the Henry Turley Company, in Memphis, explained, "When people ask about a grocery store downtown, they are really asking a more subtle question. Is there a community here? Is this really a place where we can live? Is this really a neighborhood?"[1]

In addition to "walkability," Art Lomenick, president of Workplace Urban Solutions, in Dallas, looks for areas that the city has targeted for redevelopment—where, in order to encourage "neighborhood creation," the city is more likely to be flexible about requirements for entitlements.

Where the immediate environment is weak (meaning that it is not yet an established "place to be"), or where the neighborhood is in transition or has a negative image, the developer needs to obtain enough land to create a project with critical mass—that is, a project large enough to establish its own identity and context and to make a difference in the overall character of the larger environment. Such sites must often be assembled from several different parcels. When working in declining neighborhoods, developers should locate sites at the edge of the area of decline, near more desirable uses, because such locations are more likely to enhance access to the development and to strengthen its image and sustainability.

If a particular location is highly desirable, its appeal can often overcome negative edge conditions. A good example is Old Town Village, the topic of one of the case studies in chapter 8.

Sites like the one on which Avalon Towers by the Bay was built —in San Francisco's popular SoMa (South of Market) district— are becoming increasingly difficult to find and develop. The AvalonBay Communities project was the first new high-rise housing that had been built in the city in a decade.

The project site was within easy walking distance of downtown Alexandria, Virginia, a lively historic city just outside Washington, D.C. But the site itself was an old rail yard adjacent to subsidized housing, a cemetery, empty warehouses, a busy thoroughfare, and an oil distribution facility. EYA, the development firm, believes that the site's location and relatively large size—12.3 acres—made it possible to establish a genuine sense of place and overwhelm the negative edge conditions. Similarly, the 150 St. Mary's project, in Raleigh, North Carolina, is located near railroad tracks, a prison, and a social services facility, but these factors were overcome by the project's desirable location between downtown Raleigh and North Carolina State University.

Bob Silverman, chairman of the Winter Group of Companies, in Atlanta, Georgia, typically looks for environmentally clean, well-priced sites in transitional neighborhoods that he feels are emerging as trendy places to live. One of the indicators Silverman observes to identify such places is "where gays want to live, because they are pioneers of positive neighborhood change." Silverman also likes areas that are near restaurants and art galleries, and views transit access as "desirable but not essential."

Joe Barry, president of Applied Development Company, in Hoboken, New Jersey, seeks locations where he feels he can attract market-rate buyers—meaning cities that have entertainment, restaurants, good transportation, and ambience. When possible, Barry likes to find waterfront sites, though older neighborhoods can also work well. For example, he develops in New Brunswick, which is distressed but is also a university town where "there are things to do, something to build on."

Not everyone agrees with the strategy of building in transitional neighborhoods. "It's far smarter to rebuild in stable neighborhoods than to shop for bargains in questionable areas," says Michael Lander, president of the Lander Group, in Minneapolis. "The construction cost is the same whether you build in a good or a peripheral location, but you have a far better chance of recouping your investment if you build where people want to live."[2]

Anderson Illustration Associates, Inc., 2000

Property Considerations

As with any other real estate development site, the developer will want to become familiar with the characteristics of the property and determine whether the site is appropriate and can be used cost-effectively for the proposed development. Infill sites are vacant for a reason. "Ask yourself," Eakin cautions, "Why hasn't this site been developed? Then find the answer."

Again, as with any other development, site evaluation factors include access, frontage, topography, vegetation, slopes, soil conditions, and drainage. Because urban infill sites exist within a built environment, they are more likely than greenfields to contain or be affected by easements; old utility lines; abandoned streets; historic or archaeological features; and foundations, debris, or structures from previous uses. In addition, vacant land within urban areas may be awkwardly configured or physically constrained by surrounding uses. Bruce Ross, principal *emeritus* of Backen Arrigoni & Ross, Inc., in San Francisco, notes that the shape, extent, and edges of infill sites are often constrained by the height and bulk of existing developments; rarely are such sites rectangular.

Depending on the location and characteristics of the site, a number of environmental reg-

The Mandel Group is building Trostel Square, in Milwaukee, on a remediated brownfield site that once housed the Trostel Tannery. The project will include 99 luxury apartments, 27 condominiums, public water-taxi stands, private boat slips, a public park, and business and fitness centers.

ulations can affect infill housing development.[3] Because previous industrial or commercial uses may have contaminated the site with harmful chemicals, developers must be especially cau-

tious to investigate the site's history, including potential environmental issues such as toxic wastes or groundwater contamination. Shimberg notes that his firm "walked away from the

Urban Infill on Brownfields: A Cure for Urban Sprawl?

As the rebirth of city living intensifies competition for infill land in many cities, the redevelopment of brownfields for urban housing is becoming an attractive alternative.[1] Because older industrial land is often located near employment centers, transportation, and waterfronts, such properties can present interesting development opportunities. From a city's point of view, brownfields provide a valuable land resource for needed housing or mixed-use development. Reuse of brownfields can also return idle land to productive and taxable use, remove blight, and strengthen the urban fabric. Because housing can sometimes be created through the adaptive use of industrial or commercial buildings, renovations of existing structures on brownfield sites may also help retain a community's historic, architectural, or cultural character.

Brownfield sites lend themselves to use for infill residential development because the land use requirements for housing are often very flexible: successful housing projects can be built on scattered-site lots or small property assemblages, and in locations that are far from highways or main roads and for which no other land uses may be viable.

Not all brownfield sites are practical for housing redevelopment, however. For the redevelopment of a brownfield site to succeed, the site must have market value for the intended use and meet the same site selection criteria—location, physical characteristics, cost, and so forth—as any other potential development site. In addition, the nature and extent of any contamination must be identified and the contaminants on the site must be removed, remediated, and/or contained according to the applicable legal requirements. In the past, uncer-

tainty about the time, cost, and complexity of the cleanup requirements, and concern about potential legal liability, strongly inhibited the reuse of brownfield sites.

When housing is developed on contaminated sites, substantial marketing problems may arise from deed restrictions, which limit the future use of the site in order to ensure that it remains relatively environmentally safe. However, such restrictions alert prospective occupants that some contamination may be left on the site. To alleviate such concerns, projects can be designed without underground structures such as basements or underground parking. Ground-avoiding design features, such as first-floor garages incorporated into the footprints of townhouse units, are compatible with the higher densities that are typical of urban redevelopment projects. Designing for higher densities on brownfield sites can also help make projects economically feasible (and minimize the need for subsidies), allowing the developer to spread the fixed costs of cleanup over a larger number of units.

State and local governments have actively encouraged the reuse of brownfields by clarifying the legal requirements and liabilities and by providing funds and incentives for cleanup. Currently, over 40 states have some sort of voluntary cleanup program in place, although the particular approaches to helping resolve the legal issues associated with the redevelopment of brownfields vary from state to state.[2] In addition, a number of cities, notably Chicago and Cleveland, have made major strides in encouraging the redevelopment of brownfields and other vacant industrial sites for housing. Sometimes state or local governments will proactively fund the cleanup of sites

targeted for redevelopment before any specific end user has been identified.

The U.S. Environmental Protection Agency offers comprehensive, up-to-date information on the redevelopment of brownfields through its Web site: www.epa.gov. The Northeast-Midwest Institute also provides extensive information on federal brownfields programs, resources for environmental cleanup, economic development opportunities, and options for financing cleanup and redevelopment. Its Web site (www. nemw.org) is an excellent resource. Many states also have their own brownfields Web sites.

Finally, the following recent publications include a wealth of useful information: Robert A. Simons, *Turning Brownfields into Greenbacks* (Washington, D.C.: ULI, 1998); and Todd Davis, *Brownfields: A Comprehensive Guide to Redeveloping Contaminated Property* (Chicago: ABA Publishing, 2001). ■

Source: Robert A. Simons, professor of real estate and urban planning, Maxine Goodman Levin College of Affairs, Cleveland State University.

Notes

1. Brownfields are defined here as former industrial or commercial property on which development at its highest and best use has been prevented because of actual or perceived contamination. See Robert A. Simons, *Turning Brownfields into Greenbacks* (Washington, D.C.: ULI, 1998), 3.

2. Voluntary cleanup programs typically give developers the certainty they need to move forward with development plans for brownfield sites by providing clear standards for cleanup, limitations on liability for developers and lenders, and Environmental Protection Agency and/or state certification that cleanup standards have been met. Many programs also provide assistance with funding or actual cleanup activities.

site of an old dry cleaning establishment because of potential mineral spirits contamination."

But not all environmentally questionable sites should be dismissed. Some well-located former industrial sites present excellent opportunities for reuse, and numerous public programs have emerged that limit the developer's liability. Barry has considerable experience working with contaminated sites. "We study them carefully and reflect the risk in the price we are willing to pay." Because few developers know how to assess and develop brownfields (contaminated or potentially contaminated sites), and because the cost of acquiring them is often comparatively low, this particular niche-within-a-niche can be especially profitable. The accompanying feature box describes some of the considerations involved in the identification and reuse of brownfields.

Environmental laws can affect where development may occur, what the development process will involve, what it will cost, how long it will take, and the ongoing costs of operating the completed development. Though advocates of particular regulations may rightly point out that compliance with an individual requirement imposes only modest costs, the cumulative impact of all the applicable regulations can be substantial. Therefore, developers must carefully research potential environmental requirements before committing to a site or project.

The fact that infrastructure—particularly streets and sidewalks and water, sewer, and drainage systems—is already in place is typically cited as one of the benefits of urban infill development. However, especially in older cities, existing infrastructure may be in poor repair or inadequate for the proposed use. Sewers may need to be rebuilt, and downstream capacity may be inadequate for the proposed development.

The developer must ensure that the site has sufficient sewer and water capacity, modern utilities, and good drainage. And, if open space or public parks are not available nearby, the developer may need to provide open space within the project. It is wise to ascertain infrastructure needs in advance, as well as to determine whether the local jurisdiction will pro-

The development of the Belmont Dairy, a two-block, mixed-use project in southeast Portland, Oregon, required extensive remediation of environmental contaminants in both the site and the former dairy building.

vide or fund needed improvements. For infill projects they wish to encourage, cities will often provide not only basic "public works" infrastructure but streetscape improvements such as sidewalks, lighting, street furniture, and landscaping.

Because of the many possible site-specific impediments, wise infill developers will take time upfront to investigate site development requirements. Reese Jarrett, general partner of Carter Reese & Associates, in San Diego, has confronted a variety of site development issues. "In Cypress Point, we had to excavate. In Jarrett Heights, there was a huge drainage channel and large depths of uncompacted soil. At the Village at Euclid, sewer pipes had been buried 20 to 25 feet down." While preparing the site for Old Town Village, EYA discovered archaeological remains. As Kevin Augustyn, vice president of MCL Companies, Inc., in Chicago, cautions, "You must do your homework on site conditions. On one project where the soil had lots of debris and required extensive work, we just broke even."

To avoid costly surprises later, developers are advised to complete a first-phase environmental assessment before committing serious resources to an infill site, and to conduct soil engineering studies to help estimate site preparation costs. In addition, developers should factor contingencies into their budgets to cover environmental and soil risks, regardless of the availability of funding to cover those risks.[4]

Existing buildings being considered for rehabilitation or adaptive use present both opportunities and constraints. Considerations in determining the suitability of an existing building

The 10,000 residents of downtown Dallas live in settings such as the Post Wilson Lofts, located in a renovated historic building.

for residential use include the spacing of windows; the presence of large, empty, dark spaces (which are difficult to use); and opportunities to provide parking. In addition to studying the current condition and structure of the buildings and their adaptability for the intended use, developers must investigate the possibility of contamination by asbestos or lead-based paint. In some parts of the country, developers must consider the need for seismic retrofitting as well.

While historic buildings often present exciting development opportunities, compliance with historic preservation regulations imposes additional review requirements that increase development time and cost and require a higher level of expertise. Rehabilitation projects that involve historic buildings or that are located in designated historic districts must comply with the U.S. secretary of the interior's standards for rehabilitation as well as with state and local requirements. In addition, developers must satisfy the sometimes-competing interests of local community groups, public officials, and preservationists; and the work usually requires the services of highly skilled craftspeople, who

may be difficult or expensive to employ.[5] The completed development may be well worth the extra effort; however, the developer must anticipate the requirements in advance to make an informed cost-benefit judgment on project feasibility.

The Political and Regulatory Environment

Because, as discussed in chapter 6, most urban infill projects require the cooperation, if not the participation, of the public sector, political receptiveness is an important consideration. Particularly in cities that have no recent history of urban housing development, the mayor's active interest and encouragement are crucial. For Bock, whose company specializes in transforming historic buildings into housing, criteria for selecting projects include, in addition to favorable demographics and the suitability of the property itself, "having the mayor on board, strong city leadership, city provision of free property, and the city having sources of money and a political structure that is willing to help and easy to work with."

The site's current zoning may or may not allow the proposed use. Often, sites in urban areas that developers consider for housing development are currently zoned for commercial or industrial use. Sometimes these properties present interesting opportunities. Los Angeles architect and real estate consultant Steve Fader observes, "Developers can make their own opportunities using parcels that have been overlooked because the zoning was not appropriate." In some places, commercial or industrial designations allow housing development, sometimes at even higher densities than the developer intends for the project. Other sites need to be rezoned. Clearly, it is advantageous to purchase land that is zoned to allow the intended use, so that rezoning—and the added time, cost, and risk that it entails—is not a requirement. However, where rezoning would be required—often to make possible a mixed-use or mixed-product development—developers will want to familiarize themselves in advance with the rezoning process and with community attitudes that they are likely to encounter.

Because urban infill occurs within an existing context, interested citizens will have opinions about how their community should and should not change. As discussed in chapter 7, the power of community opinion to affect project outcomes will vary among locations and projects, depending on factors such as the local political structure and attitudes and whether or not existing zoning will allow the intended use "by right." Regardless of zoning, however, developers who intend to do repeat business in the same community are wise to communicate with neighboring residents early and often and solicit their support.

Before committing to a site, prudent developers will look for hidden obstacles such as overlay districts, transit plans, potential moratoriums, traffic or infrastructure limitations, and upcoming fee increases that may affect a project's feasibility. Developers should also be aware that such information may be scattered in various public documents and not readily apparent.[6]

Size

Given the wide range of development types encompassed by urban infill housing, it is impossible to offer generally applicable criteria for the size of a site. Successful projects can consist of only a few units or many hundreds, depending on the developer's goals and resources, the nature of the local market and

regulatory requirements, and the work involved.

Developers realize different benefits from projects of different size. Large projects can transform the image of an entire neighborhood and market; enable a developer, in the later phases of the project, to reap the value created in the early phases; and allow more efficient use of upfront investments in time, money, and human resources. On the other hand, small projects enable developers to respond to specific opportunities and to test unproven markets without a long-term commitment of money and effort. Of course, in cases where a developer envisions a specific project in advance, the development program will dictate the site size required.

How to Find Good Sites

Local developers, who have the advantage of knowing their cities well, can periodically drive around in areas that they feel are established or emerging markets and identify potential sites. Developers who have deep roots in the community are also able to recall the history of the uses of various sites and to recognize changes in market dynamics that could easily be overlooked by outsiders. Brokers—and even property owners themselves—may contact local developers who are known to be interested in infill sites. "Access to sites has a snowball effect,"

Constructed within the shell of a historic brick warehouse, Oriental Warehouse, in San Francisco, features 66 two-story loft apartments.

Fisher-Friedman Associates

observes Eakin, "Landowners have emotional ties to their property and want to sell it to someone with a track record, who will develop it successfully, in a way that will make them proud." At the same time, success in identifying sites depends not only on *finding* vacant or underused property but perhaps even more on the ability to envision a new community where a blighted site or decayed, marginally useful buildings now stand. Fader cautions developers not to overlook properties that are ripe for "densification"—for example, land that is currently occupied by an aging, single-story structure and is surrounded by a higher-density environment.

Cities sometimes encourage infill development by helping developers identify and obtain sites, either by calling developers' attention to specific locations or by providing general information on vacant properties so that developers can choose among the sites available. Sometimes cities target areas for redevelopment, assemble properties, prepare them for development, and seek out private developers to build new housing or mixed-use developments, either through a request for proposals process or by inviting the participation of a specific developer whom they know and trust.

Cities often hold inventories of urban properties, such as schools, that are no longer viable for their former uses; such buildings can be transferred to developers for the creation of specific kinds of developments. Similarly, private institutions such as churches, hospitals, and universities—especially those that are closing or relocating facilities—may have excess land to sell. One of the case studies for this book, Post Uptown Square, is being developed on property formerly occupied by a city hospital in Denver.

No one knows the depth of the supply of vacant land in America's cities, but there is no question that it represents a tremendous opportunity. To take advantage of such resources within a given city, public and private decision makers must first identify the amount, location, and condition of all the vacant land within the city's borders. A recent study undertaken for the Brookings Institution revealed that many cities lack reliable means of collecting information on vacant land and abandoned structures, and that whatever information does exist is fragmented. "Information about vacant land and abandoned structures tended to reside in a variety of city agencies with varying levels of jurisdiction, responsibility, and land use powers."[7]

Computer technology presents new and more cost-effective ways for cities, developers, and other interested parties to identify sites for infill development.[8] Professor Anne Vernez Moudon, at the University of Washington in Seattle, has been creating a parcel-based land information database to help planners identify and precisely target sites that are appropriate for infill development and redevelopment. "Land monitoring with parcel-level geographic information systems seeks to identify the supply of buildable lands and to estimate the unrealized development capacity of that land to accommodate future residential and employment uses," she explains, adding that this information must be coupled with proactive programs to encourage and support the desired developments.[9]

Property suitable for urban infill housing developments may include not only vacant property but surface parking lots; historic or architecturally interesting buildings that are ripe for redevelopment; and old schools, factories, warehouses, offices, mill buildings, or other structures that can be adapted for housing. Where infill land is limited, reuse of commercial, retail, and institutional buildings for resi-

A typical residential unit in the Denver Dry Goods Building.

Shannon Sperry, Denver Urban Renewal Authority

Development of the Villa Torino apartments, in San Jose, California, required the assembly of 21 parcels of land held by six different owners.

Douglas Dun

dential purposes offers exciting opportunities for community revitalization as well as interesting architectural choices for the consumer. In some cases, developers can create innovative urban infill projects by mixing renovation, adaptive use, or both, with new construction.

Adaptive use, although hardly a novel concept, is a valuable mechanism for the kinds of infill development that can help cities regenerate. According to Washington, D.C.–area development consultant Laura Cole Reblitz, real estate investment trusts (REITs) and private developers in Washington, D.C., and Atlanta, often through the use of historic preservation tax credits, have converted former school buildings into condominiums. Similarly, in an up-and-coming arts district of Atlanta, the Winter Companies converted the site and structures of a former high school into a rental apartment and townhouse development known as Bass Lofts, and the market response has been powerful. In Los Angeles and Denver, outdated malls and strip retail developments have been transformed into "urban villages" or mixed-use projects, often through the use of tax abatements. In Pasadena, a partnership of Post Properties

and TrizecHahn Corporation is transforming an obsolete, 1970s-era shopping mall into Paseo Colorado, a mixed-use project with 387 luxury lofts and rental apartments located above street-oriented commercial space that will include shops, restaurants, and cinemas. In Baltimore and Seattle, turn-of-the-century waterfront factories have been converted to lofts and offices. In Memphis, the Alexander Company, of Madison, Wisconsin, converted Central Station, a historic downtown train station, into rental apartments, commercial space, and transit facilities. (Central Station is featured as a case study in chapter 8.) In Minneapolis, Northstar Woolen Mills, one of the original mills built near the St. Anthony Falls, downtown, has been rebuilt as loft apartments with parking on the first two floors. The project, which was finished in 1999, sold out in advance of construction.

Land Cost

Land cost is one of the key variables that determine whether an infill housing development will be economically feasible and what type

River Station, in Minneapolis, consists of 90 condominium units within three buildings on a ten-acre site, with parking underground.

of project can be built. The cost of land has to be low enough for developers to recover the acquisition price through sales prices or rents. Developers can easily determine project feasibility by factoring in construction costs per square foot and returns per unit, based on allowed density. To a great extent, land price determines project density; the higher the land price, the greater the residential density required to make the numbers work. As Craig Ross explains, "In deciding whether to purchase a site, we consider the cost of the land *vis à vis* what return it will generate when developed. Our land costs are typically 15 to 20 percent of the project's selling price."

In cities or areas where housing demand is strong and prices are high, such as Atlanta and most of California, and in markets where pioneering projects have proved demand for urban residential developments, land prices rise quickly as more developers seek to tap this market. Infill land may become scarce, as speculators hold land rather than sell it, in anticipation of realizing greater profits later as prices continue to rise. As a result of these and other factors, in many areas the cost of land poses significant difficulties for infill housing development. In Atlanta, for example, according to a recent report by Robert Charles Lesser & Co., "One of the biggest barriers to infill development is the price of land, which is eight times higher in the city . . . than in suburban jurisdictions."[10]

Escalating land costs can make it impossible for developers to create lower-density,

neighborhood-scale products—such as row-houses or three- to five-story, mixed-product developments—at prices that are affordable to anyone but the very rich. Even higher-density products may be feasible only for the luxury market. Although public subsidies are often available to help produce housing for lower-income people, middle-income people are often priced out, which creates problems for developers and consumers, both of whom have an interest in developments that serve a broader market.

In areas with high land costs, developing high-rise apartments—which distribute the cost of the land among more units—may be one way to create urban housing that is affordable to middle-income households. In many locations, however, this product type may not be acceptable to local governments, current residents, or the intended market. Furthermore, from a developer's standpoint, "High-density projects increase risk. Zoning is harder to obtain; the inability to 'buy today, build tomorrow' creates a timing risk; and longer construction cycles require huge cash outlays, gambling on solid sales in a distant and uncertain future."[11]

In softer housing markets, where demand is weak, prevailing rents or sales prices are low, or both, developers cannot pay high prices for land and still make a profit. In such cases, according to Bortz, a city that wants to encourage residential development will need to provide the property. For the six-phase development his firm is undertaking in Cincinnati—the first two phases of which are featured among the case studies in chapter 8—a land lease from the city was essential to the project's economics. However, Bortz cautions that a city's willingness to acquire properties for infill developments through eminent domain is a two-edged sword: on the one hand, it makes new development possible. On the other, it fuels speculation among landowners. (As discussed in chapter 6, cities can help developers produce infill housing—including "workforce" housing for middle-income households—in a number of other ways.)

Sometimes the price of urban land is excessive because it is based on an allowable density that is too high—a situation that most commonly occurs where land was previously zoned for commercial use and certain residential uses are allowable by right. According to Shimberg, "It's critical to understand the land economics. Brokers price land based on what the zoning allows, even though you can't meet all the other requirements—such as drainage, setbacks, and driveway widths—at that density. In our market, people like buildings in small groups, with private open space and landscaping. We figure that, realistically, you can get only 80 percent of what the zoning allows."

Cities that base property tax assessments on the current use of land rather than on its market value can inadvertently encourage speculation because the low carrying costs give owners no impetus to sell. The market value of land used for surface parking, for example, may be far above the value at which it is taxed. The parking revenue is often sufficient to pay the taxes, so the landowner can hold the property in anticipation of future increases in the land's value. This *de facto* subsidy to current land-owners makes it difficult for developers to buy land at reasonable prices. (Taxing land at market value is controversial, however, because it can also impose an economic burden on—or even force out—desirable existing uses.)

Cities can help avoid such market distortions by creating an infill development strategy as part of a larger vision for the community. They can identify and inventory sites for infill development—though such identification may also bid up the price of that land—and rezone in advance for uses consistent with their vision. And, to discourage speculators and "holdouts," it is important for cities to assess—and tax—vacant land and structures at their true market value. To that end, some cities assess and/or tax land and improvements separately.

One way to obtain reasonably priced land in a community with rising land costs is to enter into a joint venture with a property owner. As Shimberg reports, "We may joint-venture with a property owner, who puts up the land and gets a piece at the end." Another way to manage land costs is to ferret out good sites in pioneering areas, where competition is less keen. Such places are typically transitional neighborhoods close to downtown or urban locations with emerging restaurant, cultural, or entertainment identities. As noted earlier, local knowledge is a big advantage in finding such sites. Wise developers will also buy—or option—land for more than one project in the same area, so that they can capture some of the value they create. York Properties, which has purchased

Block Y, in downtown Chicago, offers a mix of product types created through a combination of new construction and the adaptive use of old industrial buildings.

Thrush Development Corporation

The 136 luxury town-houses at Ford's Landing, in Alexandria, Virginia, were built on the waterfront site of an abandoned Ford Motor Company plant.

several parcels in the area between downtown Raleigh and North Carolina State University, intends to transform the area, over time, into a stable residential community—as well as to reap the increase in value that the firm is creating by pioneering new development in the area. Jason Runnels, executive vice president and principal of Phoenix Property Company (PPC), which developed the Firestone Upper West Side project, in Fort Worth, agrees: "We are in the process of creating the market, which is why it's important to control a large portion of land."

Assembly and Acquisition Issues

Lucky is the developer who can identify a suitable site and purchase (or option) it outright. More typically, acquiring land for urban infill housing involves assembling several parcels, often from different landowners, some of whom may be reluctant to sell. Landowners may be unwilling to sell for various reasons—inertia, anticipation of higher future land prices, a desire to avoid the tax consequences of selling, and

disputes with other owners. Especially where the costs of holding land are low, reluctance to sell may well constitute a practical obstacle to infill development.[12]

One way to acquire land from a single owner is by forming a partnership with the landowner. In some cases, the partner will be a public agency—typically the city, a redevelopment agency, or perhaps a school district. In others, the partner may be a private landowner—an individual, or perhaps an institution such as a church, hospital, or university.

Where the desired property consists of a number of parcels held by different owners, the purchase process can be tricky because knowledge of the developer's objective can lead to speculative pricing. The approach used by PPC to acquire land for Firestone Upper West Side illustrates one way to acquire land from different owners. The company first held preliminary discussions with the city to determine how interested it was in supporting the project, then hired a broker to assemble the tract. To avoid setting off speculation in land prices, PPC handled purchasing quietly, with different people working with different landowners. PPC viewed certain parcels as essential; once those were obtained, the project could go forward. As PPC purchased some parcels outright and optioned others, it became heavily invested, paying between $100,000 and $200,000 per month just to extend the options. In all, PPC assembled 15 acres of land for the project from 14 different landowners over a two-year period.

As discussed in chapter 6, cities can help assemble land in a number of ways. They can forgive tax liens and help clear title to the property. They can buy the property, write down its cost, and sell it to a developer—or even swap land with reluctant landowners. Cities can also help by enticing a landowner to become a partner in the development. In some cases, developers may need assistance from public agencies that have the power of eminent domain—either through the exercise of that power or through the landowner's understanding that the power may be used. In the words of Pres Kabacoff, president of Historic Restoration, Inc., in New Orleans, having the power of eminent domain "gives you a negotiating position."[13]

Property acquisition can become complicated when landowners are difficult to identify or locate, or in cases where there are unclear titles, tax liens, or other problems. "Many urban properties have expensive liens that have to be satisfied before rehab can commence," explains David Listokin, of Rutgers University. For these "lienfields," property tax foreclosure is time-consuming and may convey a title that is weak. Bank foreclosures are similarly time-consuming, and are sometimes limited to "bulk sales." In some cases, Listokin advises, public intervention —such as city foreclosure of tax-delinquent properties—may be required.[14]

A land bank is one means of returning tax-delinquent or encumbered properties to productive use. Land banks are created to acquire and hold property for later sale or transfer to new owners, particularly to community development corporations. Typically, cities or states may endow land banks with certain powers— for example, the authority to waive liens—that enable them to fulfill their roles. In some places, cities perform the functions of a land bank without formally establishing one.

Notes

1. Speaking at a ULI Mayors' Forum on City Living, Charleston, South Carolina, June 1999.

2. Quoted in Susan Bradford, "Neighborhood Renewal," *Builder,* March 1997, 134.

3. The list of potentially applicable laws is long and includes, for example, the Clean Air Act; the Clean Water Act; the Comprehensive Environmental Response, Compensation, and Liability Act; the Endangered Species Act; the National Environmental Policy Act; the Noise Control Act; the Resources Conservation and Recovery Act; the Safe Water Drinking Act; and the Toxic Substances Control Act.

4. NAHB Economics, Mortgage Finance, and Housing Policy Division, *Producing Affordable Housing: Partnerships for Profit* (Washington, D.C.: Home Builder Press, 1999), 35.

5. Joseph A. Brown, "Saving Historic Treasures," *Urban Land,* June 2001, 28.

6. Derek Empey, "Guide to Urban Development: How to Play the Game," previously posted at http://www.multifamilyexecutive.com/Pages/MFE percent20Pages/mfelinks/mfe.currentlinks.

7. Michael A. Pagano and Ann O'M. Bowman, "Vacant Land in Cities: An Urban Resource," Survey Series (Washington, D.C.: Center on Urban and Metropolitan Policy, Brookings Institution, December 2000), 1.

8. For more information, see Anne Vernez Moudon and Michael Hubner, *Monitoring Land Supply with Geographic Information Systems* (New York: John Wiley & Sons, 2000).

9. Anne Vernez Moudon, "The Supply and Capacity of Infill and Redevelopment Lands: A Parcel-Based Geographic Information Systems Perspective" (paper, University of Washington, November 15, 2000), 6.

10. Gregg T. Logan, Todd M. Noell, and Lawrence Frank; Robert Charles Lesser & Co.; and Georgia Tech, "Mobility, Air Quality, and Development: Overcoming Barriers to Smart Growth" (draft paper written for SMARTRAQ—Strategies for Metropolitan Atlanta's Regional Transportation and Air Quality, n.d.), 5–6.

11. William H. Miller, John R. Jaeger, Gail Lissner, and Eugene W. Sunard, "Residential Resurgence," *Urban Land,* September 2000, 92–94.

12. Tara Ellman, "Infill: The Cure for Sprawl?" *Arizona Issue Analysis* 146 (August 1997): 3, 15; previously posted at http://www.goldwaterinstitute.org/ azia/146/htm.

13. Speaking at a ULI Infill Housing Symposium, Atlanta, 1998.

14. David Listokin, "Housing Rehabilitation and American Cities" (draft overview paper prepared for Housing Policy in the New Millenium, a U.S. Department of Housing and Urban Development conference, October 3, 2000).

5
Project Concept and Design

This chapter discusses general considerations that developers need to address as they create an overall project concept and decide what elements to include in a given project. ULI's *Density by Design: New Directions in Residential Development,* second edition, and *Multifamily Development Handbook* provide more specific design ideas and examples of the many types of higher-density housing products that can be built in urban infill locations.

When creating a concept and design for a market-rate urban infill housing development, developers follow many of the same principles that would apply to any housing development but take other considerations into account as well. The history, development patterns and policies, politics, and culture of the city will affect the design of the project. The project and its design must be appropriate to local economic and market conditions. The level and nature of the city's involvement in the project are other important factors because the city may have its own development agenda, which must be respected in return for financial or other support.

At the site-specific level, because infill housing is developed within a built environment, the existing physical and political landscape will constrain and

Block X, in Chicago, features contemporary exterior design, large windows, and both private and common outdoor space.

On a small lot in the heart of Santa Monica's low-rise commercial and retail district, the developer used terracing, variations in facades, and contrasting colors to set back the upper levels—a design that made it possible to achieve the density ratio of a high-rise apartment in a five-story multifamily project.

Van Tilberg, Banvard & Soderburgh Architects

partly determine not only what can be built on the site but what it will look like. Often, the characteristics and configurations of the infill sites themselves limit project design options, as considerations of density, parking, and access come into play. If the project involves the rehabilitation, adaptive use, or historic preservation of an existing structure, that structure will largely define project design. In many cases, urban infill sites have view opportunities or constraints, or are near a feature that can be exploited, such as water frontage or transit access. The design of an urban infill development may also require careful planning for a number of concerns that do not greatly affect the design of suburban projects, including noise mitigation, waste disposal, access (within the existing street pattern), and the location of utility meters.

Of course, developers of infill housing want to create housing that will appeal to the target market. Because the people who choose to live in urban locations are often drawn to unique housing types—and to interesting, or even quirky, living environments—the range of salable (or rentable) design possibilities, for both the overall project and the individual units, is typically greater than it is for suburban tract developments, where design tends to be less varied. The challenge for the designers of urban infill housing is to be realistic as well as creative.

An urban locale demands a different type of development than a suburban one. The typically higher price of urban land generally dictates a higher-density product. At the same time, because urban residents tend to own

fewer automobiles than people who live in the suburbs, they require less parking.

The Project Concept: What to Build

The first step in project design (after determining the target market) is deciding what type of project to build and determining the general parameters: size, uses, tenure type, unit types and mix, and pricing. Often, developers decide the general parameters of the project early in the planning process—perhaps even before the property is acquired—and then refine them as circumstances dictate. This section outlines some of the considerations specific to developing an overall project concept for an urban infill site.

Size

Given the diversity of potential urban infill housing developments, there are no rules governing project size. Developers interviewed for this book built projects ranging in size from six to 1,000 units, depending on the particular opportunity and their own business preferences and requirements. Monty Hoffman, president of P. N. Hoffman Construction Development, in Bethesda, Maryland, which is developing a 46-unit project in the Tenley Hill section of Washington, D.C., finds that a project of that size yields a good profit and does not compete with the high-density projects of "big-box" developers. In his opinion, 150-unit projects cannot be constructed "close to the neighborhoods where people want to live"; Hoffman also finds that larger projects are more likely to provoke resistance from neighbors and are more difficult to match to the existing historic architecture.[1]

Other developers feel that, given the difficulties, risks, and expense involved in getting urban infill projects underway, large projects are preferable because the upfront costs can be spread across more units. According to Al Neely, group senior vice president, Charles E. Smith Residential Realty, Inc., in Arlington, Virginia,[2] his firm prefers rental projects of 300 to 400 units or more because that scale makes it possible to include a variety of amenities, including on-site personnel and services.

In transitional urban neighborhoods, infill housing developments should be of sufficient size, or "critical mass," to create their own environment, and thereby signal a positive transformation of the area's physical and investment environment. Large, phased projects also assure residents, other developers, and the investment community that the city and the project developer have made a long-term commitment to revitalizing the area.

Mixed-Product Developments

A number of developers interviewed for this book hedge their market risk by including a mix of product types in their infill developments. Mixing product types in a single location has other advantages as well: it is consistent with the varied development patterns that make cities interesting, and it can make possible more creative architecture.

In developments that include both for-sale and rental components, however, the different tenure types should be physically separate (to avoid conflicts arising from their differing purposes and goals), although they can share architecturally compatible elements. In some developments, such as Old Town Village, in Alexandria, Virginia (featured in chapter 8), the for-sale townhouses and the condominium products were built by different developers.

In Site 17, a 97-unit apartment development in Seattle, a variety of materials, colors, and forms break the block-long structure into smaller components, yielding a rich visual palette that appeals to the project's young urban market.

Eduardo Calderon

Mixed-Use Projects

One aspect of urban housing that appeals to prospective residents is convenience—easy access to facilities that meet their daily needs. In some cases, infill sites may be within walking distance of shops and services. If not, depending on the size of the project, developers may want to consider including space for retail shops and/or other commercial uses within the project. How much retail to include depends on project circumstances; there is no formula. Bruce Ross, principal *emeritus* of Backen Arrigoni & Ross, Inc., in San Francisco, says that 80 percent housing, 20 percent commercial (retail and/or office) is a typical mix, though in some cases the housing component may be as little as 60 percent.

Even where neighborhood-type stores and services are available, it may be desirable to include retail space in order to create a sense of energy and provide transparency from the street into the building. Most urban infill sites exist in areas that already have a mix of uses, in which case first-floor retail can provide continuity with the surrounding environment. In addition to hedging market risk, a mix of uses creates opportunities for architectural variety and richness. Furthermore, many local jurisdictions require it, and some city zoning ordinances prohibit residential uses on the first floor. In other cases, cities may provide incentives to encourage developers to include uses that meet various neighborhood needs.

Of course, if retail spaces are included simply to enhance the marketability of a housing project, they may prove difficult to lease. For retail to succeed, the site must also be a good market location. The retail leasing strategy should be tailored to the specific project and location—but, generally speaking, convenience stores, delis and restaurants, health clubs, video rental stores, dry cleaners, barber shops and beauty salons, and banks are among the uses that are most compatible with urban infill housing developments.

Bob Silverman, chairman of the Winter Companies, in Atlanta, believes "retail is critical—and also the most difficult part of a project." Done well, it can also be a profit center. For example, the Louisiana Redfish Restaurant, located on the first floor of Towne Properties's Groton Lofts development, in Cincinnati, has proved extremely successful and generates significant rental income for the developers.

Retail tenants require foot traffic, visibility, and easy customer parking. Provision must be made for deliveries, trash pickup—and sometimes, additional ventilation or noise mitigation. Retailers will also be concerned about security and will want to ensure that their customers, vendors, and employees feel safe, particularly at night. While shopkeepers will want streets and parking lots illuminated at night, the developer must ensure that the lighting is placed where it will not disturb the project's residents.

In the case of a high-rise housing development in a densely populated area, it may be possible to attract a much-needed community-serving retail use, such as a grocery store. When the John Buck Company, of Chicago, built a high-rise apartment building in a densely populated area of downtown Evanston, Illinois, it reserved the first-floor commercial space for a Whole Foods grocery store.[3]

Balconies placed above rear-entry garages partially shelter the driveways of these townhouses and provide private outdoor space for residents.

Maureen McAvey, senior resident fellow for urban development at ULI, cautions that "mixed use is very complicated, and retail is not a panacea" in infill housing developments. Retail space in housing developments may be difficult to lease because chain stores generally have criteria for site selection that cannot be met by urban infill sites. As a result, retail tenants in infill developments are typically small local merchants who are often undercapitalized and whose leases banks are often unwilling to finance. Mixed use is also difficult to finance because lenders cannot define the exit strategy. "Our investors need to have parcels that you can sell off individually," Silverman explains. Natalie Bock, development manager of the Alexander Company, in Madison, Wisconsin, adds that in the Midwest markets where her firm operates, "It's hard to lease retail. We never underwrite income from retail. We prefer to do residential on the first floor because when we do, it leases and makes money."

Mixed use may involve uses other than retail shops and services. Incubator office space, offices, or other kinds of businesses can also be first-floor tenants. In Cincinnati, Towne Properties redeveloped the old Shillito's department store into the 97-unit Lofts at Shillito Place; Shillito Center, the first-floor commercial space, is anchored by an advertising agency and a weekly newspaper.

Within the bounds of market reality, the possibilities for mixed-use development are limited only by the imaginations of the city and the developer. For example, the Alexander Company, working as part of the Central Station Limited Partnership, redeveloped Memphis's historic Central Station to include 63 rental apartments, 28,000 square feet of retail space, an Amtrak rail station, a bus station, a police substation, and public parking.

Mixed-Income Projects

"Mixed-income housing is an important component in all neighborhoods and all communities," explains Ron Terwilliger, national managing partner of Trammell Crow Residential, in Atlanta, "because it creates diverse housing opportunities for people of different incomes,

Fugleberg Koch Architects

ages, races, and ethnicities, and it enables the city's workforce to live near places of employment."

Mixed-income housing developments may be a desirable option for infill housing sites, especially in transitional neighborhoods where the local jurisdiction requires that a portion of all housing developed be affordable to existing residents. Not-for-profit developers may choose mixed-income projects because such projects are often consistent with their missions and, at the same time, compatible with community goals. Some public programs that fund housing development, such as the Department of Housing and Urban Development's HOPE VI public housing transformation program, encourage mixed-income development. Other public funding sources include setaside requirements for affordable housing. For example, developers

Bilevel loft design can create a feeling of volume and grandeur through use of a transparent handrail, higher ceilings, and more expansive window heights.

Lorig Associates, LLC

The individual patios of Broadway Place Apartments, in Eugene, Oregon, face an interior courtyard highlighted by a large fountain.

who fund projects with tax-exempt bond monies typically must impose income restrictions on at least 20 percent of the units. In other cases, a mix of incomes may be required as a part of public/private agreement—in return for a city's provision of land, for example.

In designing mixed-income housing, the general rule is that a passerby should be unable to point out the affordable units. Even if the affordable units are smaller, or are rental apartments in a development that is largely for-sale townhouses, they should be so similar on the outside—in architectural style, design, and materials—that they are virtually indistinguishable from the market-rate homes. Inside, the affordable units typically include less luxurious features and finishes.

To attract market-rate residents, mixed-income developments must be as nice as, or nicer than, competing developments, incorporating the same careful attention to planning, community design, architectural features, and amenities that characterize a well-designed market-rate community.[4]

Redevelopment Opportunities

Some of the most exciting new infill housing being built today results from the rehabilitation, adaptive use, or historic preservation of existing buildings. The examples are much too numerous to detail, but include the transformation

of previous uses such as schools, breweries, factories, YMCAs, flour mills, dairies, office buildings, and train stations into interesting and unique living spaces. (A number of the case studies featured in chapter 8 include the redevelopment of existing structures.) While such developments pose special risks and requirements, as noted in chapter 2, they also have the potential to create the one-of-a kind, signature developments that spark civic pride, generate their own markets, and give developers the special thrill that comes from creating something uniquely valuable in their local communities.

In addition to creating urban infill housing through the reuse of existing buildings, developers can expand existing development. Especially in cities such as Portland and Seattle, where urban growth boundaries have created "densification" pressures, innovative additions to traditional developments and to other existing land uses present opportunities for infill housing development. To create the Macadam Village development, for example, three miles from downtown Portland, the developer built apartments above and behind retail strip centers. Northrup Commons, a four-story, 20-unit townhouse development a mile northwest of downtown Portland, was built in the air rights over the parking lot of a medical clinic. The first two levels of the former parking lot were used for parking for both the residents and the clinic. In other cases, the addition of more levels to existing buildings has yielded new housing units.

Project Design

Once the general parameters of a project have been established, the development of a site plan and the design of the individual buildings and units can proceed. According to Bill Kreager, managing partner of Mithun Partners, in Seattle, Washington, the design of urban infill projects must satisfy three markets: the neighbors, the planning bureaucracy, and the buyers. Kreager notes that neighborhood concerns center on how the project fits in with its surroundings; city planners "labor under a healthy fear of elected officials and the massed anger of the public"; and buyers want quality housing.[5] As with any development, the design of an urban infill housing project must take into account these and numerous other considerations, such as the need to sustain financial feasibility and to address the opportunities and constraints of the project's location and site.

Donald Carter, managing principal of UDA Architects, in Pittsburgh, has outlined several general principles his firm has developed for designing housing projects in infill settings:

- First and most important, involve the existing residents, through focus groups and neighborhood meetings, to determine their concerns and aspirations;
- Study the context, including neighborhood history and surrounding development;
- Focus on the street—for example, by using porches and uniform setbacks;
- Provide linkages to other neighborhoods and city amenities;
- Combine infill with restoration of existing housing;
- Provide a variety of housing choices;

- Develop a pattern book to ensure that developers and builders conform to design guidelines;
- Construct or enhance amenities, such as landscaping, parks, recreation centers, and neighborhood stores and services.

Kreager advises developers to create a context inventory and create a focal point for the project, such as a courtyard, fountain, or park. He also cautions that to avoid the need to retrofit later, it is important to plan early in the design process for details such as waste storage and pickup, and the location of utility meters, utility holes, and fire hydrants.[6]

Because each urban infill development is unique, design must be individualized for each project, which makes infill developments more costly and risky than more standardized real estate products. As Terry Eakin, chairman of Eakin/Youngentob Associates, Inc., of Arlington, Virginia, notes, "We spend a lot of time going through an elaborate design process; these are not cookie-cutter projects."

At the same time, experience shows that there are general guidelines developers can follow. As discussed in chapter 6, many cities have established design guidelines for urban infill housing developments that ensure harmony with the neighborhood context; such guidelines address issues such as setbacks, modulation of facades, street-level uses, and building materials. The sections that follow discuss a number of design issues specific to creating an urban infill housing project.

Fitting in with the Context

Because infill developments are created within an established environment, they must respect both the physical character of surrounding neighborhoods and the existing residents' desires and goals. According to Ross, communities are aggregates of buildings; in the best communities, all the buildings are well-behaved and respect the prevailing style and character of their neighbors. Good infill projects, he explains, "add to the total community aesthetic rather than shout out their own presence." Using similar scale, massing, and building forms; materials and textures; fenestration;

Some urban residential developments include security features such as fences. Gates provide access to individual units.

colors; and architectural details helps to reinforce the existing neighborhood character. Scott Shimberg, executive vice president and co-owner of Hyde Park Builders, Inc., in Tampa, Florida, says that he knows his project designs are successful when people tell him the homes fit in so well that they look as if they have always been there.

Though urban infill developments must be good neighbors and fit in well with their surroundings, the project design should be distinctive enough to get the market's attention and establish the project's unique identity. As a rule, when developing within an urban setting, build-

Reserve at Park Central, developed in Dallas by Trammell Crow Residential, contains four different product types, two separate garage structures, and a centrally located facility with a swimming pool, recreation center, and spa.

ings should shape the street. Careful building placement, along with well-designed courtyards, variegated structures and massing, and a network of open spaces, can create interesting urban places while respecting local context.

In urban developments, public and private spaces interface at the street level. The design of streets and parking should focus on the pedestrian, deemphasizing (though of course still accommodating) the automobile. The streetscape can be given added visual interest and pedestrian appeal through elements such as paving enhancements; street trees and other landscaping; benches; and lighting.

If the context and site will allow, infill housing can be designed with parking or retail on the street level and housing above. When residences are placed above commercial uses or parking, developers need to ensure that living spaces are adequately protected from odors, noise, and other externalities that may emanate from the nonresidential uses. When properly designed, such an arrangement can provide the second-story residents with even more privacy and quiet than they would enjoy if they lived on the first floor of an all-residential development. Townhouses or rowhouses are typically at grade level, with individual garages and entrances from the street or a rear alley.

In larger projects, a mixture of unit types—some at street level; some above retail or parking, perhaps with retail on a corner; and some accessible through a *porte cochère* entry—can be used to break up a large expanse of building along the street. A high-density project can be visually softened if it is designed as a series of connected components, with variations in massing, rather than as a large box. In Paseo Plaza, in San Jose, projecting stoops and planter boxes, as well as deeply inset townhouse entries, are used to articulate the street-level facade; on the upper stories, the recessed balconies of the condominium flats break up the plane of the building and create a pattern that evokes the appearance of a series of individual structures.

Where there are no separations or setbacks to provide visual variety and interest, the use of different kinds of construction materials and a palette of colors, and the addition of other kinds of architectural details (varied rooflines, distinctive window and entrance features, and corbeling) can enliven the design. Creative landscaping and streetscape design can also help produce a more pleasing appearance. Nonetheless, cautions Settle Dockery, vice president of York Properties, Inc., in Raleigh, North Carolina, "If you have a bad design, the best details can't save it."

Density

The density of an urban infill development will be determined by a number of factors, including the price of the land, the developer's perception of the local market's preferences and willingness to pay, the project's compatibility with surrounding land uses, the opinions of the neighboring community, and decisions about how to accommodate on-site parking. As a rule, urban housing developments are denser than those in the suburbs, and people who choose city living appear to be comfortable with that. Although consumer preferences vary with the particular market, David Mayhood, president of the Mayhood Company, in McLean, Virginia, notes that "the developer tends to be more concerned about density than the consumer."

The project's density should be consistent with that of surrounding land uses—even if, as is true in many cases, the site's zoning will allow greater density than good design (or market demand) would dictate for the site. As noted earlier, successful infill housing developments weave seamlessly into the neighborhood fabric. "Remember," cautions Ross, "allowable density is a limit, not a prescription." For example, Jason Runnels, executive vice president and principal of Phoenix Property Company (PPC), in Dallas, notes that his firm designed the Firestone Upper West Side project to be less dense than other new infill housing developments being built in downtown Fort Worth so that it would fit in well with its immediate surroundings. Land price was also a factor. "We were able to get a lot of land at a fairly low basis," he explains, "which made it possible for us to create the kind of project we wanted—one that had a neighborhood feel and identity."

Especially where high-density housing development is allowed by right, parking may prove to be the most telling determinant. In most cases, there's a natural fit between the number of units and the accommodation of parking: "How many cars we can get in the basement tells us how many units we can build," Ross explains. His firm does a density analysis, which involves trying different parking scenarios to see what works: "If we do it this way, we will have a two-level garage; if that way, it will need a three-level garage, which means we will be at the water table or have to go through bedrock and it won't work."

Security

Developers interviewed for this book felt that, on the whole, people who choose to live in urban settings are less concerned about security than suburban buyers. Nonetheless, to ensure that security does not become an issue, most incorporate some security features into their urban infill housing developments.

There is a tension between the goals of making an infill development distinct and secure and integrating it into the existing neighborhood. Arranging the homes so that they face a secured interior courtyard is one way to make a development secure. Kreager cautions, however, that "a new project that turns its back on existing neighbors with unattractive rear elevations and fences is an unwelcome neighbor."

High ceilings, exposed ductwork, and large windows offering views of the Cleveland skyline all add to the appeal of Bridgeview Apartments.

Wrought-iron gates separating the street from a project's interior courtyards can provide residents with security while maintaining some visual access for passersby.

A more typical configuration, in which the building facades are brought to the sidewalk, creates not only an urban streetscape, but, in effect, a limited-access "security fence" of building walls around the perimeter of the project. In the case of condominiums and apartments that have this configuration, residents' access is typically limited to a few doors and driveways, which can be secured with keys and electronic devices.

Where buildings are set back from the street, the developer needs to decide whether to install security perimeter fencing and entry gates. Although the gating of pedestrian and vehicular access points is fairly standard, the decision to gate the entire development is an individual one. In Eakin's opinion, "Gating creates a negative edge." His firm prefers to achieve a secure environment through exterior lighting, visible entrances, secured parking, and a watchful security staff.

In the Firestone Upper West Side apartments, residents are issued "clickers" that, when triggered, send out an audible alarm and call a security company, identifying both the person and his or her location. Other, more commonly used forms of security include security guards, surveillance cameras, card access systems for elevators and lobbies, community policing and crime-watch programs, the enclosure of first-floor balconies, and local police patrolling on foot, bicycle, or horseback.

Parking

Parking requirements are dictated by both market expectations and the local jurisdiction's requirements. Some cities require fewer than one space per unit, especially if the development is near public transportation, and others one per bedroom. Parking standards sometimes differ even within a city. Daniel Hunt, a partner in HuntGregory LLC, in Minneapolis,[7] explains that in Minneapolis, the required parking ratio depends on the project's price point.

Beyond legal requirements, wise developers want to satisfy the demands of their market: people who select homes in urban infill housing developments do not want to wrestle with the inconveniences of urban life. "Consumer research shows that many suburbanites identify culturally with cities but are frustrated by the daily problems of living at higher densities, such as having to fight for a parking space. Developers of urban infill housing seeking to expand their market to suburbanites should make creative provisions for automobiles."[8] The accompanying feature box illustrates a creative approach to providing parking for a historic preservation project on a tight urban site in Washington, D.C.

Summit Grand Parc: Historic Restoration and State-of-the-Art Parking Innovation

When Charlotte, North Carolina–based Summit Properties, Inc.,[1] purchased the United Mineworkers' Building, on McPherson Square, in Washington, D.C., the company saw an opportunity to offer luxury residences in a market where the idea of "downtown living" was experiencing a renaissance—and where supply was limited.

Originally built in 1912 as the University Club, the property offered outstanding features for residential use, including wood-paneled rooms, ornate moldings, high ceilings, and parquet floors. When it opens as Summit Grand Parc in spring 2002, the project will feature 105 luxury apartments located in the historic building and in the adjacent new tower, as well as 15,000 square feet of Class A office space. To address historic preservation requirements, preservation architects Martinez & Johnson designed the tower so that both its massing and its residential character would distinguish it from the historic structure and from the surrounding office buildings.

This rare opportunity for a niche residential development in the central business district arose because the existing building's small floor plates and tight adjacent parcel did not offer the expansion space necessary to attract office developers. Additional restrictions against rooftop additions further limited the floor/area ratio. Subsidies, in the form of federal historic preservation tax credits and D.C. transferable development rights, allowed this real estate investment trust, which develops multifamily housing, to compete for a prime downtown site two blocks from the White House—but finding a solution to parking required a bold step: pioneering an automated parking system in the market.

Although the historic building was exempt from current parking requirements, satisfying market demand for parking in a downtown residential project required a minimum parking ratio of 60 percent. The tight site prohibited a conventional garage. Many options were explored without success, including full valet service, a sharing arrangement with neighboring buildings, and several automated systems.

The developer opted for the pioneering Wohr Parking System, a racking system developed in Germany and used extensively in Europe and Asia. The system allowed Summit Properties to

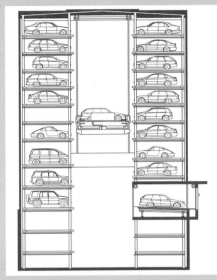

A typical storage-retrieval unit used in the SpaceSaver Parking Systems Multiparker 700 Series. Patrons vacate their locked cars and leave the entry area, after which the entry doors close, and the system takes the car into the below-grade vault and places it in its assigned rack.

secure 74 spaces—a 70 percent ratio. The racks, which will be installed in a four-story vault space under the new apartment tower, maximize the number of cars that can be stacked in the small floor area available. Two elevators and a horizontal transporter allow for quick access to the parking vault. Residents enter the garage, drive into the elevator parking bay, step out, and park their cars automatically, using a magnetic key-card system. When retrieved, the cars are turned for easy exit from the garage. Electronic display boards in the garage and in the building's Terrace Room will allow residents to monitor their retrieval requests in comfort. Average delivery time is projected to be four minutes, faster than most valet operations in the area. ■

Source: Adrienne Teleki, development manager, Summit Properties, Inc., Bethesda, Maryland.

Note

1. NYSE: SMT.

Summit Grand Parc.

In projects where buildings front the sidewalk's edge, parking is typically provided underground or within interior portions of the block, either on the surface or in structures. For both security and privacy, amenities such as courtyards and swimming pools are also often placed within the protective wrap of perimeter buildings. In some cases, amenities may be placed on the top deck of a parking structure.

In municipalities that permit shared parking arrangements, developers may negotiate parking for urban housing developments at large nearby facilities, such as hospitals or municipal lots that have excess capacity.[9] For example, Jack Buxell, chief executive officer of J. Buxell Architecture, Ltd., in Minneapolis,[10] the developer of the LaSalle project, an adaptive use of an old YMCA building in downtown Minneapolis, found that tenants in only 10 percent of the 125 units owned cars. The project included no parking, but the developer negotiated with the city to lease spaces in a municipal lot for a monthly rate, and negotiated with a nearby office tower for night parking.

Where structured parking is required because of land costs or the size of the site, costs can soar, and city funding may be needed to make the project feasible. In the Paseo Plaza development, for example, the city redevelopment agency funded the cost of structured parking. At the Gramercy on Garfield development, in Cincinnati, the city owns and operates the garage, which serves both project residents and the public. In San Antonio, to attract development to targeted areas, the city used long-term financing to build parking structures.

Privacy

When developing in cities, where there are people on the streets and living or working in adjacent buildings, it is important to design buildings to ensure residents' privacy. As noted earlier, one way to create transparency without sacrificing residents' privacy is to locate retail or office uses on the street level, with housing units above. Placing common open space, such as courtyards, gardens, and recreational facilities, within an interior area or plaza creates a private gathering place. Units overlooking interior open space enjoy both views and privacy, and command premium rents or prices.

Homes that must be located on street level along the buildings' perimeter can be designed as rowhouses or townhouses, with garages on the first level and living space above. If the living space is at street level, some developers build brick-walled courtyard entryways that are typically entered through a locked door, provide a small private open space, shield residents from the view of passersby, and create an extra layer of security. To mitigate noise, street-level walls typically include extra insulation, and street-level windows have multipane glass.

Amenities and Public Spaces

As with other types of projects, developers of infill housing typically select amenities for a specific project by surveying competitive projects and undertaking focus groups with prospective consumers. Generally speaking, amenities typical of urban infill projects include, in addition to security features, garage parking; shops and services (which were discussed earlier); health clubs or fitness facilities, which may be open to the public as well as to residents; gathering spaces, such as clubrooms and outdoor courtyards or rooftop gardens, sometimes with swimming pools or spas; concierge services; high-speed Internet access; laundry and dry cleaning facilities or pickup services; and programmed social activities.

Location, target market, and price point are the key determining factors in the selection of amenities. In many locations, the city itself is a sufficient amenity. In lower Manhattan, amenities typically include concierge services, on-site dry cleaning, free health clubs, and party rooms—"to compensate for the fact that lower Manhattan lacks the off-site neighborhood amenities that are commonly available to developments in the competing Upper East Side and Upper West Side real estate markets."[11] Neely, who operates largely at the high end of the market (predominantly high-rise, high-end rental products in Boston, Chicago, Washington, D.C., and southeast Florida), describes his firm's offerings as "an amenity package on

In the Firestone Upper West Side apartments, PPC created a community center in the restored Firestone Building, which had formerly been an open-air tire company and garage. The glass-walled, high-ceilinged space fronting the street was the perfect setting for a half-court basketball gymnasium; an array of state-of-the-art fitness equipment was installed on the floor above, overlooking the action on the court. The community center also includes a living room–style television lounge with a pool table, bar, and kitchen; and a business center with two conference rooms, one of which contains computers, high-speed Internet access, and a printer, fax machine, and copier.

Courtyard areas should be designed to encourage residents to socialize; in addition to attractive landscaping and tables and chairs, they often include swimming pools and spas. Some also provide features such as barbecue grills, fountains, artwork, and outdoor fireplaces.

Project amenities are commonly clustered in a private, secure area. Neely says that his firm is now giving more thought to how the components of the amenity package relate. In One Superior Place, an 800-unit project in Chicago, amenities occupy the entire seventh floor, including a walkout to the sun porch that sits atop the roof of the parking lot. "We want to create a resortlike atmosphere and promote socializing," he explains. "We also think about how the amenities relate to the leasing experience, and create a 'marketing trail' for prospective tenants."

The public realm immediately surrounding an urban infill housing development creates the project's setting and contributes to its overall image. This area may need to be upgraded or redesigned to reflect the site's new use, particularly through improvements in streets and sidewalks, crosswalks and access points, street furniture, covered transit stops, landscaping, and lighting. Such improvements are typically undertaken by, or at least funded by, the city, and are designed to be consistent with both the project's needs and the surrounding context. For aesthetic reasons and to strengthen community relations, developers should make an effort to save existing trees where possible.

Placing the first floor of living space one level above the street and adding partial privacy walls helps to minimize noise and visual intrusion.

steroids." The package typically includes a 24-hour front desk, 12- to 16-hour concierge service, a top-notch health club, a business center, and a cyber-café. "We like to be near a luxury hotel," he adds, "where we can negotiate a deal regarding the use of room service."

The latest entry into the high-amenity infill housing category is Millennium Partners, which is building luxury condominium developments with—and in—luxury hotel settings: the idea is that each use will benefit the other. Like the hotel guests, condominium residents have access to all the hotel's luxurious facilities, amenities, and services. The hotel benefits from the additional vitality and from increased income for fee-based services. In Washington, D.C., adjacent to Georgetown, the company is building the Residences at the Ritz-Carlton in the West End, which will include 162 residences, a 300-room Ritz Carlton Hotel, and a 100,000-square-foot sports club, as well as retail uses.[12]

Projects that target young people will want to include amenities that catch their attention.

Unit Design

Depending on various location-specific factors, new or redeveloped urban infill housing may take the form of small, single-family homes; rowhouses or townhouses; lofts; flats above retail or townhouses; or low-rise or high-rise condominiums or apartments. Some projects, like Post Uptown Square, may also include some "corporate apartments"—short-term furnished rental units. As evidenced by the case studies in chapter 8, different product types are often mixed with one another or with commercial uses in innovative ways to produce a unique urban housing form.

To offer both the singularity and variety valued by the urban market, some infill developers create numerous floor plan options, even within a single product type or building. For example, the LaSalle project, in downtown Minneapolis, which has 24 different floor plans for its 125 units, was fully leased 30 days after completion. Central Station, a 63-unit adaptive use project, features more than 30 floor plans. Offering numerous choices makes possible a broad range of prices, creates urgency to buy (because there is a limited number of each type), and enables buyers to select a more "personalized" unit. On the other hand, Mayhood notes that including many different unit types in a single development is expensive for developers, particularly if the project is small; for that reason, some prefer to offer a small number of unit designs.

To attract tenants and command higher rents than those for similar suburban products, urban housing must be competitive in terms of size, finishes, and amenities. "Suburbanites now are coming back to town in unison, in search of everything they are leaving behind except the work that goes with it. They want the same roominess in their homes and the same frills they have grown accustomed to; in fact, many want even more. . . . They demand state-of-the-art appliances, bath fixtures, and window treatments; walk-in closets; and high-tech wiring. They want to be pampered with concierge services, fitness facilities within walking distance, panoramic views, private entrances, garages, controlled access, security, and plenty of nearby recreational opportunities."[13]

Of course, not all suburbanites can afford the roominess they desire. One of the challenges for infill developers, according to Mayhood, is "designing a product for consumers who are accustomed to 40 percent more space." As a result, he cautions, "You have to be very sensitive to the proper use of space and design each room so that it can be used for multiple functions."

As noted earlier, parking, security, and privacy are especially important considerations in urban housing design. Ensuring adequate light is another. In dense developments in urban settings, placing windows where they provide light without compromising the residents' or neighbors' privacy can be challenging. As a rule, to counterbalance the density of urban living, developers should also try to incorporate some private open space into unit plans—patios or small courtyards in the case of rowhouses or townhouses, balconies in the case of condominiums or apartments. "Because of the light," Neely advises, "put balconies on the south side of the building, even if it makes the building asymmetrical."

Lofts

A unique, cutting-edge urban form, and one of the hottest new project types in urban housing developments, is the loft—a product for which there is no suburban equivalent. Mayhood defines lofts as "space, height, and light." At one time, lofts were created from old industrial space for artists who wanted to combine living and working space. Reflecting their roots, loft units typically have open ductwork on the ceilings; few room partitions; and minimally finished, industrial-style walls and floors. Lofts' open spaces and large walls are unconventional and permit residents' freedom of expression, which is a major selling point.

According to Robert Koch, president of Fugleberg Koch Architects, in Winter Park, Florida, lofts are especially popular with the D (for "digital") generation—kids "who were brought up with computers as a second language, are self-centered, independent, live a social, active lifestyle, work long, nontraditional hours, and come and go at unconventional times." This generation likes lofts, Koch explains, because lofts—with their high ceilings, undraped windows, and partial room dividers —"represent an extension of the open, unrestricted, uncensored lifestyle they prefer."

Lofts are so "cool" that well-conceived loft projects create their own markets: people will buy the product rather than the environment. Lofts appeal not only to urban pioneers but to a broad urban market that cuts across age, gender, income, and lifestyle. According to Mayhood, "Loft production in a pioneering area can overcome the environment." In many areas, the market for lofts appears to be deeper than many developers anticipated. Says Atlanta developer Michael Loia, "We are stunned by the market acceptance of lofts." In cities across the country, developers are scrambling to fill the demand.

Because lofts appeal to such a broad market, developers can construct a loft project to meet the demands of a targeted market segment. "Hard" lofts have cement floors and minimal, industrial-style finishes, and tend to appeal to young singles and couples. "Soft" lofts—often created through new construction rather than through rehabilitation or adaptive use—appeal more to hip, affluent, empty nesters and have luxury finishes and features such as hardwood floors, stone fireplaces, granite countertops, and top-of-the-line appliances.

Silverman has been very successful in envisioning and creating successful loft developments from previous uses such as schools and factories. His list of the features that make loft developments "cool" includes

- High ceilings, large windows, volume spaces, and open spaces;
- Great places to hang art or display sculpture;
- Wood floors (if possible), or stained concrete;
- Interior brick;
- A "*Seinfeld* kitchen" (one that is open to the living room);
- In old warehouse buildings, circular columns with flared capitals;
- Exposed ductwork and painted pipes;
- In an adaptive use, heavy timber;
- "Neat" features in bathrooms;

- Stainless steel in the kitchen—"if we can afford it."

David Chase, principal of Thrush Development, in Chicago, points out that an important issue in transforming old industrial buildings into lofts is finding a way to get light and ventilation into the interior core. One solution, according to Chase, is to use the center core for storage space rather than living space; another is to build interior courtyards or skylit corridors.

Koch observes that volume for loft apartments can often be carved out from attic space, using the building's sloping windows to define the ceiling and skylights to admit natural light. In some cases, creating an attic loft can enable developers to "steal volume from the structure while adding another floor."

According to Koch, when building a for-sale loft product, developers typically include more variety in floor plans—both because loft buyers like to customize their units, and as a means of creating urgency by offering a very limited supply of any one product. For rental loft

In the Cypress Hills development, the use of river rock, wrought iron, and woodwork recalls the classic Craftsman-style architecture of San Diego.

Van Tilberg, Banvard & Soderburgh Architects

Design that pulls the standard elements of a house inward and upward reduces land use by one-half or more, as shown by these three-story homes in an urban infill project on the beach in Santa Monica, California.

properties, Koch explains, developers generally produce less variety.

In cities where loft development has been successful, few well-located properties suitable for loft conversion remain, and some developers are using new construction to meet the demand. New loft construction gives developers the freedom to create what they feel are the most desirable aspects of the loft product. "We wanted Buckhead Village Lofts to be *avant-garde,* cool, and hip, but a place where you could park your BMW," explains Loia. Because it was new construction, he adds, "We could incorporate quality construction, energy efficiency, and great finishes. And, we could put parking under the building."

Unit Size

Most of the developers interviewed for this book indicated that their buyers or renters tend to prefer large units. To keep rents low, Bortz built Gramercy on Garfield, the first phase of a multiphase project, with 129 of the 148 units as studios and one-bedroom apartments. He found, however, that the market actually wanted more room and was willing to pay for it, so in the next phase, Greenwich on the Park, he increased the proportion of two-bedroom units to 60 percent.

Urban infill developers are finding that empty nesters, in particular, like larger units. Loia learned from his experience with Buckhead Village Lofts that empty nesters from the suburbs tended to buy several units and com-

bine them. As a result, when he built Matheson Exchange Lofts, his second new-construction loft development, he reserved the top three of 13 floors as penthouse floors. On these floors, units can be customized and buyers can take as much square footage as they want. The ten floors below feature standard floor plans with few partitions.

Unit Features

Unless the unit is a loft, design considerations will be similar to those for other projects targeted to singles and childless couples.

Opinion is mixed regarding the level of luxury needed to attract buyers or tenants to urban infill housing developments. Some developers feel that the product should be more than competitive with suburban alternatives, and include high-end finishes and amenities as standard. Others, who work in more established markets or tailor their products to a less affluent market segment, offer a basic package of finishes with opportunities to upgrade. As with other aspects of design and development, developers must know their market.

Based on what his firm has learned about design and features in developing high-end rental products, Neely offers the following recommendations for unit design:

- Offer a diverse mix of units;
- Include efficiency units, which are the most costly to develop but yield the highest per-square-foot rates;
- Include washer-dryers, especially side by side;
- Design foyer space to create a sense of arrival;
- Try to achieve a minimum height clearance of 8 feet 4 inches, preferably 9 feet;
- Use stone or Corian countertops rather than laminate;
- Include a gas range when possible—even though "People don't cook";
- Use trim and moldings consistent with local style (e.g., a contemporary design in Chicago, traditional in Washington, D.C.);
- Install deep, oversize (at least 5½ feet long) bathtubs;
- Include walk-in as well as reach-in closets —preferably both;

- Try to move away from the standard "white box": introduce some variety, such as an angled vanity wall in the bathroom or a rounded wall in the living room;
- Make the garage safe, well-lit, clean, and easily accessible;
- In cold-weather areas, include fireplaces in 30 percent of the units; these must be planned from the outset or they will create problems with construction requirements and unit designs;
- Design two-bedroom units as split master suites;
- Build a small piece of the market for empty nesters, preferably on the top of the building;
- Create large, comfortable lobbies decorated with art.

The Design Process

Two aspects of the design process have special relevance for urban infill housing development: one is the desirability, where feasible, of involving neighborhood residents in planning the project design; the other is the need to maintain control of the design process in order to avoid cost overruns that could damage the project's financial feasibility.

As explained in chapter 7, involving community residents in at least some aspects of project design can help build needed community support for the project and strengthen the developer's reputation with both the immediate and larger community. Because current residents understand local history and development needs —and may well buy (or rent) some of the project's units—community input may help to create a more marketable product.

Most developers interviewed for this book emphasized the importance of controlling the design process. Bortz, for example, says that his firm's designs have been successful in part because "We are confident of our knowledge of the market and give clear direction to the architect. We do not let the architect run the job." The Alexander Company works with its own experienced in-house design team, which helps manage construction risk and makes the firm more competitive. As Bock explains, "Third-party architects charge 6 percent of construction costs, plus change-of-scope fees. Our design staff understands the kind of projects we do and is accustomed to working with state historic preservation organizations and the federal government. They design buildings we can afford to build and calculate a guaranteed design fee. If we have to redesign many times, we'll do it. We manage the process."

Notes

1. Buzz McClain, "Residential Developer Discovered in DC—Species Survives!" *Regardie's Power,* May-June 2000, 59.

2. Speaking at ULI's Spring Council Forum, Minneapolis, May 2001.

3. Jane Adler, "Everyone Goes Downtown," *Journal of Property Management,* May/June 1999, 80.

4. For more information on mixed-income housing, see Diane R. Suchman with Margaret B. Sowell, "Mixed-Income Housing," in *Developing Infill Housing in Inner-City Neighborhoods* (Washington, D.C.: ULI, 1997). Current information on mixed-income housing produced through HUD's HOPE VI program is available on HUD's Web site, http://www.hud.gov.

5. William H. Kreager, "Infill Housing Design: Winning Over Neighbors, Public Officials, and Buyers," *NAHB Smart Growth Resources,* http://www.nahb.net/growth_issues/infill/infill_design.html, 1 (members-only site).

6. William H. Kreager, "Developing Infill Housing," *Land Development,* winter 1996, 10–12.

7. Speaking at ULI's Spring Council Forum, Minneapolis, May 2001.

8. Karen A. Danielsen, Robert E. Lang, and William Fulton, "What Does Smart Growth Mean for Housing?" *Housing Facts & Findings* 1, no. 3 (fall 1999); previously available at http://www.fanniemaefoundation.org/research/facts/fa99s1.html.

9. Adler, "Everyone Goes Downtown," 80.

10. Speaking at ULI's Spring Council Forum, Minneapolis, May 2001.

11. Lawrence O. Houstoun Jr., "Urban Awakening," *Urban Land,* October 1998, 35.

12. David C. Dozier, "Room with a View," *Urban Land,* November/December 1999, 55.

13. Ibid.

6

The Role of Public Sector Partners

Successful urban infill housing developments frequently require an active partnership between developers and local governments.[1] In fact, says Art Lomenick, president of Workplace Urban Solutions, in Dallas, "The city's attitude and its understanding of what it takes to do a infill project successfully are key to a project's success." Though public policy cannot create demand for urban infill housing, it can "help accelerate potential into action—by educating, providing incentives, and removing regulatory obstacles."[2]

Because each urban infill development and the challenges it poses are unique, the kinds of public participation required will differ for each project. With this in mind, local governments, through their various agencies and designees, can encourage urban infill housing through combinations of the wide variety of resources that they control. These resources include

- Leadership;
- The power to shape the public domain;
- Planning and coordination;
- Regulation of land use;
- Site assembly, acquisition, and preparation;

Memphis is redeveloping its downtown by following the draw of the Mississippi River—and by building housing first.

71

©Tony Glasgow

Historic Renovation, Inc., converted an 1882 New Orleans cotton mill into 249 rental apartments and 18 condominium units organized around a landscaped interior courtyard.

- Infrastructure and public services;
- Tax policy;
- Information;
- Financing incentives for developers and buyers;
- Advocacy.

Furthermore, by facilitating housing that is affordable to moderate-income working households as well to the rich and the poor, local governments can make their cities home to a more economically diverse population.

At the same time, local governments should be aware that some of their actions and regulations may have unintended negative effects on the feasibility of urban infill housing development: such actions might include, for example, certain transit policy decisions, independent scheduling of public works projects, the imposition of development fees, and the assignment of priority to uses that produce city revenue; extreme sensitivity to community objections may be another influential factor.

Maureen McAvey, senior resident fellow for urban development at ULI, cautions developers, "If you're going to partner with the public sector, you need a true partner. The developer needs to know that it will take longer, cost more, and the public sector will be in your face, in your books, all the time. The public entity must advocate for the project, and mitigate political risk. It needs to understand the criteria for success—what the developer needs to achieve their mutual goals."[3]

The accompanying feature box summarizes the ways in which some cities that are participating in the Building Homes in America's Cities program are encouraging infill housing. The program was created jointly by the Department of Housing and Urban Development (HUD), the National Association of Home Builders, and the U.S. Conference of Mayors.

Leadership and Vision

Effective change can be accomplished only through the vision and leadership of a mayor who makes housing a priority and brings together city government and key downtown stakeholders to create a positive, proactive housing policy that will encourage downtown housing development. As Michael Jones, executive director of the Greater St. Louis Regional Empowerment Zones, observes,[4] unless the city's housing policy is based on a vision, "You respond to the projects that walk in the door. If it's a good project, you get a good project. If it's a bad project, you get a bad project."

The mayor's leadership must be communicated into action by city departments. For example, after Denver's mayor worked with the Denver Downtown Partnership (an association of business leaders) to make housing the city's priority, he organized city resources to facilitate urban housing development. In Pittsburgh, the mayor made a policy decision to encourage investment in Pittsburgh's poor urban neighborhoods; he then appointed himself chairman of the board of the housing authority, an institution that he believed to be in need of fundamental changes.

Building Homes in America's Cities: A Progress Report

A dozen cities pursuing development of market-rate, in-city homes have invented imaginative, effective programs that demonstrate the feasibility and benefits of building new homes in urban environments. An October 2000 progress report on the Building Homes in America's Cities initiative, launched in 1999 by the U.S. Department of Housing and Urban Development (HUD), the National Association of Home Builders, and the U.S. Conference of Mayors, describes a broad array of local incentives for in-city homebuilding.[1] The programs and activities undertaken by the dozen cities whose programs are profiled here can be roughly categorized into seven types of incentives:[2]

1. *City assemblage and cost write-downs of housing sites:* This strategy focuses on seizing tax-delinquent properties, preferably clustered, and reselling them at very low cost;
2. *City assistance in development financing and tax reductions:* Often using tax increment financing (TIF) and tax abatements, this strategy may also incorporate location-efficient mortgages (offered by HUD to account for transportation alternatives), first-time homebuyer mortgages, and low-cost renovation loans;
3. *City reduction of infrastructure costs for new housing:* Cities using these programs may reimburse developers for off-site utility costs, waive impact fees, or use sales tax allocations for infrastructure improvements;
4. *Mayoral "summits" and housing agency reorganizations:* This strategy requires a highly proactive government and mayor, and involves forums between city government and the development community identifying key means by which the development process can be simplified;
5. *Education and information campaigns:* Using tools such as the Internet, residential market studies, and tours of homes, these programs are aimed at informing the greater pub-

lic about homes and neighborhoods where redevelopment is targeted;
6. *Regulatory relief:* Streamlining or expediting the zoning and permitting processes through various means;
7. *Neighborhood conservation programs that create a positive development climate.*

The first major section of this feature box describes each city's programs and lists best practices engaged in by a number of cities. The second major section lists incentive programs in each of the seven categories described above.

Many programs offer multiple incentives and assistance. In addition, program categories build on longstanding experience; thus, the *types* of incentives are not as new as the specific *applications* of these ideas by individual communities. Furthermore, these programs usually operate in tandem with or as part of broader, ongoing city housing and neighborhood conservation programs, including HUD housing assistance programs. City housing programs also have taken full advantage of low-income housing and historic preservation tax credits to attract private-market housing investments in these areas. In addition, HUD regional and local staffs and Community Builders have helped identify potential funding opportunities and shaped program objectives.

The experiences of these cities so far have demonstrated the value of certain approaches, summarized as follows:

- Nurturing partnerships among the public, nonprofit, and private actors in the development process;
- Recycling of tax-delinquent, abandoned, and surplus properties;
- Targeting rebuilding efforts in neighborhoods where developable sites can be made quickly available, locational advantages are strong, and resident cooperation and support are forthcoming;
- Expecting the need for public infrastructure investments;
- Responding to the gentrification issue through inclusion of affordable

housing units and/or setasides for neighborhood residents.

Summary of Pilot City Programs

Chicago

HomeStart program finances market-rate housing development through developer request for proposals (RFP) process.

New Homes for Chicago provides home-construction subsidies for moderate-income families.

New Homes for Chicago/ Condominium Rehabilitation focuses "New Homes" subsidies on housing rehabilitation.

City Lots program provides city-owned land and noncash subsidies.

Note: Above programs benefit from city recycling of tax-delinquent, abandoned, and surplus properties.

TIF for Housing provides gap financing and infrastructure improvements.

TIF Neighborhood Investment provides grants for improving owner-occupied homes.

Building Permit Self-Certification authorized for new construction based on approved prototype designs.

Houston

Mayor-Led Homeownership Campaign in collaboration with homebuilders to stimulate in-city housing construction.

Neighborhoods to Standard program targets selected neighborhoods for improved infrastructure and city services.

Builders Association White Paper recommends actions to remove obstacles to in-city housing construction.

Tax Increment Reinvestment Zones reimburse developers for improvements to city-owned utilities.

Housing Manager Appointed to oversee implementation of homeownership initiative.

continued on next page

Building Homes in America's Cities: A Progress Report (continued)

Land Bank of Tax-Delinquent Properties to be managed by newly created redevelopment authority.

Reimbursement for Developer-Provided Infrastructure similar to reimbursements available in suburban jurisdictions.

Model Homes Park to showcase in-city homes and offer homeownership information.

City Parade of Homes similar to annual suburban event.

Third-Party Building Inspectors to expedite housing construction.

Cincinnati

Cincinnati Homeownership Partnership created by mayor to market city neighborhoods as desirable housing locations; sponsors Web site and published a neighborhood guidebook.

Real Estate Ambassador training program for real estate agents about in-city housing opportunities.

Homeownership and Neighborhood Revitalization focuses redevelopment and rehabilitation activities on selected neighborhoods.

Homesteading program recycles vacant or deteriorated properties through annual lottery.

CitiRAMA city/builder annual program to develop new homes for sale.

Housing Round Investments through developer RFPs.

Homeowner Counseling for new homeowners.

Low-Cost Renovation Loans, including repair guidance.

Freddie Mac Alliance arranges flexible mortgages for first-time homebuyers.

Sacramento

City Housing Strategy (1991) provided 65 recommendations for expanding in-city home construction.

City/County Redevelopment Agency assists developers in building in-city housing.

Boarded and Vacant Homes program recycles dilapidated housing for rehabilitation.

Painted Ladies Home Improvement Program provides low-interest financing for improving historic homes.

Capital Mall housing development on state surplus land in this special district.

San Antonio

Community Revitalization Action Group formed by mayor and council to initiate housing and other efforts.

Incentive Tool Kit for core area, including impact-fee waivers, tax abatements, expedited permitting, one-stop permitting.

Affordable Showcase of Homes similar to upscale showcases elsewhere in the city.

Tax Increment Reinvestment Zones to reimburse homebuilders for infrastructure improvements.

HOPE VI project through city/homebuilders collaboration.

Citywide Reconstruction Program provides city-funded low-cost loans for rebuilding deteriorated homes.

Neighborhood Sweeps targets city cleanup and improvement efforts to selected neighborhoods.

Affordable Housing Task Force of city council members identifies redevelopable land for city purchase, conveyance to homebuilders association for development.

Surplus Property program conveys surplus city properties to nonprofit housing agencies.

Neighborhood Improvement Challenge program provides small grants for neighborhood improvements.

Downtown Alliance Redevelopment Study will identify housing opportunities and needed incentives.

Seattle

Housing Summit convened by mayor to identify ways to increase market-rate, affordable housing in the city.

Creation of Housing Office within the executive office to increase supply of housing for middle-income residents.

Multifamily Housing Tax Abatements promote market-rate housing in target neighborhoods.

First-Time Homebuyers' Loans to reduce mortgage costs.

Hometown Home Loan program provides low-cost loans for employees of major in-city institutions.

Location-Efficient Mortgage program lowers downpayment, provides 25 percent discount on transit passes.

Transfer of Development Rights (TDR) and Housing Bonus programs provide incentives for low/moderate-income housing in or near downtown (proposed changes include middle-income component, other locations).

Fast-Track Permitting increased 24-hour reviews from 30 percent of project applications to 65 percent.

Seattle-Specific Housing Designs were solicited through a citywide competition to promote compatible infill housing.

Parking Reduction Ordinance to lower parking standards in densely built neighborhoods with transit service, thus reducing development costs.

Best Practices

Baltimore, Maryland: Class B office building conversion to increase supply of downtown market-rate housing.

Columbus, Ohio: Residential market study to identify in-city housing development opportunities.

Dayton, Ohio: City assembly of tax-delinquent, abandoned houses and vacant lots for rebuilding as market-rate homes.

Denver, Colorado: Mayoral summits on downtown revitalization, including housing.

St. Louis, Missouri: Half-cent sales tax to fund capital improvements, including housing infrastructure.

Tampa, Florida: Permit streamlining and follow-up monitoring process through city/homebuilder collaboration.

Types of Incentive Programs

City Assemblage, Cost Writedowns of Housing Sites

Chicago: HomeStart, New Homes, City Lots programs

Cincinnati: Homesteading program

Dayton: Program to recycle tax-delinquent, abandoned, vacant properties

Houston: Land Bank of Tax-Delinquent Properties

Sacramento: Redevelopment and Capital District Properties

San Antonio: Affordable Housing Task Force, Surplus Property programs

City Assistance in Development Financing, Tax Reductions

Baltimore: Tax abatement, state gap financing for Class B office building conversion

Chicago: HomeStart, New Homes, TIF for Housing, and TIF Neighborhood Investment programs

Cincinnati: Housing Rounds, low-cost renovation loans, mortgage assistance

Sacramento: Redevelopment financing assistance

San Antonio: Tax abatements

Seattle: Multifamily housing tax abatements, first-time homebuyer loans, location-efficient mortgage program, transfer of development rights, and housing bonus incentives

City Reduction of Infrastructure Costs

Chicago: New Homes for Chicago program offers fee waivers, off-site facility construction

Houston: Tax Increment Reimbursement Zones, city reimbursement of developer costs

San Antonio: Tax Increment Reinvestment Zones, impact fee waivers

St. Louis: Sales tax allocation for infrastructure improvements

Mayoral "Summits" and Housing Agency Reorganization

Denver: Mayoral summits on downtown revitalization, including housing

Houston: Homeownership campaign, new redevelopment authority

Sacramento: City Housing Strategy

San Antonio: Community Revitalization Action Group

Seattle: Housing Summit, mayor's Housing Office

Education, Information Campaigns

Cincinnati: Homeownership Partnership sponsors Web site and neighborhood guidebook; Real Estate Ambassadors; CitiRAMAs; homeownership counseling

Columbus: Residential market study

Houston: Homeownership Campaign, Model Homes Park, City Parade of Homes

San Antonio: Affordable Showcase of Homes, Downtown Alliance Redevelopment Study

Regulatory Relief

Chicago: building permit self-certification of preapproved designs

Houston: Builders Association white paper on streamlining recommendations; authorization of third-party building inspectors

Seattle: Fast-track permitting, Seattle-Specific Housing Designs, parking reductions

Tampa: Permit streamlining, city/builder monitoring of application process

Neighborhood Conservation

Cincinnati: Homeownership and Neighborhood Revitalization program

Houston: Neighborhoods to Standard program

San Antonio: Neighborhood Sweeps, Neighborhood Improvement Challenge programs ∎

Source: Douglas R. Porter, with Anita Kramer, Terry Lassar, and David Salvesen, "Building Homes in America's Cities: A Progress Report," (paper prepared for the U.S. Conference of Mayors, the U.S. Department of Housing and Urban Development, and the National Association of Home Builders, October 2000).

Notes

1. By making home development as attractive to builders in cities as in suburban areas, the initiative is intended to promote construction, over a ten-year period, of 1 million market-rate homes in urban areas throughout the nation. To accomplish this goal, the partnership has selected 18 pilot cities where collaborative public/private programs and activities will be used to spur the development of market-rate homes. In the next phase of the initiative, the partnership will make available the results of these efforts—including "best practices"—to cities across the nation.

2. This report describes the programs of six pilot cities and presents selected "best practices" from six additional pilot cities.

Developments like Firestone Upper West Side, in Fort Worth, are attracting new residents to America's downtowns.

Shaping the Public Domain

Across the country, cities that have invested in the revitalization of their downtowns are seeing a resurgence of interest in city living. The most obvious examples are New York and Chicago, where the mayors have led major public investment efforts to recreate their cities as safe, clean centers of economic vitality, entertainment, and culture. As a result, demand for urban housing has exploded.

Smaller cities—even those that, until recently, have had no new urban housing for many years—have had similar success. In Fort Worth, for example, city leadership has transformed what was once a dusty "cow town" into a business, cultural, and entertainment destination. Today, a varied array of shops and restaurants line its landscaped brick streets. The center of the entertainment and shopping district, where the city has focused its attention and resources, is Sundance Square, a multiblock area in the city's core. Now that downtown has become "a place to be," housing developments are springing up within walking distance of the center city.

To support these new investments, cities must make people feel safe in their homes and

At the project level, mayoral leadership can be critical, especially if the project is a pioneering one. To facilitate development of the Firestone Upper West Side apartments, in Fort Worth, the mayor's office arranged for the developer to meet with the heads of city departments before submitting plans, to make sure that the project's needs would be met, that requirements would be coordinated, and that everyone understood that the mayor wanted the project.

Denver's Strategy for Reviving Its Downtown Housing Market

One of the first things I did after taking office in 1991 was to convene a downtown summit focused on housing. Up to that point the emphasis downtown had been on retail, not on housing. I was convinced that if a residential population could be established downtown, retail would follow. Out of the summit came several housing-oriented initiatives.

We created a downtown housing office to market our inventory of vacant buildings to housing developers and to provide developers and investors with accurate information on properties and market conditions. We also made sweeping changes in downtown zoning to encourage housing and transit-oriented development and to protect historic buildings. The land use regulations

in place at the time actually inhibited housing. We used higher density to encourage housing and created design standards and review. As a result, we were able to save a critical mass of our older buildings downtown. They may not have been functional for office space, but they worked as housing.

In addition, we eliminated parking as a "use by right," which further strengthened our effort to preserve historic buildings and stimulate residential development. We know that once a downtown is more than one-third parking lots, it loses its character and sense of place.

We provided housing financing on unconventional projects. Once these projects were successful, they were

supported by conventional lenders. We directed all our private-activity bond allocations toward downtown housing projects for three years. And we created a multimillion-dollar revolving loan fund for housing, which we continue to increase. And, a final key to our downtown revitalization has been a constructive partnership between the public and private sectors. ■

Source: Excerpted from Wellington E. Webb, "What Cities Can Do: Revitalizing Denver's Downtown," *Brookings Review* 18, no. 3 (summer 2000): 50–53, available at http://www. brookings.edu/press/review/summer2000/webb.htm.

on the street through effective police protection and crime-prevention measures, and must ensure prompt delivery of public services such as street maintenance, waste collection, and removal of blight.

Based on a study of residential development in downtown Denver, Milwaukee, New York, Philadelphia, and other cities, Lawrence O. Houstoun Jr. has developed the following list of factors that contribute to a city's success in attracting residential development to its urban core:

- The setting often requires a substantial upgrade. Milwaukee's streetscape investment was essential to converting an entire district.
- Goals must be set, progress monitored, and changes in strategies adopted when required.
- Downtowns have to be better—and be *perceived* as better—a marketing challenge requiring deep pockets; high-quality, professional marketing campaigns; and substantial commitment.
- Having someone in charge—whether affiliated with government, a nonprofit organization, or both, is vital.[5]

Planning and Coordination

Cities, through their planning departments, can translate the mayor's vision and policy directives into a planning framework that encourages the development of urban housing. One way to do so is to target specific geographic areas for new housing development. Within those targeted areas, cities can use various legal, regulatory, and financing tools (explained in a later section) to facilitate the development of housing; assist developers with land acquisition; make needed infrastructure improvements; enhance the streetscape; encourage the development of supportive neighborhood services; and so forth.

Creating the planning framework means not only incorporating the vision into the public plans and documents that guide future development but ensuring that the implementation process facilitates—rather than impedes— achievement of the desired goals. Guiding im-

Located in the historic renovated Riverside Casino, in Reno, the Riverside Artists Lofts offer 35 live/work studios on the upper levels, with an arts foundation, an art gallery, and retail space below.

plementation includes, among other things, reconciling and coordinating the goals, plans, and policies of different public agencies, such as the planning, public works, and transportation departments.

Often, developers report that in working with city governments to obtain support and gain approvals for proposed projects, they get caught in a bureaucratic muddle characterized by inadequate information, lengthy delays, rigid requirements, competing (and sometimes conflicting) demands, and other problems.[6] To remedy these difficulties, cities can review and coordinate their procedures and requirements to eliminate duplication and excessive red tape. They can also provide prompt and complete information, impose tighter deadlines for departmental decisions, and allow more flexibility in meeting their requirements. Other commonly recommended strategies for simplifying the development approval process include

- Consolidating permit processes;
- Waiving or reducing fees for projects (like affordable housing) that benefit the public;
- Minimizing changes to previously approved plans and eliminating conflicts between requirements from different city departments;
- Holding a single, consolidated public hearing for all approvals;
- Streamlining the review process.[7]

A number of cities have incorporated these and other ideas into their programs and procedures. Denver, for example, has imposed strict timelines for staff reviews, and if an infill project meets the city's design standards, approvals come quickly. (However, if a development firm wants to do something different—that is, outside the standards—the project must go through a more extensive design review process.) Tampa has taken several steps to streamline its approval and permitting processes, holding quarterly meetings with developers to assess the progress of their permit applications and using permit-fee increases to acquire technology—including e-mail, cell phones for all inspectors, and the capacity to receive applications electronically—that will facilitate plan reviews. In Chicago, developers can self-certify preapproved home designs.[8]

While many cities have succeeded in easing developers' regulatory burdens through changes in the approvals process, progress has generally been piecemeal; in most cities, wholesale revision—to rationalize, streamline, and coordinate the approvals process—is generally not a reasonable or achievable option. However, it may be possible to create an organizational entity, such as a quasi-public redevelopment authority, to manage all the city's development initiatives, including the development of infill housing. Such an entity would be separate from, but accountable to, the city. It could create and institutionalize the necessary capacity; pro-

vide continuity over time; and, employing powers delegated to it by the city, direct the infill housing development process in a proactive and entrepreneurial manner. To protect the public interest, the entity would operate according to clear and consistent city policies directing how choices are made—especially those concerning the use of financial incentives.[9]

A good way to coordinate and expedite the approvals process is for the responsible entity to designate a project manager to be the developer's single point of contact for all public actions affecting a particular project. He or she would be responsible for initiating, coordinating, and monitoring all project reviews in a timely manner and for solving interagency disputes. This approach eliminates the need for developers to scamper from office to office trying to figure out the components, requirements, and timing of the process.

Regulation of Land Use

The types of land use control that most directly affect infill housing development include zoning, subdivision regulations, building codes, and design guidelines and reviews—although, depending on the jurisdiction, other legal issues and requirements may also be important. In general, government regulation of infill development tends to be more demanding (and therefore more costly to the developer) than government regulation of new development in newly developed places. In urban areas, the myriad requirements of the approvals process can take a significant amount of time, impose additional costs, and constrain innovation—and, the outcome may be unpredictable. As a result, experienced infill developers allow extra time—and funds—to identify legal requirements in advance and navigate the approvals process.

Zoning

Many infill parcels are zoned for uses that are obsolete or have become economically infeasible. In many cities, inflexible and antiquated zoning codes—many of which are designed to separate different land uses—are not suited to

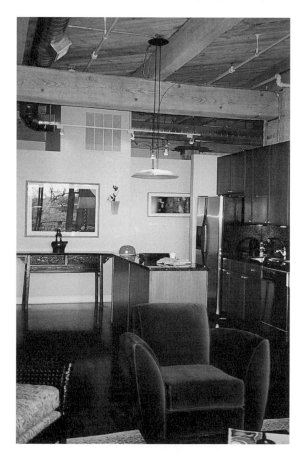

In the Block Y development, in Chicago, luxurious floor and kitchen finishes contrast with the exposed beams and mechanical elements of the "heavy timber" loft apartments.

Urban Design Associates

In the shadow of downtown's office towers, Crawford Square, in Pittsburgh, has reclaimed a portion of the Hill District, a traditional urban residential neighborhood, and restored much of what was lost to urban renewal efforts of the 1960s.

the higher-density, mixed-use, urban development form that is often the most appropriate means of producing housing in urban settings. For example, flexible standards are needed to allow the variations in setback and parking requirements among commercial and residential uses. Rigid zoning specifications often force the developer either to revert to older, less desirable development types or to obtain variances, which takes time and money and increases risk.

One approach that maximizes flexibility and encourages innovation is the use of performance-based zoning, under which projects are evaluated according to how well they satisfy specific criteria (which can be developed with the participation of community groups), and any projects that meet enough criteria qualify for approval. A performance-based zoning ordinance might use questions such as the following to evaluate a project: "Is the project consistent with the local land plan for the area? Does it meet local architectural guidelines? Does the site plan preserve open space? Is it easily accessible to transit?" One advantage of performance-based zoning is that it can "depoliticize the development process."[10] Alternatively, a city might establish overlay zones, which emphasize design criteria and conformance with the approved master plan.

Denver has encouraged downtown housing development by changing its zoning code to eliminate parking as a use by right. Before the zoning change, property owners had been tearing down marginal historic buildings, which generated little revenue, and using the land for surface parking lots, which require little investment to produce income. With the change in zoning, this practice became uneconomical. The city also shifted the way it awarded density bonuses: instead of encouraging the inclusion of plazas and atriums in office buildings, the new system encourages the inclusion of housing. The change was made partly to provide an incentive to create housing and partly to improve the streetscape by encouraging the construction of buildings at the edge of the street rather than behind a plaza.[11]

In some places, city governments compensate for rigid zoning requirements with informal, individually negotiated variances granted through vehicles such as "planned development" designations. While more flexible, such approaches can prove costly and time-consuming for developers, and the outcomes—which often depend more on politics and personalities than on deliberate public policy—are typically unpredictable.[12]

According to Adrienne Schmitz, ULI's director of residential community development, some communities use their zoning ordinances to encourage higher-density development. "Instead of prescribing maximum allowable height and lot coverage and minimum setbacks," she explains, "they are taking the opposite approach, and specifying minimum height and lot coverage and 'build-to' lines that minimize setbacks."

Subdivision Regulations

Subdivision regulations may also make urban infill housing difficult. For example, lot patterns in older areas may be inappropriate for modern developments: because most zoning laws emphasize development within a property, as opposed to the integration of the development with other properties, they employ setbacks from the street and from adjacent properties to ensure the separation of uses. By pushing buildings back from the social sphere of the sidewalk—and moving stores away from potential retail customers on the street—these setback requirements limit developers' ability to create pedestrian-oriented developments and to integrate land uses (by, for example, locating apartments over retail). Numerous variances

In downtown Atlanta, the Winter Companies redeveloped Muses Block, a group of deteriorated buildings overlooking Woodruff Park (above), into loft residences above ground-floor retail (below).

are required to bring buildings closer to the street, which cost developers time and money. In addition to creating barriers for some developers, these added costs—which are ultimately passed on to residents—can translate into housing prices that are beyond reach of many potential consumers.[13]

Building Codes

In many cities, housing development is impeded by strict building codes (especially fire codes) that are intended for office structures and that are sometimes excessive for residential construction. In addition, building codes designed for new construction may be unrealistic for rehabilitation projects. To help facilitate desired housing developments, Rochester, New

York, helps developers obtain state waivers that make renovations less costly. Cities can also help by building in some flexibility. In Denver, a tool known as Chapter 31, developed 20 years ago, enables developers to obtain variances or waivers "to balance the often unintended and harsh effects on housing redevelopment wrought by standard codes."[14] A recent HUD report, "Smart Codes in Your Community: A Guide to Building Rehabilitation Codes," provides advice and examples for communities seeking to create and adopt construction codes that encourage the reuse of existing structures.[15]

Typically, older buildings being redeveloped must be brought up to current building codes. Although adaptive use exemplifies the use of sustainable development practices, helps meet market demand, and contributes to the preservation of historic structures, the costs associated with bringing some older buildings up to current standards may render such redevelopment economically infeasible. Loft developers in Atlanta, for example, in attempting to convert existing institutional or industrial buildings into loft residential uses, found themselves burdened by the added expenses associated with meeting the accessibility requirements of the Americans with Disabilities Act, as well as fire and other codes instituted well after the buildings were originally constructed. In some cases, the added costs are so great that it makes more sense financially to simply tear the building down and rebuild new.[16] In many cases, if standards could be applied more flexibly to buildings built before such requirements were anticipated, it might be possible both to facilitate reuse and to achieve the goals of the standards.

The good news is that building codes that apply to rehabilitation projects are changing at the local, state, and federal levels. In 1999, to make its requirements for the redevelopment of downtown buildings built before July 1, 1974, more realistic, Los Angeles eliminated parking requirements and permitted more flexibility in the size and layout of living spaces, among other changes. In 1998, New Jersey developed an entirely separate state building-code system to govern the rehabilitation of existing buildings. The new code follows a "ladder system":

the more changes that are made, the higher the level of code requirements. The ladder encompasses (from least to most) repairs, renovations, alterations, reconstruction, change of use, and additions.

The revised New Jersey code was developed between 1995 and 1998. During that time, HUD was developing rehab standards that could serve as a model for adoption nationwide. The New Jersey regulations are technically referred to as the Uniform Construction Code, Rehabilitation Subcode (commonly known as the New Jersey Subcode), while HUD's regulations are called the Nationally Applicable Recommended Rehabilitation Provisions. HUD now has a demonstration program underway called Model ReModel. States that have adopted variations of the New Jersey Subcode include Maryland, Rhode Island, and Vermont.[17]

Design Guidelines and Reviews

One way cities can ensure that infill development is compatible with the character of the neighborhood is through design guidelines, which address aspects of development such as building scale; the placement of garages and parking; window placement and design; roof shape; building materials; facade features; sidewalks; landscaping; buffering; and the relationship of buildings to the street. Though design guidelines may appear to add another layer of requirements and complexity to the development process, they can save developers time, money, and frustration by reassuring the community in advance that the proposed development will be attractive and compatible with the existing neighborhood, especially if local residents are involved in creating the guidelines.

Properly structured, design guidelines can achieve their goals without adding significant costs to development. For example, the San Jose Redevelopment Agency developed a set of straightforward areawide principles to guide the design of redevelopment projects. "We learned that if we let developers know what we expect in terms of design and construction quality, the developers will do it," says Tom Aidala, principal architect and urban designer

for the redevelopment agency from 1980 to 1997. "Problems arise only when requirements are not consistent or are unpredictable." In San Jose, the redevelopment agency worked with developers early on to discuss design expectations. Developers of redevelopment projects were required to meet with the urban design review board three times during a project's planning. The function of the board—whose members, selected by the city's board of supervisors, included local businesspeople, an architect, and a supervisor—was to identify needed design changes at a stage of the process when it would be least difficult and expensive for the developer to make them.

Land Assembly and Acquisition

One of the most important ways the public sector can encourage infill housing development is by assisting developers to assemble and acquire land and to prepare it for development. As discussed in chapter 4, in addition to the availability and cost of well-located, appropriately sized parcels, issues include the time and cost involved in (1) clearing title (which can sometimes exceed the value of the land), (2) identifying and finding the landowner, and (3) dealing with encumbrances on the property, such as tax liens.

Heritage Landing, in downtown Minneapolis, includes 229 residential units, two floors of underground parking, and retail space.

Although some of the most potentially attractive infill sites are publicly owned, developers often it difficult to acquire and develop these properties. For example, the public agencies or authorities that own the land may have acquired it in the course of pursuing various objectives and may have no well-considered plans for its development or disposal. Cities can facilitate infill housing by making a descriptive inventory of publicly owned property and assigning priority to sites for redevelopment.

Cities can use condemnation to obtain and reuse blighted properties, and can use eminent domain, on a selective basis, to assist in acquiring key parcels for developments that will generate public benefits. Often, the mere possibility that such powers may be used will be sufficient to persuade owners to sell underused property. On the other hand, extensive use of eminent domain can encourage speculation and drive up land prices. Cities can also create a land-bank authority to hold and dispose of redevelopable properties, especially if those properties will be used for affordable housing in the future.

In some cities, especially those with soft housing markets, where unit prices do not justify the development costs associated with infill housing development, the city (or the redevelopment authority or other public agency) can write down or provide the land to stimulate housing development in targeted areas. A variation of this technique is for the city (or other public entity) to acquire the land and lease it to the developer for a specific number of years for a given development. This approach, which was used in the Central Station and Gramercy on Garfield/Greenwich on the Park case studies in this book, enables the city to retain some control while reducing the costs associated with development. In both of these projects, the public partner receives a portion of the development's cash flow.

Developer Arn Bortz, a partner in Towne Properties, in Cincinnati, describes the constraints his firm faced in developing the Gramercy on Garfield/Greenwich on the Park project. "The economics are challenging: Even a friendly lender who accepts your projections will not write a loan that will cover all you need. There's

a 'feasibility gap' because rents are so low and land costs so high—the classic cost-to-value issue." For that reason, the city had to acquire site control. "We had no acquisition costs in any of the four phases. If we had been required to buy the sites, we couldn't have done it."

Cities can also help developers acquire properties that are ripe for redevelopment, either directly or by negotiating for acquisition on the developer's behalf. According to Jennifer Moulton, director of community planning and development for the city and county of Denver, the mayor's office worked with the owner of a vacated downtown hospital property (Columbia Health One) to help market the abandoned campus of St. Luke's Hospital for redevelopment. The owner had offered to give the property to the city. Instead, the mayor's office—recognizing that the hospital did not understand the real estate business, or how to dispose of land assets—brought in the Denver Urban Redevelopment Authority (DURA) to help prepare the 11-acre site for sale. DURA began by working with neighborhood groups to determine what the community wanted and did not want and to identify potential issues. Because the vacant buildings were a blight on the neighborhood, the community was supportive of the sale and of the property's reuse. Columbus Realty Trust (now Post Properties) was looking for land in the area and called DURA. Because its vision was compatible with the community's, DURA made the match.

Cities can be especially helpful in removing legal barriers to acquisition. Depending on state law, they can forgive tax liens, use condemnation, combine the powers of different agencies to acquire land, and create a land-banking system. In Pennsylvania, for example, counties have the legal authority to undertake spot condemnation for redevelopment as well as the ability to forgive liens. However, in tax sales, where liens are forgiven, the public agencies must often bid against private speculators. In Norfolk, Virginia, the city cannot forgive back taxes but may use public funds to repay them. In Atlanta, unpaid taxes may be forgiven for land-bank properties that have financing for redevelopment, especially when the redevelopment is undertaken by nonprofit community development corporations (CDCs). To help clear titles—a process that typically takes about a year—the San Antonio Development Agency has a title analyst on staff. In Atlanta, some of the 1960s redevelopment laws were brought back into use to help speed up title clearance for Olympics sites.

Land Development

One of the thorniest issues impeding development of some urban infill properties is environmental contamination. Though environmental problems can be complex, highly technical, and expensive to manage, and can require specialized expertise, some developers have found a profitable niche in redeveloping contaminated sites.[18] Potential environmental issues include the contamination not only of the site itself but of structures being considered for renovation or preservation.

HUD and the U.S. Department of Commerce have developed programs to encourage the redevelopment of brownfields, and most states now offer financial and technical assistance to encourage the cleanup and remediation of such sites. Local governments can actively promote brownfield redevelopment by providing incentives, helping to fund remediation, and assisting developers to identify reusable sites and to work with federal and state environmental agencies. In some cases, to make development of key sites possible, cities have acquired brownfield sites, assumed responsibility for environmental cleanup, and marketed the sites to developers for the desired reuse.

Some sites contain items of historic or archaeological significance. For example, when preparing the site for the Old Town Village project, in Alexandria, Virginia, Eakin/Youngentob Associates unearthed a Civil War privy containing various objects of historic interest. To ensure that the exploration and preservation of this find would not make the project infeasible, the city and the firm agreed to a cost cap for working through the archaeological issues.

Often, cities that contribute land for a project will also prepare it for development. For

example, they may demolish existing structures, remediate environmental contamination, install supportive infrastructure, and make streetscape improvements. In some cases, they may even build underground parking to serve the project, and, typically, the public as well.

Infrastructure

The term *infrastructure* covers public facilities such as streets; water, sewer, and drainage systems; parks and open space; and, more broadly,

A landmark beaux arts hotel in Atlanta was rehabilitated as the Georgian Terrace, with 294 luxury apartments. A 19-story addition complements the original structure.

Some sections of the Pointe at Lincoln Park, in Chicago, share common garages under the residences. Residents have direct private entrances to the units from the garages.

Roy H. Kruse & Associates/Robert J. Heidrich

schools. Infrastructure that makes the city as a whole more accessible, functional, and attractive encourages infill housing development. And, in areas specifically targeted for infill development, parking facilities, streetscape improvements, and landscaping—along with services such as good maintenance and security—can also increase the attractiveness of neighborhoods and create a more receptive development environment. Mass transit systems, bridges, and improved access points can make a downtown more attractive overall as a place to live and work. Rochester, New York, for example, is rebuilding its major streets as gateway streets and has implemented a policy in which street improvements are coordinated with residential and commercial construction.

As a rule, cities provide the streets and the water, sewer, and drainage systems that serve the site, but the developer is responsible for on-site infrastructure. The city can also work with local utility services to have utilities placed underground and to ensure that services will be adequate. Cities can facilitate infill housing development in targeted areas by coordinating infrastructure improvements with development needs so that there are no surprises or infrastructure impediments.

In Norfolk, the redevelopment and housing authority functions much like a developer, making infrastructure improvements to individual properties that it owns and then reselling them. Other local governments have learned that they can require certain concessions from developers in exchange for infrastructure improvements—including affordable housing setasides, specific design elements, and the provision of public amenities.[19]

Information

Cities amass various kinds of information that can be valuable to developers, and they can encourage infill housing by creating an easily accessible system for sharing that information. Such information includes demographic and economic statistics; data on housing sales and starts; information about local, state, and federal funding programs; information on environmental issues; and recent public and private studies and reports. In addition, some cities collect information specifically to encourage certain types of development. For example, Columbus and San Antonio have commissioned market studies that they use to attract residential developers to the city.[20]

Because land is such a critical factor in developing urban infill housing, perhaps the most important kind of information cities can make available to potential infill housing developers is an inventory of vacant land and of buildings suitable for rehabilitation. Ideally, the inventory should be mapped and, for each property, include information on ownership, current use, and current tax value and status. The inventory should also highlight publicly owned properties whose redevelopment the city wishes to encourage.

Cities can also help by providing a single, centralized source of information about the city's regulating agencies and development requirements, the approvals and permitting process, and the entitlements process.

Finally, the public sector can help developers to identify potential funding sources and to apply for private loans and government funding, and can offer to work with lenders and brokers to encourage their support of specific projects.

Tax Policy

How a city structures its tax policies—particularly policies regarding property taxes and special tax districts—can either spur or impede infill housing development. Property taxes can influence infill development in a number of ways. As noted in chapter 4, taxing land and improvements at a single rate can be a disincentive to improving land. Taxing land at a significantly higher rate than that applied to property improvements, however, can promote the development of vacant infill parcels and spur

the redevelopment of underused land and obsolete buildings.[21]

Cities that tax land according to its current use rather than its market value may encourage speculation and fuel the escalation of land prices. High prices for infill land have two undesirable effects. First, for a project to be financially feasible, its density must be increased to a level that is often unacceptable to neighboring residents; second, home prices (or rents) become unaffordable to most of the market. For this reason, cities wishing to encourage infill housing development need to ensure that their property assessments and property taxes are based on market value rather than current use.

How a city handles arrears in property taxes for vacant or underused properties can make those properties easy or difficult for developers to obtain and develop. As noted earlier, depending on the city's legal framework, various policies and procedures can be established to assist developers to acquire properties encumbered with tax liens.

Some cities use various forms of property tax abatement to encourage the development of infill housing, especially if that housing is tied to other city goals. Within its urban enterprise zones, for example, Atlanta offers a ten-year tax abatement on housing developments in which 20 percent of the units are set aside for low-income residents. Baltimore offers a ten-year tax abatement for Class B office space that is converted to housing. Seattle abates taxes on multifamily developments in the city.[22]

Tax abatement can be especially important in two circumstances: (1) where development costs are high and (2) where it is necessary, during the early stages of a city's housing renaissance, to stimulate rehabilitation and new construction. According to Hamilton Rabinowitz and Altschuler, a New York City real estate consulting firm, the city's willingness to abate existing taxes and taxes on improvements for 15 years was crucial to the office conversion projects in downtown New York City. "The present value of these tax savings can be in the range of $30 to $50 a square foot, depending on current taxes and the scope of improvements." Two other important factors: some pre-1939 buildings have earned federal investment tax credits, and 1996 zoning changes reduced regulatory impediments. All three elements were essential in overcoming the early reluctance of lenders to participate in residential development, which lacked both a well-established market and a track record.[23]

In the course of acquiring land for the Firestone Upper West Side project, the developer, Phoenix Property Company (PPC), realized that despite relatively low land costs, the project would not be financially feasible. PPC responded by seeking tax abatements, documenting how the project would likely stimulate additional development and increase land values in the area. In Fort Worth, where the project is located, land and structures are appraised separately, and separate taxes are levied by the city of Fort Worth, Tarrant County, and the Fort Worth Independent School District. All agreed to allow PPC to pay taxes only on the land value of the project's 11 acres, and abated taxes on the structures for ten years. PPC agreed to pay full taxes on the remaining property it owned in the area and to initiate another development on the non-tax-abated portion of the land.

In some places, preservation of historic properties will automatically qualify developers for tax abatements. For example, Bob Silverman, chairman and chief executive officer of the Winter Companies, in Atlanta, reports that in Georgia, any property on the National Register of Historic Places enjoys a property tax freeze at the pre-renovation level for eight years; in the ninth year, taxes increase up to half the added value; and full taxes are due in year ten.

Special taxing districts, such as tax increment financing districts or public improvement districts, enable cities to use marginal tax increases within those districts to fund public improvements that support desired forms of development. In "payment in lieu of taxes," or PILOT programs, developers pay the local government a negotiated fee instead of property taxes for a specified period of time. Cities can also offer homebuyers time-limited abatements on their property taxes. Typically, the taxes are phased back in.

In addition, as noted later in this chapter, funding sources that have tax benefits attached to them can be valuable sources of project financing. These include tax credits, such as federal and state low-income housing tax credits

The Denver Dry Goods Building, once a landmark department store in the heart of downtown, has been reborn as a mixed-use, mixed-income development. The renovation required financing from 23 different public and private sources.

Shannon Sperry, Denver Urban Renewal Authority

and historic tax credits, and tax-exempt bond financing, which can be used to help fund qualified urban infill housing developments.

Advocacy

The city can play an important role by working with community groups to help generate support for desired urban infill housing developments. As discussed in chapter 7, the city can begin by building consensus for plans that include urban infill housing. Later, the city can work with community groups to advocate well-conceived individual projects that are proposed within those plans.

Financing

Whether developers of urban infill housing will need financial help from the public sector, and how much and what kind of help they will need, will depend on the local market. Because housing is "market rate" does not mean it will be financially feasible to develop. Each development and its goals and context are unique, so the financing requirements will vary among projects. In most—though not all—cases, some combination of public and private financing will be required. As Donald Carter, managing principal of Urban Design Associates, in Pittsburgh, points out, "Downtown housing of any kind will not happen without some public involvement. Much of that housing now targets middle-income or upper-income residents, making public officials who support such housing susceptible to criticism. However, nearly all new downtown commercial development has some public investment. Housing is just part of the overall equation."[24]

Developers can obtain financing for urban infill housing projects from a wide variety of public and private sources. Private sector financing, as noted in chapter 2, may include developer or investor equity as well as bank financing. Depending on the project's characteristics, other private sources include financial intermediaries, foundations, pension funds, utilities, and special-purpose private lenders, such as bank CDCs. Sources of public sector

financing may include federal, state, or local funds, particularly if the planned project will benefit low-income households or neighborhoods.

The primary federal funding sources directly available to developers are the low-income housing tax credit and the historic tax credit.[25] Federal low-income housing tax credits and HUD's HOPE VI public housing transformation programs can both be used to help finance mixed-income infill developments. Community Development Block Grants, another HUD program, can be used to fund certain site improvements. HUD's Section 108 loans can be used to help finance housing rehabilitation, public facilities, and certain large-scale developments. In addition, the PATH program (Partnership for Advancing Technology in Housing) offers financial incentives for projects that use environmentally friendly and energy-efficient construction. The Environmental Protection Agency offers incentive programs for urban infill developments that meet its "smart growth" objectives. And the requirements of the federal Community Reinvestment Act may spur some lending institutions to invest in urban infill housing developments.

State and local governments can choose from a wide range of financial incentives to assist urban infill housing developers, including the following:[26]

The 170-unit Broadway Place Apartments, in downtown Eugene, Oregon, is a public/ private development that features a shared parking arrangement: the city owns the land and the 70-stall parking garage, and a private company—Broadway Apartments LLC— owns the apartments and ground-level retail space.

Lorig Associates, L.L.C.

The development of Mizner Park sparked new life in Boca Raton's downtown. The mix of uses includes a public park and mid-rise residential apartments located above street-front retail shops and restaurants.

- Allocation of city program funds; assistance in identifying and obtaining federal and state program funds;
- Tax credits for historic properties or low-income housing;
- Taxable and tax-exempt bonds;
- Housing trust funds;
- Predevelopment grants and loans;
- Land acquisition loans;
- Loans made against committed (but not yet funded) equity or loans;
- Construction loans;
- Gap financing;
- Soft second mortgages;
- Credit enhancements;
- Assistance to buyers (e.g., downpayment assistance; first-time buyer programs).

Public soft money is especially important. Joe Barry, president of Applied Development Company, in Hoboken, New Jersey, reports that New Jersey, through its statewide Downtown Initiative program, will provide an accruing, low-interest, soft second loan that does not amortize until the project is generating sufficient cash flow. If, for example, a project costs $100,000 per unit to build, Barry will obtain a $60,000 loan from a bank and a $25,000 second mortgage from the state, through the Downtown Initiative, then put in $15,000 of his own equity. Thus, "You only have to carry a mortgage of $60,000 per unit, which you can demonstrate to the banks that you can carry. Then you immediately start amortizing (paying off) the state loan. We agree to share the cash flow with the state—after operating expenses and once we earn 12 percent on equity." The state typically gets 20 to 50 percent of the cash

flow. The Downtown Initiative has been in place for about five years. "It's a small program, about $7 to $10 million per year," Barry explains, "but it gives us lots of leverage."

Often cities attach *quid pro quo* requirements to the receipt of public assistance. These can range from requiring a developer to build facilities for public use, such as a park or plaza, to requiring that a portion of the housing development be affordable to lower-income households, to requiring that a certain percentage of subcontractors be minority-owned firms. In Minneapolis, for example, in exchange for the city's contribution of land, a developer must set aside 20 percent of the housing units as affordable (income-restricted) housing.

While it is wise for cities to consider creative ways of ensuring that public investment will yield public benefits, putting too much weight on fragile development deals can cause them to collapse. Mayor John O. Norquist, of Milwaukee,[27] cautions, "Many of the most sophisticated developers will not come into a city because of all the tangential social issues that must be addressed in development. We're taking our eye off the ball when we have to address so many different social issues."

How much subsidy is enough? Opinions differ and markets differ. Ron Terwilliger, national managing partner of Trammell Crow Residential, in Atlanta, suggests that "the overall economics have to give the developer a free and clear yield that can be financed and is competitive with suburban uses."

Workforce Housing

The definition of *workforce housing* varies from city to city. Generally speaking, however, the term refers to housing that is affordable to households with incomes that are between 60 and 80 percent (and in some places, as high as 120 percent) of the area median. Depending on the specific project, local housing market conditions, and the project's location within the local market, workforce housing may or may not be income restricted.

It is often easier for cities to encourage the production of low-income housing than workforce housing. Public subsidies, such as low-income housing tax credits or tax-exempt bond financing, require that a portion of the housing produced be set aside for low-income households. For example, because its financing included tax-exempt bonds, 20 percent of the units in the Gramercy on Garfield/Greenwich on the Park development (featured in chapter 8) are restricted to households earning up to 50 percent of the area median income. It is more difficult to produce workforce housing for people with incomes that are too high to benefit from public subsidy but too low to afford market-rate urban housing prices.

Producing workforce housing can be an issue in both "hot" and "cold" markets. In hot markets, where the economy is expanding, demand for housing is vigorous, and the costs of doing business are generally higher, infill housing is more costly to build. Higher costs for land acquisition and site development, for example, translate into higher housing prices: often, choice infill properties were snapped up long ago, and those still on the market may be available only because they are being held by speculators, who expect exorbitant prices, or because they present expensive development problems, such as environmental contamination or difficult infrastructure issues. Higher development and construction costs, combined with high prevailing home prices and rent levels, mean that without a subsidy, new homes in urban infill areas will be unaffordable to moderate or even middle-income households. And in cities with growing economies, a shortage of intown workforce housing will eventually choke economic growth: if the supply of workforce housing cannot keep pace with increases in the number of jobs, workers will eventually migrate to cities where they can live in reasonable proximity to their employment.

In soft markets, land costs and building costs tend to be lower, but so are home prices and rents. Typically, in order to make a profit, developers of infill housing must charge higher prices than the moderate-income market can afford. Moreover, even in soft markets, land prices are sometimes high, especially where the city has used eminent domain to acquire land in the past. Overuse of eminent domain

The architecture of the Townhomes of Capitol Hill, a mixed-income, limited-equity co-op in downtown Washington, D.C., reflects the character of the surrounding neighborhood.

Cities can help create the setting for urban infill housing through investments such as street improvements. In the case of the Huntington, the city of St. Petersburg, Florida, improved and beautified adjacent Second Street with parallel parking spaces, median dividers, and attractive landscaping.

can encourage speculators to hold property in anticipation of future public acquisition, or to sell it only at inflated prices.

Meeting the demand for urban workforce housing typically requires partnerships among for-profit and nonprofit developers, city government, and private funding sources, including lenders, institutions (such as hospitals, universities, or churches), foundations, insurance companies, and pension funds. In some cases, employers may participate in producing housing that is affordable to their workers.

In addition to the public sector tools and subsidy sources listed earlier in this chapter, some common approaches to creating workforce housing include the following:

- Higher-density housing, which can often be made possible through density bonuses;
- Mixed-income housing (including HOPE VI public housing transformation projects);
- Inclusionary zoning programs, which mandate that a certain percentage of units in developments over a specified size be "affordable" (a term that is defined differently in different jurisdictions);
- Employer-assisted housing programs;
- Demand-side incentives, such as assistance for first-time buyers.

From a city's point of view, some of the other challenges in devising a workforce housing strategy include ensuring the long-term afford-ability of the lower-cost units produced; preserving the existing stock of affordable housing in markets where demand for upscale urban housing is strong; and, if workforce housing is to attract families with children, addressing the problems of urban public schools.[28]

Notes

1. Though numerous federal and state laws also affect urban housing development, this chapter focuses primarily on the role, resources, and effects of local governments. Another good source of information on the role of local governments is Nancy Bragado, Judy Corbett, and Sharon Sprowls, *Building Livable Communities: A Policy-Maker's Guide to Infill Development* (Sacramento, Calif.: Center for Livable Communities/Local Government Commission, 1995).

2. Jennifer Moulton, "Ten Steps to a Living Downtown" (discussion paper prepared for the Center on Urban and Metropolitan Policy, Brookings Institution, October 1999), 9.

3. Speaking at ULI's Spring Council Forum, Minneapolis, May 2001.

4. Speaking at a ULI workshop, "Encouraging Moderate-Income Housing Development in the District of Columbia," June 2001.

5. Lawrence O. Houstoun Jr., "Urban Awakening," *Urban Land,* October 1998, 41.

6. Much has been written about developers' frustrations with procedures for obtaining development approvals for all types of projects, and the reader is encouraged to seek out such materials for ideas.

7. Rick Cole, Nancy Bragado, Judy Corbett, and Sharon Sprowls, "Building Livable Communities: New

Strategies for Promoting Urban Infill," *Urban Land,* September 1996, 37–40, 63

8. Richard M. Haughey, *Urban Infill Housing: Myth and Fact* (Washington, D.C.: ULI, 2001), 13.

9. This recommendation was made at a ULI workshop, "Encouraging Moderate-Income Housing in the District of Columbia," June 2001.

10. Gregg T. Logan, Todd M. Noell, and Lawrence Frank; Robert Charles Lesser & Co.; and Georgia Tech, "Mobility, Air Quality, and Development: Overcoming Barriers to Smart Growth" (a draft paper written for SMARTRAQ—Strategies for Metropolitan Atlanta's Regional Transportation and Air Quality, n.d.), 18.

11. Jennifer Moulton, director of community planning and development, city and county of Denver.

12. Tara Ellman, "Infill: The Cure for Sprawl?" *Arizona Issue Analysis,* no. 146 (August 1997); previously available at http://www.goldwaterinstitute.org/azia/146.htm, 6.

13. Logan et al., 4–5.

14. Moulton, 17.

15. This guide is available at the HUD USER Web site, http://www.huduser.org/publications/destech/smartcodes.html.

16. Logan et al., 5–6.

17. David Listokin, "Housing Rehabilitation and American Cities" (draft overview paper for "Housing Policy in the New Millenium," a U.S. Department of Housing and Urban Development conference, October 3, 2000).

18. For detailed information on the development of brownfield sites, see the U.S. Environmental Protection Agency's Web site, http://www.epa.gov, and Robert A. Simons, *Turning Brownfields into Greenbacks* (Washington, D.C.: ULI, 1998).

19. Haughey, *Urban Infill Housing,* 17.

20. Douglas R. Porter, with Anita Kramer, Terry Lassar, and David Salvesen, "Building Homes in America's Cities: A Progress Report" (paper prepared for the U.S. Conference of Mayors, the U.S. Department of Housing and Urban Development, and the National Association of Home Builders, October 2000), 10.

21. Municipal Research & Services Center of Washington, "Infill Development Strategies for Livable Neighborhoods," Report No. 38 (June 1997), previously available at http://www. mrsc.org/textfill.htm, 23.

22. Haughey, *Urban Infill Housing,* 10.

23. Lawrence O. Houstoun Jr., "Urban Awakening," *Urban Land,* October 1998, 36.

24. Donald K. Carter, previously cited in http://www. uli.org/member/Urban_Land/2000/07/hudnut.cfm.

25. Investors can obtain federal historic tax credits by investing either in designated historic properties or in older properties that do not have an official historic designation.

26. An excellent compendium of state and local affordable housing initiatives is Michael Stegman, *State and Local Affordable-Housing Programs: A Rich Tapestry* (Washington, D.C.: ULI, 1999).

27. Speaking at a ULI Mayors' Forum, "Bringing Community Back to the City," Washington, D.C., 1997.

28. A good resource for developers on ways to produce workforce housing in a variety of settings is National Association of Home Builders, Economics, Mortgage Finance, and Housing Policy Division, *Producing Affordable Housing: Partnerships for Profit* (Washington, D.C.: Home Builder Press, 1999).

7

Working with the Community

From a developer's standpoint, working with current residents to obtain their input—and to ensure that their objections will not impede or halt a proposed project—is an integral part of the process of developing almost any housing project. Because urban infill housing development takes place within an established environment, there will always be people who live, work, or own property nearby. Many may be longtime residents or businesspeople with deep roots in the community, and they are sure to have—and to voice—concerns and opinions regarding any proposed development in the area.

A classic tension exists between the interests of developers, those of the community, and those of the larger society, as represented by the market and by the public sector. Developers want to create salable, profitable developments that they will be proud to claim as their own. Local residents want to protect the value of their homes and often want to maintain the social and political *status quo*, though they would often be happy to see some physical improvements to their neighborhoods. The market wants certain kinds of housing products in certain kinds of locations. Politicians want to serve their constituents, take actions that will benefit their communities and engender

Villa Torino, a 198-unit apartment development in San Jose, California, incorporates high-quality features and amenities to attract residents to a formerly deteriorated part of the city.

Douglas Dun

93

civic pride, and get reelected. Public officials charged with representing societal interests respond to myriad needs—ensuring that housing is available to households with a variety of interests, maximizing tax revenues, guiding development into rational patterns, promoting economic development, providing equitable public and social services, redeveloping blighted areas, and protecting the environment, among others. Though all parties want high-quality developments that will be assets to their communities, their differing interests often collide when a specific infill development is proposed.

Some developers avoid the hassle by choosing to develop only where they are welcomed by the community, or where their projects can be developed "by right," thus bypassing the need for community involvement. In such instances, the developer may nevertheless choose to solicit community input, especially if he or she intends to develop additional projects in that community.

However, in most cases, community participation is an important part of the development process. The power that local community groups exert over proposed developments varies among cities and depends on the politics and legal requirements of the local development process. In some places, like Atlanta, Chicago, or Minneapolis, either by law or custom, proposed urban housing developments cannot go forward without the local community's approval.

Robert Harris, executive partner of Holland & Knight, LLP, in Bethesda, Maryland, points out that working with neighbors has become more challenging. People are more sophisticated today, and they have more tools with which to hinder a project. In addition to having better communication and access to information, via e-mail and Web sites, neighbors often hire attorneys who can use an array of ever-expanding rules and requirements to threaten litigation, stop a project, or both.

When considering a project that requires neighbors' approval, wise developers will seek to understand the interests and attitudes of local neighborhood groups and assess the likely level and nature of potential community opposition early in the process—even before preparing or filing plans and certainly before committing to the project. Hyde Park Builders, Inc., in Tampa, Florida, takes this approach, as executive vice president and co-owner Scott Shimberg explains: "We get an option on the land first, then talk to people in the neighborhood to assess the likely neighborhood issues before going forward." In determining whether to proceed, the developer must balance the cost of accommodating (to some extent) neighborhood demands versus the costs of not accommodating. Choosing not to meet neighbors' demands may result in project delays or create problems later in the development process—problems, which, at worst, may force the developer to abandon the project and forfeit the money, effort, and opportunity expended in its pursuit.

Often, developers need to work closely with community leaders not only to meet legal or political requirements but to show their respect and acknowledge the leaders' legitimacy and importance—and thereby avoid unnecessary confrontations.

Key Concerns

Community concerns typically center on two types of issues: (1) physical development issues and (2) the displacement of existing lower-income residents by more affluent newcomers, a process known as *gentrification*. In addition, neighbors may be concerned about how they will be affected during the construction process.

When an infill project is proposed for an established neighborhood, current residents may object even if the development will improve the neighborhood. Though the range of potential objections is extremely broad, residents will typically be concerned about the following issues:

- The project's design—including its architecture, massing, scale, landscaping, overall quality, compatibility with the neighborhood context, and siting (for example, whether the buildings will block valued views);
- The amount and location of parking for the project's residents (e.g., whether adequate on-site parking will ensure that the new res-

The Winter Companies

Apartments in Bass Lofts, an adaptive use project in Atlanta developed by the Winter Companies, feature expansive windows and soaring ceilings.

idents will not park on the street; how the parking will be designed and integrated into the development);

- The amount of traffic that will be added to local streets;
- The proposed project's density, especially if it would be greater than that of land uses in the immediate area.

In addition, some current residents will want to preserve any vacant property as open space. And in some places, residents will object to any change in the *status quo,* even if it would be a positive change; this is what Norman Coleman, the mayor of St. Paul, Minnesota, has referred to as "the CAVE [citizens against virtually everything] mentality."[1]

While it is often true that, as Harris observes, "the more desirable the neighborhood, the less the neighbors desire change," community opposition to a proposed infill housing development can also be strong in lower-income neighborhoods, where residents may be concerned about a project's potential impact on home values, property taxes, and the ability of current resi-

dents to remain in their homes. In addition, there may be concerns (often unstated) about political displacement or change in the neighborhood power structure.

The flip side of this situation occurs when neighbors in more affluent parts of the city become worried about the inclusion of lower-income residents in a proposed mixed-income project. However, because people who choose to locate in urban settings are generally more tolerant—and often even welcoming—of diversity, the inclusion of lower-income households in a mixed-income development in an otherwise affluent setting is rarely an issue. Often, when developers include a certain proportion of income-restricted units, it is because they are legally required to do so as a condition of project financing or other city assistance. Such requirements would likely affect any housing developed on the project site. Thus, developers can often address community objections through excellence in overall project quality and design and by pointing out alternative development possibilities for the site.

Eakin/Youngentob Associates, Inc.

Old Town Village fits seamlessly into the existing fabric of Old Town Alexandria, Virginia.

Strategies for Building Community Support

Perhaps the best way for developers to minimize community opposition in any neighborhood is to become involved in the planning process for that area. For example, in California, the preparation of a "specific area plan" is one mechanism that can be used to convene all stakeholders to plan for a neighborhood's future. A specific area plan is a detailed plan for the development of a delineated geographic area, and ideally includes a master environmental review. Specific area plans are proactive; involve local residents at an early stage; and provide residents, public officials, and developers with "a predictable framework for making trade-offs so that neighborhoods evolve in a balanced way."[2] By bringing all stakeholders together, the process makes it possible to reach consensus on core issues before specific development projects are proposed.

Cities can also help forestall concern about design quality and compatibility by involving community groups in the creation of design guidelines for infill housing development. Enabling local residents to express their concerns about design and quality considerations

such as density, massing and scale, architecture, construction materials, and parking before developments are proposed can help developers anticipate and avoid many potential problems in working with the community on project design.

According to Debra Stein, president of GCA Group, in San Francisco, the three factors that are the most important causes of community opposition are (1) lack of adequate information, (2) fear of being ignored, and (3) conflict of goals. As a result, successful community relations strategies should involve public information, public participation, and a process for resolving disputes.[3] The following general rules apply:

- Communicate early and often;
- Educate the community—and allow yourself to be educated by the community;
- Identify the community's core concern and "embrace the issue";
- Seek and nurture potential project supporters within the community, especially within the community leadership;
- Negotiate a solution;
- Create a common vision.

To avoid problems from the community, the basic rule is "Never blindside the neighbors."[4]

Developers should involve neighborhood groups early in the development process, keep them informed, hear their concerns, and actively listen to their suggestions regarding what kind of development is needed and desired. Through early and ongoing dialogue, current residents can often be transformed into advocates for the proposed development. The ideal outcome would be a negotiated process through which each party gains something that is important to it but becomes open to giving up other things. No one party would be entirely satisfied—or entirely frustrated.

Wise developers take the time to educate themselves about the history and environment of a site. Harris cautions that a developer who is going into a negotiating process must know the issues as well as the neighborhood does: he or she must read the local paper, learn who the players are and what concerns them, and discover what their potential objections might be—as well as "what turns them on." And, because current local residents often make up part of the market for urban infill housing developments—as well as participate in public hearings—some developers will, as part of the project planning process, conduct focus groups of community residents to discuss desired features for the project and for unit design.

According to Lee Quill, principal of Cunningham + Quill Architects, in Washington, D.C., one of the most important things developers can do in working with community groups is to listen. At large-scale public meetings, his firm makes a one-hour presentation, then responds to questions from the community and invites informal comments while community residents examine drawings and models of the proposed development. The drawings and models enable residents to understand the intended design, massing, and scale—to visualize the proposed project and how it would fit onto the site and into the community. In addition, the firm establishes a Web site where local residents can download presentation images and transcripts of meetings, and send their comments by e-mail. In this way, even those people who could not attend a scheduled meeting can feel—and be—involved.

When neighbors raise an issue concerning a proposed development, it is important to acknowledge, understand, and consider the group's position and the reasons behind it. Often, a core issue becomes an organizing point for community opposition, and developers must be prepared to negotiate and make concessions on that issue. And, because local residents understand the history and character of their neighborhood, they may be able to offer suggestions that will improve the design and quality of the ultimate product.

When explaining the intended development, it can be helpful for developers to point out less desirable "by-right" alternatives—that is, other uses that could be built on the site under the current zoning, such as a warehouse or a big-box retail store. Matthew Birnbaum, vice president for development at AvalonBay Communities, Inc., of Alexandria, Virginia, notes that drawing up a by-right plan can also create important political cover for public officials. Birnbaum also suggests that to engage the community in finding solutions and to forestall a yes-no decision, developers offer options in the form of different sets of plans.

Above all, developers should not lie or embroider the truth. In many areas, residents can recite one story after another of unfulfilled promises—and, as a result, no longer trust either developers or the government. The best advice for developers is this: Do the necessary studies. If the proposed housing will, for example, add traffic to the streets, acknowledge that this is the case, and work with the community to find acceptable ways to minimize the traffic impact. Stein cautions that it is "absolutely vital that all statements be true and defensible and that public information materials only include commitments you are certain can be kept."

Developers also need to identify potential allies and marshal support to offset the opposition—in part to protect decision makers who are inclined to support the project yet who may be politically vulnerable. Potential sources of support might be organizations that focus on specific issues, such as affordable housing, smart growth, mass transit, or historic preservation. In some places, groups collaborate to support projects that advance their land use agenda. For example, the members of Smart Growth Alliance, in Washington, D.C., which is composed of local homebuilders, the Chesapeake Bay Foundation (an environmental group), smart-growth proponents, and the Board of Trade, will throw their collective support behind smart-growth projects. Similarly, the Housing Action Coalition, in the Santa Clara Valley, was formed by a broad range of organizations and interests to promote housing and mixed-use developments that meet its criteria.[5]

In working with the community, developers must expect to make changes in order to address residents' issues. How far to go in accommodating community concerns will, of course, depend on the circumstances of the individual project—especially its economics. However, making concessions can often be in the developer's best interest. For example, according to Jim Kane, development manager for the Charles E. Smith Companies, in Arlington, Virginia, neighbors of the upscale Alban Towers project in Northwest Washington, D.C., asked the firm to pay for their legal counsel. "We agreed to pay for part of the costs," he explains, "because we wanted to have an educated negotiator on the other side."

To avoid misunderstandings, Harris suggests that once the community and the developer have reached consensus, the developer obtain a written agreement that declares the community's support for the project in exchange for certain actions to be taken by the developer.

Gentrification

In low-income and transitional neighborhoods, community opposition to new, market-rate housing developments tends to focus on the issue of gentrification—"the process by which higher-income households displace lower-income residents of a neighborhood, changing the essential character and flavor of that neighborhood."[6]

Langham Court, in Boston, includes a mix of apartments that range from subsidized low-income to market-rate units.

© Steve Rosenthal; Courtesy of Goody, Clancy & Associates

When new development occurs in a transitional or low-income neighborhood, gentrification is not inevitable. Some cities, for example, that have lost population in the past can accommodate many new residents without displacing existing ones. In some instances, however, new housing development can result in higher rents and real estate taxes, changes in community leadership and political character, and involuntary displacement—and can also catalyze other physical, economic or social changes that transform the neighborhood's overall character and image. How much displacement occurs depends on how tight the local housing market is:[7] generally, renters and the poorest residents, many of whom are elderly and all of whom have few alternatives, are the most affected.

In addition to raising concerns, gentrification—and the general, neighborhoodwide improvements it brings with it—can provide benefits. A new, market-rate development can be the impetus for long-needed infrastructure improvements, help create a more attractive living environment, draw needed stores and services, and help increase safety. Tax revenues generated by the new housing development can help support government programs and services that benefit all residents. Current homeowners can benefit from the appreciation in property values, and all residents can enjoy improvements in the neighborhood's physical, social, and economic condition.

Often, people who live in low-income neighborhoods do not understand that negotiating with developers can create the opportunity to gain benefits. Notes Harold Barnette, president of Heak Associates, Inc., in Atlanta, the challenge for developers is "to harness the intellectual capacity within the community to help them achieve their goals to rebuild their neighborhoods, create new opportunities, and create wealth for themselves and others." Specifically, he advises developers to become involved in the neighborhood planning process and to help educate residents about concepts such as mixed use, smart growth, and value creation.

Mossik Hacobian, executive director of Boston's Urban Edge Housing Corporation, observes that in places where community devel-

Computer imagery shows a strip development (top) transformed into a high-density, mixed-use main street (bottom). Such simulations can be used to help residents and public officials visualize the benefits of higher-density infill development.

opment corporations have created significant amounts of housing that will remain affordable to low- and moderate-income households, residents are not threatened by the introduction of market-rate housing and higher-income residents. Instead, they welcome the benefits that such development will bring. On the other hand, Hattie Dorsey, president and chief executive officer of the Atlanta Neighborhood Development Partnership, observes that improvements in lower-income neighborhoods resulting from nonprofit development activity can also affect citywide housing markets. "Nonprofit developers create value in the neighborhoods where they build," she notes. "We did not anticipate that one result of our efforts would be an inflation in housing costs that would affect the overall affordability of intown housing."

Where the threat of displacement is real, the key is for cities and developers to "spend more time developing strategies to avert or address the adverse consequences of gentrification and less time opposing or supporting the market-driven process itself."[8] Cities can help by addressing the effects of gentrification in any number of ways.[9] In addition to involving existing residents in planning the future of their communities, local government strategies might include the following:

■ Stabilizing existing renters through rental assistance programs, nondiscrimination laws, "just cause" eviction controls, mandatory relocation payments (when rental units are eliminated), and condo conversion controls.

The design of Victoria Townhomes, in Seattle, disguises the fact that the units were built above a two-level garage.

Robert Pisano; Courtesy of Mithun

■ Creating preservation programs to stabilize existing market-rate housing.

■ Developing new housing in which all or some of the units are set aside for low- and moderate-income households through long-term affordability restrictions.

■ Using tax policy to reduce the cost to developers of producing and operating infill housing. Tax deferment programs, for example, can be used to defer a portion of property taxes until the property is sold; tax increment financing can be used to fund project-related improvements. If tax increment financing programs are used, a portion of the funds generated by the new development can be set aside for affordable housing.

■ Using public assets, such as city-owned land and school buildings, "to spur development consistent with the neighborhood's vision."[10]

The loss of minority-owned property can often be addressed by involving the community in the planning process, encouraging ownership by African Americans and other minorities, working with minority partners, and seeking to achieve an economically, ethnically, and racially diverse occupant mix.[11]

Construction Issues

The process of constructing a housing development within an existing urban setting requires special care if neighbors are not to be unnecessarily disturbed or inconvenienced. To maintain good community relations, developers need to think about and plan for these issues ahead of time.

Considerate developers will inform the neighbors in advance of the construction schedule, explain what provisions have been made to minimize disruptions during the construction process, and provide the name and phone number of a contact person whom residents can call to resolve any problems or conflicts that may arise.

To minimize traffic on neighborhood streets, developers may need to limit the number of vehicles that workers can drive to the site, perhaps by arranging for workers to use public transportation or by providing shuttles from public parking lots. The developer may want to coordinate activities and deliveries to minimize the number of trips required, locate project access points where they are least intrusive, and create on-site staging areas for operations, storage of materials, and construction parking. Access points for trucks and other large vehicles must be planned for maximum safety. Construction vehicles should be kept clear of neighbors' access, driveways, and landscaping. During construction at the Alban Towers site, the Charles E. Smith Company hired a uniformed police officer from 6:30 to 9:00 each morning to handle traffic and parking issues. For safety as well as security, the site should be fenced during construction. Where residences are immediately adjacent to the site, fencing should block visibility as well as provide security.

To prevent drainage from the site from affecting nearby properties during construction, stormwater management must be planned in advance. Noise abatement measures may be needed during construction. Noise can be less troublesome if loud activities are planned in the middle of the day, when most residents are at work. Out of consideration for the neighbors, developers will often agree to restrict their hours of operation.

Other issues sometimes arise during construction. According to Kane, his firm installed seismic monitors in some of the homes surrounding Alban Towers to allay fears of construction damage, and hired rat experts to control what residents believed was an increase in the rat population resulting from the construction activity. When a building is demolished, site treatment to control vermin is essential because "tear-down sites are luxury resorts for large rodent populations."[12]

Developers can keep sites clean by storing building materials in confined areas, providing adequate trash disposal containers, and scheduling regular trash pickups. Neighborhood streets must also be kept clean. "When foundations and slabs are pumped from the street

and deliveries made from there as well, road conditions become problems," writes Kent Dougherty, of *Builder* magazine. "Spread two-inch stone and set up wheel-wash stations at access points. A regular Friday evening street washing can impress residents and officials alike. Making the effort is sometimes all that is needed."[13]

Notes

1. Speaking at ULI's Spring Council Forum, Miami, 2000.

2. Kate White, "Specific Area Plans: Building Consensus for Infill Housing," http://www.spur.org./infill.html, 2.

3. Debra Stein, *Winning Community Support for Land Use Projects* (Washington, D.C.: ULI, 1992), 7.

4. William H. Kreager, "Developing Infill Housing," *Land Development,* winter 1996, 10.

5. The endorsement criteria that projects must meet in order to obtain the Housing Action Coalition's support are provided on the group's Web site, previously available at http://www.svmg.org/htm/housing_hac.htm.

6. Maureen Kennedy and Paul Leonard, "Dealing with Neighborhood Change: A Primer on Gentrification and Policy Choices" (discussion paper prepared for the Center on Urban and Metropolitan Policy, Brookings Institution, and PolicyLink, April 2001), 5.

7. Ibid., 15.

8. Ibid., 3.

9. For more detailed suggestions, the reader is encouraged to visit PolicyLink's Web site, http://www.policylink.org/gentrification, which includes the "Beyond Gentrification Toolkit," a comprehensive array of strategies for addressing gentrification issues.

10. Kennedy and Leonard, "Dealing with Neighborhood Change," 36.

11. Summary Report, ULI Infill Housing Development Symposium, Atlanta, 1998.

12. Kent Dougherty, "The Adventurer's Guide to Infill," *Builder,* July 1998, http://www.builderonline.com.

13. Ibid.

Case Studies

Marston Point Place
San Diego, California

Queen palms, other extensive landscaping, and varied setbacks and architectural features enliven the streetscape of the Rowhomes.

Marston Point Place, a 42-unit development of suburban-style, for-sale homes in an urban setting, is located on Sixth Street in Park West—an older, mixed-use neighborhood in San Diego. Just across from the cultural attractions of Balboa Park and only ten blocks from downtown, the development includes four different product types on a single city block and is the first major new homeownership project developed in Park West in 20 years.

Founded in 1993, the development firm, Carter Reese & Associates, focuses on the creation of market-rate homeownership opportunities in the city of San Diego. During the savings and loan crisis, the firm bought, rehabilitated, and sold apartment buildings—but, in the words of general partner Reese Jarrett, "After a while, we found that that was not a lot of fun. So we decided to try a more interesting

challenge, one where we could make a difference: for-sale residential development opportunities in older neighborhoods."

The firm's first development, Jarrett Heights, brought 23 new, single-family homes to Lincoln Park, a struggling neighborhood where no one else was building for-sale housing. The project, named for Reese Jarrett's father, has stimulated additional investment in the neighborhood. Among the firm's other projects are Cypress Hills, a 30-unit townhouse development in Bankers' Hills; the Village at Euclid, a 23-unit single-family development in Lincoln Park, just one half-mile east of Jarrett Heights; and Mission Hills Commons, a mixed-use project now under construction along Washington Street in Mission Hills.

In response to substantial pent-up demand for urban living, a great deal of infill residential development is taking place in San Diego today, with approximately 8,000 new housing units currently planned or underway in the downtown redevelopment district. Under the auspices of the Centre City Development Corporation (CCDC), residential developments within that district receive various kinds of support, including expedited approvals and permits—and, if they qualify, additional financial support in the form of grants, loans, and tax credits. In Jarrett's opinion, however, the primarily high-priced mid-rise and high-rise development within the redevelopment district differs markedly from Carter Reese developments in terms of market, product type, and architectural style.

The 52,000-square-foot Marston Point Place site was selected because of its uptown location: across from Balboa Park and on high ground that commands views of the park, San Diego Bay, and downtown San Diego. With museums, the acclaimed San Diego Zoo, and other cultural amenities on its grounds, Balboa Park is not only an oasis of open space and recreational facilities but the cultural center of the city. The site is easily accessible to I-5 and State Highway 163, Lindbergh Field International Airport, the train station, the Gaslamp Quarter, shopping in Mission Valley, and the restaurants of Old Town and Little Italy; local shopping, restaurants, and professional services are just steps away. The project's name reflects its location on Marston Point, which was named for George W. Marston, a civic leader and one of the creators of Balboa Park.

Though the project site had previously been developed for residential and office uses, at the time the land was purchased it was vacant and had become a trash-strewn eyesore. Another developer had bought the site some years earlier and demolished the structures, planning to build a hotel, but the market changed and the site eventually reverted to the lender through foreclosure. Carter Reese &

Associates bought the site from the lender. The site was essentially clean, and site development posed few problems.

The design challenge was to create a full-block development that was neither monolithic nor monotonous and that matched the proportions and scale of nearby structures. To that end, Marston Point Place includes four three- and four-story product types on a single city block: Rowhomes, Court Homes, Lane Homes, and the Marston, a condominium building. The combination of different residential products made possible a varied yet harmonious project design that reflects the historical development patterns and architectural character of the Park West neighborhood. And, by including different types of homes, Carter Reese broadened the range of potential buyers and created a project that could be built in phases rather than all at once, thereby lessening its market risk.

The homes range in size from 1,000 to 2,400 square feet, with sales prices from $199,000 to $545,000. Lot sizes differ, with Rowhomes on 1,400-square-foot parcels, Court Homes on 1,200-square-foot lots, and Lane Homes on lots averaging 1,100 square feet. Per-square-foot construction costs were $70 for the Rowhomes; $80 for the Court Homes, $85 for the Lane Homes, and $95 for the Marston condominiums.

The Rowhomes portion of the project built on the success of an earlier Carter Reese rowhouse development on an adjacent block. That project, called Sixth and Ivy, was designed by Bruce Dammann, Marston Point's land planner and one of its architects, and consisted of six rowhouse units fronting Sixth Street, across from Balboa Park. Although the Sixth and Ivy project required considerable effort, Jarrett explained, "It was worthwhile to experiment with the product to see if it worked." Market response was so enthusiastic that, as Jarrett says, "I don't think we could ever find the bottom of demand for that particular housing type in the city."

Marston Point Place's 11 Rowhomes are also on Sixth Street, facing Balboa Park, and include features normally associated with suburban homes—such as large two-car garages; two or three stories of living space; and a patch of yard. To avoid creating a common wall between homes, the company leaves a two-inch separation between each pair of homes and then covers the separation with a flange to create a seamless facade. The units have either two or three bedrooms and between 1,900 and 2,400 square feet of living space.

The inclusion of garages dictated a home design in which living areas were elevated above street level, minimizing street noise and visual intrusion—an important concern on busy streets in urban neighborhoods. Even though they require more curb cuts, Dammann prefers front-loaded garages: because they require homes to be set back a bit from the street, they make it possible to include some private open space in front of the homes. In addition, when garages are located in the front of the units, the design

Garage parking for the Court Homes is provided off an interior common driveway.

allows for rear patio yards in the space that would otherwise be consumed by alleys and garages. Dammann includes the driveway pavement, plantings, and designs as part of the project's landscaping plan.

The two- or three-bedroom Court Homes front either Ivy Street or a semiprivate walkway with a private motor court that provides entry to the garages. Each of the 16 two-story cluster homes has a two-car garage and a storage room on the street level; the entry, kitchen, and dining areas are on the floor above, and the bedrooms are on the third level.

The seven Lane Homes are similar in design to the Court Homes but have three levels of living space. In addition, because their entrances are at street level, off a common entry lane, the design allows the inclusion of a private enclosed yard.

The Marston, the development's "crown jewel," occupies the site's highest elevation and presents wonderful opportunities for views. A stacked, four-story condominium structure built over parking at the northwest corner of Sixth and Juniper streets, the building includes eight units: four townhouses on the first level, all with living areas on the second floor so that residents can enjoy the views; and two units on each of the third and fourth floors.

Homes include features such as wrought-iron balconies; high ceilings; marble countertops; large, double-pane picture windows; fireplaces; and telecommunications wiring. Most have some private outdoor space, and all are prewired for optional security systems. Because Marston Point is located along the flight path of airplanes traveling to and from nearby Lindbergh Field airport, noise was a potential problem. To mitigate noise, the units were designed with double-paned windows and air conditioning, and the exterior walls and ceilings were upgraded with extra insulation and resilient channels for sound attenuation.

The project was built in two phases: the first consisted of six Rowhomes and half of the Court Homes. At the lender's urging, the Rowhomes were priced 20 percent over their appraised value; nevertheless, the homes in the first phase sold before they were built, on the first weekend they were offered. The Rowhomes cost more to build than anticipated. Though prices were increased on the remaining Rowhomes and Court Homes, they too sold out quickly, and home values have continued to rise rapidly. For example, prices for Rowhomes sold in 1998 and 1999 averaged in the mid-$300,000s; one recently resold for $570,000. Jarrett himself lives in one of the Rowhomes.

Community concerns, which influenced the project's final design, focused on the development's relationship to its surroundings—in particular, the numerous driveways. Carter Reese maintained the old sidewalk grid, but added more landscaping (such as a double row of queen palms along Sixth Avenue, and vines over the garages) to soften the visual impact of the intersection between the elevation and the street. In addition, the texture of the pavement blocks was varied to reduce the visual impact of the driveways.

The project was financed with conventional bank financing (at a low loan-to-value ratio) and private equity (totaling approximately 15 percent of the project cost). Carter Reese raised over $1,500,000 in equity and also invested its own cash as equity. San Diego National Bank financed the land, and First National Bank provided construction financing. Because the market for these homes was not proven, First National Bank required equity from Carter Reese in the form of a secondary lien on its existing assets.

The project was marketed primarily to people driving by (through on-site signage); through word of mouth; and to a list of prospects, including people who had bought homes in earlier Carter Reese projects. According to Tom Carter, general partner of Carter Reese & Associates, competition was not really an issue because the project was unique.

The target market included people without children—young people seeking starter homes, singles, DINKs (double income, no kids), and empty nesters (although Jarrett, who has a five-year-old daughter, was an exception). The residents represent a mix of incomes, racial and ethnic backgrounds, and lifestyles. Carter observes that people who decide to move into

Every unit has some private open space that is protected, either by its location or by a physical buffer, from the view of neighbors.

city locations readily accept demographic and economic diversity.

In retrospect, Carter feels that the homes could have commanded higher prices. And, "it would have helped to have models to show what we were building, because it was a long time between sales and closing."

The toughest challenge in developing Marston Point Place was obtaining development approvals for the project, largely because of the city's attempt to legislate design through the Planned District Ordinance (PDO), a city law that applies to a zoning overlay district within which the project site is located. Adopted in response to poor-quality developments in the 1970s and 1980s, the PDO is well-intentioned but very specific in its requirements. According to Carter, the PDO requirements' strict limitations on project design tend to yield self-contained, inward-turning developments; the result, he fears, will be "a lot of homogeneous, monolithic developments that will ruin the character of the old city." Carter Reese, in con-

The elegant simplicity of the design of this corner townhouse is accentuated by decorative railing and nontraditional windows.

site. To meet the requirement for visitor parking, the negotiated solution was to include an unfinished "bonus room" adjacent to the rowhouse garages. This space met the PDO parking requirement because it could be used for additional parking, but actually buyers can also refinish it as a recreation room, bedroom, or other living space.

To some extent, California's strict construction-defect legislation also dictated project design—specifically, the small separation between units in the Rowhomes, Court Homes, and Lane Homes. In California, a homeowners association (HOA) can sue a developer, contractor, or subcontractor for damages for poorly built units for up to ten years, holding them to the same standard as a manufacturer. According to Jarrett, because the law is so favorably biased toward HOAs, it has been exploited, and law firms seek out HOA clients. As a result, small developers like Carter Reese do not want to risk that kind of liability for small condominium projects. Instead, they build "air space condos," configurations in which a small envelope surrounds each house, making it a separate unit without an active HOA. The homeowner is responsible for the home's exterior, landscaping, and so forth; and, although there is a "dormant HOA," it owns nothing. When the firm must create an active HOA, Jarrett explains, "We don't create a size that will attract the attention of law firms." Thus, Marston Point's 42 units are governed by three different HOAs, one of which—that for the Rowhomes—is dormant. The HOAs for the Court Homes and Land Homes own common driveways, walkways, landscaping, and lighting, but no living areas. Only the association for the Marston owns common areas within a residential building.

The condominium liability issue creates other problems as well. To avoid potential liability, high-production subcontractors prefer to work on commercial or single-family suburban construction. As a result, developers of projects (especially small ones) that have a condominium component have fewer choices in subcontractors and must pay higher prices.

Coordinating the different—and sometimes conflicting—requirements posed by various city

trast, strives to create developments that maintain the character of the neighborhoods in which they are located. To build Marston Point, the firm had to obtain 33 deviations from the PDO, which took 18 months. Yet, in Carter's opinion, the project's innovative yet contextual design was essential to its success.

Carter Reese worked with the community to obtain support for changes to the PDO's requirements for setbacks, parking ratios, and transparencies. For example, the PDO required windows on the ground floor. For both parking and privacy, Carter Reese sought permission to include garages instead. The PDO required—and the city wanted—visitor parking on the

agencies is also difficult. And, as is the case with many regulations, the city's engineering requirements are the same for urban and suburban projects. In Dammann's opinion, some of these standards, such as required road widths and turning radii, are excessive for an urban infill development.

Carter cautions that infill development requires time, patience, and perseverance. In all, it took four years to complete the 42-unit Marston Point Place development, partly because the development approvals process is inherently difficult, and partly because city staff are not trained to understand infill development. (Redevelopment projects within the purview of the CCDC respond to a separate planning department and follow a different,

expedited approvals process.) Because of the tortuous regulatory process, Carter Reese plans to diversify its operations and work in other cities. "If it takes 18 months to obtain approvals for this kind of project in San Diego," comments Jarrett, "we can't do another Marston Point."

Carter, who is a former mayoral candidate, also emphasizes that developers involved in infill development need to be politically active and maintain a good relationship with the city and community groups. In this way, they can better anticipate and adjust to changes in the environment for real estate development and respond to neighbors' concerns by creating developments that will succeed—both in the marketplace and within the larger community.

Street-level garages enhance security and privacy as well as provide parking.

Site plan.

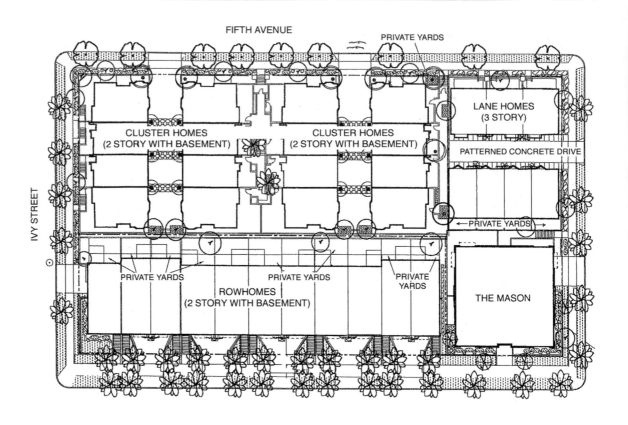

Floor plans—row-homes and court homes.

Project Data: Marston Point Place

Land Use Information

Site area	1.2 acres
Total dwelling units	42
Gross density	35 units per acre
Total parking spaces	83

Residential Unit Information

Unit Type	Total Number	Square Feet	Sales Prices
Rowhomes	11	1,900–2,400	$325,000–$370,000
Court Homes	16	1,300–1,500	$215,000–$280,000
Lane Homes	7	1,000–1,200	$199,000–$212,000
The Marston	8	1,500–2,000	$399,000–$545,000

Development Cost Information

Land acquisition	$1,856,123
Site improvement	928,334
Construction	5,486,040
Total soft costs	2,308,879
Total hard and soft development costs	$10,579,376
Average development cost per unit	$251,890

Financing Information

Source	Purpose of Financing	Amount
Developers/investors	Capital	$3,079,376
First National Bank	The Marston	2,100,000
First National Bank	Rowhomes, Court Homes, and Lane Homes	5,400,100
Total		$10,579,476

Development Schedule

Site purchased	October 1997
Planning began	April 1997
Site work began	September 1998
Project completion	January 2001

Phase I: Rowhomes, Court Homes, and Lane Homes

Number of units	34
Planning started	April 1997
Construction started	September 1998
Construction completed	December 1999
Sales started	September 1998
Sales completed	December 1999

Phase II: The Marston

Number of units	8
Planning started	April 1997
Construction started	October 1999
Construction completed	January 2001
Sales/leasing started	December 1999
Sales/leasing completed	January 2001

Project Award

In 2000, Marston Point Place received the Planning Project Award from the San Diego section of the American Planning Association.

Development Team

Developer
Carter Reese & Associates
3636 Fifth Avenue, Suite 300
San Diego, California 92103
619-232-2200

Land Planner/Architect
Bruce Dammann
3636 Fifth Avenue, Suite 100
San Diego, California 92103
619-699-1113

Architect
Jon Ebert
4916 Everts Street
San Diego, California 92109
858-272-8181

Project Address

2200 Sixth Avenue
San Diego, California 92101

General Information

Thomas F. Carter or Reese A. Jarrett, general partners, Carter Reese & Associates
619-232-2200

All information in this case study is current as of January 2001.

Old Town Village

Alexandria, Virginia

The two-story court-yard homes, with their private front and rear yards and covered entrances, offer suburban-style living in an urban setting.

The development of Old Town Village transformed an old and abandoned railroad yard close to the heart of historic Alexandria, Virginia, into a 285-unit community of townhouses, courtyard homes, and condominiums. Developed by Eakin/Youngentob Associates, Inc. (EYA), of Arlington, Virginia, the project demonstrates the combined power of a terrific urban location, excellent project design, and critical mass in overcoming negative factors on and immediately around a site. In all, the project has won 25 local, regional, and national awards.

Founded in 1992 by Terry Eakin and Bob Youngentob, EYA is an innovative, entrepreneurial residential development firm that specializes in high-quality infill communities in premium locations in the Washington, D.C., metropolitan area. Among the other EYA developments are Ford's Landing, 136 luxury townhouses on the waterfront in Alexandria, Virginia; Palisades Park, 128 townhouses in North Arlington, Virginia, overlooking the

Potomac River near Key Bridge; Monument Place, 17 luxury townhouses overlooking the Iwo Jima Memorial, also in North Arlington; and Harrison Square, 98 townhouses in the Shaw community of northwest Washington. EYA has become known for its creative, high-density site plans and architectural design, and has won more industry awards in its first nine years as a company than any other Washington-area builder. EYA has approximately 100 employees, delivers about 250 homes per year, and in 2000 was designated America's Best Builder by *Builder* magazine.

EYA was attracted to the Old Town Village site because of its location just a few blocks from the center of Old Town Alexandria, a lively historic district on the Potomac River, just four miles outside of Washington, D.C. Settled in 1688, the city of Alexandria offers a rich variety and concentration of historic buildings, most of which have been restored. The boutiques, restaurants, art galleries, and colonial ambience of Old Town Alexandria draw visitors from throughout the Washington area, and the city is one of the most sought-after and expensive residential addresses in the region.

The Old Town Village site is a short walk from the commercial and residential core of the city and just five blocks from the King Street Metro (subway) stop. However, the uses immediately surrounding the site include a busy traffic thoroughfare, low-income housing, a cemetery, empty warehouses, and an oil distribution facility. The site itself had been used as a railway switching yard during the Civil War, and at one time contained brick office buildings used for railroad research. At the time of purchase, oil tankers from the adjacent distribution facility were often parked on a portion of the property.

In 1995, the site's owner, Norfolk Southern Railroad, was looking for a buyer for the site. A local broker contacted EYA—which, after many months of negotiations, contracted to purchase the site for $12 million, subject to city approval of the proposed development. The seller liked EYA's vision of a low-rise residential community that would reconnect the rail yard site with the grid pattern of the city streets. To avoid competing with a nearby infill project owned by the seller, EYA agreed, as part of the purchase agreement, not to develop apartments on the property.

Working with the city's planning office and with neighborhood groups, EYA created a detailed plan for Old Town Village that included 285 homes: 130 condominiums, 116 townhouses, and 39 courtyard homes. The plan for the site offered different types of units and a variety of architectural styles, creating an appearance that would be consistent with the historic character of Old Town. EYA developed the master plan for the entire project, created all the architectural designs, and obtained all development approvals.

Site development and planning were complicated by a number of problems. First, legal issues regarding roads, easements, and plats had to be resolved through negotiations with the city. For example, the site included four abandoned "paper streets," which many in the community wanted reopened—though they did not want the through-traffic that would likely result. In addition, oil from the adjacent distribution facility had leached onto the site; and arsenic, which had been sprayed on the railroad lines to kill vegetation, remained in the soil. The city required EYA to haul away the top four inches of the site, encapsulate the soil, and make sure that each unit's backyard was covered with 18 inches of clean new topsoil. Finally, because the soil on a portion of the site included 20 feet of uncompacted fill, EYA had to sink piles at one end of the site, where the condominiums were built, in order to establish buildable pads.

Townhouse units come in a range of sizes and offer a variety of colors, materials, and architectural styles.

Other interesting—and expensive—surprises surfaced before actual construction. To meet the city's requirements for archaeological finds, EYA hired an archaeological contractor to map the site, identify key resources, and negotiate with the city to determine which parts of the site had to be excavated. In the course of this work, EYA uncovered a buried, 20-foot octagonal privy—with a rifle, boots, razors, buttons, and so forth dating back to the Civil War, when the site was used as an encampment by the

Union Army and as the headquarters for its railroad operations. The city of Alexandria proved very cooperative, agreeing to a cost cap and a deadline for working through the archaeological issues. Though the archaeological work delayed development, EYA president Bob Youngentob and chairman Terry Eakin describe this part of project development and planning as memorable and exciting. It also illustrates the very time- and management-intensive nature of infill development.

Obtaining a special-use permit from the city of Alexandria—which required the approval of city staff; positive recommendations from the planning commission and the board of architectural review; and, in a highly political process, a final vote by the mayor and city council—posed a major challenge for EYA. To work through various issues, EYA participated in more than 20 meetings with civic groups; city staff; and members of the planning commission, the board of architectural review, and the city council. For example, the Old Town Civic Association's concerns, which the company accommodated in its final plans, centered around the compatibility of the overall

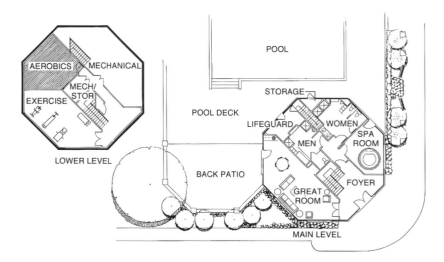

The community center is located within a large village green in the center of the development.

site design with existing streets, signage, and architectural style. For structures in the small portion of the property that fell within the Old Town historic district, the city's board of architectural review had to approve the authenticity of EYA's architectural designs and building materials.

Using neotraditional planning principles, EYA designed the site plan for the project as an integral part of the fabric of the existing urban neighborhood rather than as a self-contained unit. Blocks of homes face the public streets, reestablishing the community's historic grid pattern and reconnecting the property to adjacent residential neighborhoods. Interior private streets are generally located on historic rights-of-way, reconnecting them visually with the neighboring streets—a connection that had been severed in the early 1800s, when the site was first occupied by railroad uses. The complex internal road system and a single, one-way exit onto the adjacent major road minimize through-traffic. To ensure the integrity of the streetscape, all garages are rear-loaded and face the alleys behind the homes. Tree wells, brick walkways, and period streetlights create streetscapes that echo patterns in the larger community environment. Although an early consultant had recommended a perimeter wall to separate the development from its less attractive neighbors, no special security measures were included in the final project design. EYA believes that the relatively large size of the 12.3-acre site helped create the critical mass necessary to establish a sense of place, thereby overwhelming negative edge conditions.

EYA included different types of homes in Old Town Village to expand the potential market (in terms of both size and price range), to maximize sales absorption, and to reduce the financial risk. To further lessen its risk, EYA and its investors sold a portion of the site to Pulte Corporation to build the condominium component of the project. Given the unproven demand for infill residential sales properties in the mid-1990s—and the questionable character of the land uses immediately surrounding the site—EYA and its investors and lenders were understandably concerned about risk.

The courtyard homes are two-story, 32-foot-wide, attached single-family homes—generously sized (over 2,600 square feet), and with what Fakin describes as a "very unique design." More like a suburban home than a traditional urban rowhouse or apartment product, the courtyard home draws its design theme from the "side yard houses" of Charleston, South Carolina. The home's entry is right on the street—through a solid "front door" into a private enclosed courtyard, within which are a small front yard and a covered front porch. A second solid front door leads from the covered porch into the home. Off the breakfast room, at the back of the home, is another private enclosed courtyard.

Two courtyard architectural styles were offered: one, designed to appeal to empty nesters, features a master bedroom suite on the first floor and two other bedrooms, a family room, and a computer loft on the second level. The second style is similar, but the family room is on the first floor instead of the master suite and all three bedrooms and the computer loft are upstairs.

Before the models were built, this innovative product was hard to sell, but once sales prospects were able to see the homes, they were snapped up quickly at escalating prices. Interestingly, three-fourths of the buyers (even empty

Garage parking off rear alleys is provided for all townhouses and courtyard homes, and each townhouse has a deck above the garage.

Interiors are characterized by open floor plans and high-quality finishes.

nesters) preferred the style in which all the bedrooms were upstairs, although Eakin cautions that this pattern could be attributable to the fact that the model home was decorated so attractively.

The townhouses were built in four sizes, ranging in width from 16 to 24 feet and ranging in size from 1,840 to 2,820 square feet—again, in order to reduce risk by appealing to the widest range of potential purchasers. All the townhouses are four stories high, with similar, richly detailed facades and high-quality finishes. However, the varied elevations of Federal, Georgian, and Victorian architecture and the range of colors and materials offered ensured that no two townhouses or courtyard homes would be exactly alike. Though home types are mixed throughout the site, architectural styles are grouped in three- to four-unit sections, echoing the development pattern of the Old Town area.

All courtyard and townhouse units (except the 16-foot-wide townhouses, which provide space for tandem car parking) feature two-car garages off a rear alley. Each townhouse has a large outdoor deck above the garage. All EYA

homes include double-hung wooden windows with insulated glass; professional landscaping; master bedroom suites with cathedral ceilings and soaking tubs; gourmet kitchens; gas fireplaces; and living areas enhanced with hardwood floors, crown molding, and chair rails in selected areas.

The five-and-a-half-story condominium buildings were designed to resemble Alexandria's Old Cotton Manufacturing Building, a historic structure on Washington Street complete with cupola and colonnaded entrance. All the condominiums are duplex units, offering the feeling of a townhouse but at a more affordable price.

The focal point of the community—what a visitor sees upon entering—is a town square, a central gathering place that includes, within a large village green, a community center with a year-round spa, an outdoor swimming pool, and an antique clock. To reflect the site's history, the community center was designed to look like an octagonal railroad roundhouse of the early 1900s. The community center contains a health club and a furnished clubroom.

Initial prices for the courtyard homes and townhouses ranged from $259,000 to $420,000, with a target market made up primarily of young professionals and empty nesters. Though the development appealed to a broad range of buyers, few have children living at home. An EYA study in 2001 indicated that the homes' resale prices increased an average of about 16 percent per year in the roughly three years after construction. The firm attributes the appreciation to two principal factors: the vitality of the Washington-area real estate market and strong consumer interest in infill properties.

Presales took place in an onsite trailer, and initial home sales were tremendous: between 20 and 30 units in the first month, and 136 in just over a year, at an average rate of 8.5 per month. This rapid pace enabled EYA to, in Eakin's words, "march through the project." Initially, homes along busy Duke Street were priced only slightly lower because of the noise and traffic, but Eakin notes that "even they were gobbled up." Prices for courtyard and townhouse units rose by approximately 20 percent over the sellout period. All were presold within 22 months, and the developer built them as fast as it could.

At the time Old Town Village was developed, a few smaller infill townhouse developments were underway in Alexandria—but, Youngentob notes, "Our competitors were forced to slow down and wait for Old Town Village to sell out." In his opinion, Old Town Village had the competitive advantages of a better location, products, and prices.

Significant investment in marketing is one reason for the project's success. For example, even though EYA knew that it would have to be torn down later, the firm chose, early in de-velopment, to build a streetscape—complete with curbs and gutters, brick pavers, and landscaping—so that prospective buyers could see the "Old Town" image that the development would create. "We are willing to commit and invest," explains Youngentob, "which gives our market a feeling of confidence."

In retrospect, because of the tremendous market response to this development, the principals at EYA feel that, were they developing the project today, they would retain the condominium piece and develop it themselves. And they would have sold the homes more slowly and raised prices more quickly.

However, as EYA's experience illustrates, pricing infill developments can be difficult because each project is unique—and, typically, there are few real comparables on which to base judgments. To price Old Town Village, EYA hosted a series of luncheons to ask the advice of top Old Town brokers. Because of the negative factors in the immediate area, the brokers were generally very cautious. "We initially charged 25 percent more than they recommended, and we were still too low," Eakin explains. "The project created a frenzy of demand." A difficult issue for a project of this nature, according to Youngentob, is "determining at what level to raise prices to slow sales to the pace of construction, without pricing yourself out of the market."

According to Youngentob, a good working partnership with the city was essential, and the success of this project can be explained in part by "the city of Alexandria's cooperative and flexible approach to working with us. Everyone wanted to see something happen on this property; we were working toward a common goal."

Site plan.

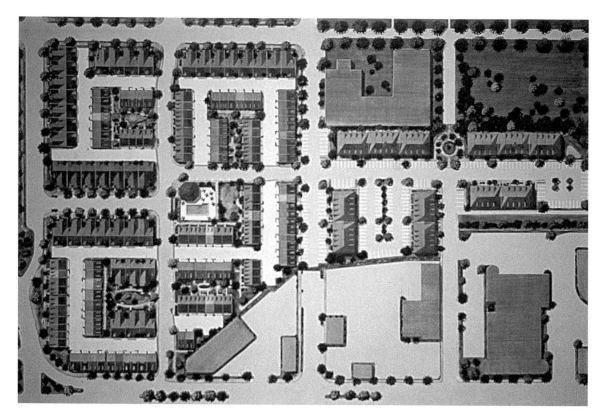

Floor plans.

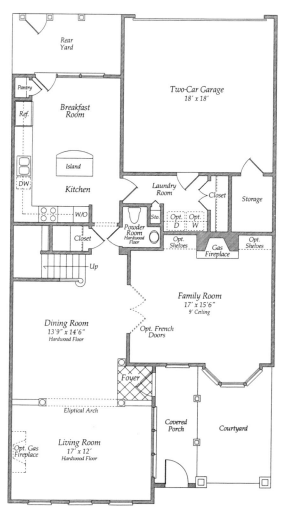

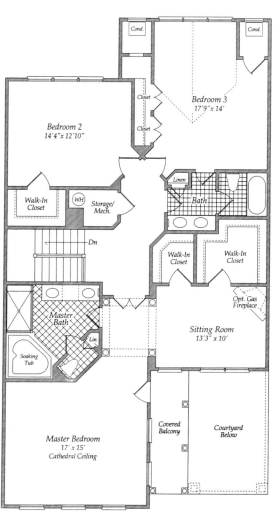

Project Data: Old Town Village

Land Use Information

Site area	12.3 acres
Total dwelling units	285
Gross density	23 units per acre
Amenities	0.5 acres
Clubhouse	2,900 square feet
Total parking spaces	585
Indoor and garage spaces	310
Outdoor lot spaces	275

Residential Unit Information

Unit type	Total Number	Square Feet	Initial Sales Prices
Courtyard homes	39	2,636	$420,000
Townhouses	116	1,840–2,820	$259,000–$369,000
Condominiums	130	1,350–1,400	$190,000

Development Cost Information

Land cost	$12,000,000 (for 285 units)
Site improvement	5,656,000 (for 285 units)
Construction	19,673,000 (for 155 units)
Amenities	328,000 (for 285 units)
Total soft costs	12,586,000 (for 155 units)
Total hard and soft development costs	$50,243,000 (for 285 units)

Financing Information

Source	Type of Financing	Amount
First Union Bank, McLean, Virginia	Acquisition and development loan	$16,900,000
First Union Bank, McLean, Virginia	Revolving construction loan	$7,897,000

Development Schedule

Site contracted for purchase	April 1996
Planning started	April 1996
Construction started	May 1997
Construction completed	December 1998
Sales started	February 1997
Sales completed	May 1999

Project Awards

Old Town Village received 25 local and national awards, including the 1999 Aurora Awards for Best Residential Development and Best in State, conferred by the Southeast Builders Conference. The project was also a 1999 finalist in ULI's Awards for Excellence.

Development Team

Developer
Eakin/Youngentob Associates, Inc.
1000 Wilson Boulevard, Suite 2720
Arlington, Virginia 22209
703-525-5565

Land Planner/Architect
Lessard Architectural Group
8603 Westwood Center Drive
Vienna, Virginia 22182
703-760-8704

Landscape Architect
Studio 39
6416 Grovedale Drive, Suite 100-A
Alexandria, Virginia 22310
703-719-6500

Project Address

Duke and Henry Streets
Alexandria, Virginia 22314

General Information

Contact Information
Terry Eakin, chairman, Eakin/Youngentob Associates, Inc.
703-525-5565

All information in this case study is current as of January 2001.

Buckhead Village Lofts
Atlanta, Georgia

Terraces, balconies, and large windows bring outdoor space and sunshine into the lofts' interiors.

© 2000, Don Rank Photography, Inc.

Buckhead Village Lofts is the first newly constructed loft-style multi-family residential project in Atlanta. Located in the Buckhead neighborhood of northern Atlanta, the 104-unit development, developed by Roddy White and Michael Loia, is designed to resemble a reused factory structure. Targeting high-income singles and couples, Buckhead Village Lofts offers a creative solution to meeting the high demand for a product in limited supply.

To develop Buckhead Village Lofts, White and Loia, both of Atlanta, formed Buckhead Village Lofts, LLC. Loia engaged his architectural firm, Loia Budde & Associates (LB&A), and general construction company, Neal & Loia

Construction Company, to develop the project; White's property management firm, White & Associates, handled marketing and sales. Combining these three areas of expertise in a design-build approach made direct architect-contractor communication possible, shortened delivery time, allowed design modifications to be made on the fly, and enabled the development team to make decisions quickly. And, because his two firms handled both design and construction, Loia was able to exert significant creative control as the project's architect and codeveloper.

LB&A is a full-service architectural, interior design, and planning firm. Before it became involved in Buckhead Village Lofts, in 1997, much of LB&A's architectural work had been in hotel, office, and some residential condominium design, but the firm had not taken on anything as risky as introducing a new product into an untested market. Since then, LB&A has designed other high-quality high-rise multi-family residential loft-style projects, and is now involved in designing both new and renovated loft-style projects throughout the Southeast.

Developed in the 1930s as a suburban residential enclave for Coca-Cola executives and other members of the city's business elite, Buckhead is a third-generation portion of the metropolitan core, some ten miles north of downtown. Thanks to an explosion in real estate investment that began in the 1970s, Buckhead now boasts numerous high-end, super regional malls; an enormous share of new office construction and absorption; and high levels of new, attached, luxury residential construction. Buckhead is also home to the region's entertainment district. Sitting on the northern edge of Atlanta but still within the city limits, Buckhead is "uptown" as well as "intown."

Originally, the Buckhead Village Lofts site had been partially cleared for a proposed extension of Georgia Highway 400, but it was not used when the new road project was completed in the early 1990s. A restaurant also stood on the site, which backs up to a well-established, high-end, low-density neighborhood and is surrounded by boutiques, upscale restaurants, and personal and professional services. Retail and commercial uses that residents can walk to are rare amenities in Atlanta, which has had relatively little mixed-use or high-density development in comparison with other large cities.

Because Buckhead developed rapidly during the 1970s, it was never an industrial core and therefore lacked the older downtown commercial and industrial structures that can be retrofitted for loft living. In Buckhead (as well as in other submarkets, like downtown and mid-town), Atlanta's loft and condominium markets have been booming since the 1990s, and demand for units in adapted structures has nearly exhausted supply. "Neoindustrialism"—recreating the look and feel of older industrial buildings—is one creative design strategy to accommodate the tastes of the young, hip, upscale urban market.

After searching for more than a year to find a property suitable for conversion, White and Loia concluded that no such structure existed. Their decision to construct a new, loft-style condominium building from the ground up established a new concept in the Atlanta high-rise residential market. The site, within easy walking distance of Buckhead's cultural amenities, was exactly what they were looking for.

Sharing a gut feeling that there was substantial demand in the Atlanta market, and particularly in Buckhead, for a high-end loft project, the developers began the project without undertaking a formal market study or consumer research. Loia had noticed that the move back into the cities from the suburbs had been accompanied by popular television shows set in brick-walled lofts and in upscale attached housing. Loia and White believed that Buckhead was ready for the urban lifestyle that had become popular in the 1990s in midtown.

To minimize their exposure, the developers planned to construct Buckhead Village Lofts in two phases. Equity financing was provided through the development partners' personal equity. To obtain debt financing, the developers had to educate lenders about the product. Although Atlanta had examples of successful rental loft developments, none were for sale. So, Loia and White cited examples of successful for-sale loft developments in New York and Chicago, and supplemented this with published information about for-sale lofts in other cities. Regions Bank, of Birmingham, Alabama,

Luxurious fixtures and countertops traditionally are not associated with lofts, but the high-end market at Buckhead Village wanted them.

© 2000, Alan McGee

agreed to underwrite the first phase of the project with no presale requirements. The bank underwrote the project as an apartment development, with the understanding that the developers would offer the lofts for sale but would rent them out if sales did not materialize. Phase I sold briskly in its first three weeks, at which time the developers began work on

© 2000, Don Rank Photography, Inc.

The buildings step back from the parking deck at the base, a design approach that accommodated changes in grade and made it possible to create terraces at the fifth-floor level.

the second phase and the bank provided the remainder of the financing.

The site comprises five adjacent parcels totaling 2.9 acres, with four different zoning classifications. After land use restrictions were addressed, the building was designed to maximize buildable and sellable area while providing desirable views, and amenities such as terraces and balconies. The developers' sensitivity to the natural environment resulted in the preservation of a creek and 1.5 acres of heavily wooded forest in the heart of a dense urban area, producing a wooded buffer on one side of the project and an urban street scene on the other.

Buckhead Village Lofts contains three levels of partially below grade parking and seven levels of one- and two-bedroom residential units. With a density of about 36 units per acre, the project has 182 parking spaces in the three-level, gated-access parking deck that is constructed partially aboveground on the downhill side, fully within the building's footprint. There are 30 one-bedroom units, 60 one- or two-bedroom units, and 14 two-bedroom units. Initial sales prices ranged from $200,000 to $400,000, and units range in size from 1,000 to 1,720 square feet. The pro forma was designed to achieve sales exceeding $200 per square foot.

After researching what consumers wanted and liked about loft living, the development team "deconstructed" what a loft building retrofit is all about—determining what the important elements were and what attracts people to loft living—and then recreated it from scratch. The defining characteristics were high ceilings, exposed utilities, an open floor plan, numerous windows, and lots of light. Ceiling heights vary from 12 to 14 feet within each floor level.

Loia and White's experience with speculative office space helped inform the design process for Buckhead Village Lofts. Beginning with a floor plate and a corridor, Loia custom designed each unit to meet buyers' needs and specifications—for window styles, overall size, balcony size (some units even have multiple balconies), and the placement of plumbing, for example. As a result, no two units are the same size, and the final architecture—interior and exterior—bears the creative stamp of its residents. Allowing buyers not only to upgrade and customize finishes but to determine structural layout proved to be a popular practice.

Originally, the concept for the interior finishes at Buckhead Village Lofts was below what the Buckhead market desired. In response, the developers upgraded the quality of the windows, added more hardwood floors, and offered more luxurious fixtures and countertops. Such high-quality interior finishes are not traditionally associated with lofts, but the high-end market desired them: the result is, in effect, a hybrid product that fuses the basic characteristics of lofts with the finishes of luxury condominiums. On a per-square-foot basis, constructing a loft to appear retrofitted is more expensive than constructing a traditional luxury condominium unit. Additional costs associated with the loft included spiral ventilation ducts; larger heating, ventilation, and air-conditioning units to serve more space (traditionally, loft ceilings are ten to 14 feet high, while those in luxury units are closer to nine feet); aesthetically pleasing electrical conduits; brick (as opposed to plasterboard) interior walls; and precast concrete windowsills.

The market absorbed the project quite rapidly, partly because of pent-up demand for a loft product not otherwise available in the Buckhead area. Sales began in the spring of 1998, the first closing was in March 1999, and the project was 99 percent sold by January 2000.

Most buyers were between the ages of 30 and 45 and had no children. More singles than couples have purchased homes in the project. During the presale period, the developers created a virtual tour of the units' interiors, incorporating computer-generated "walk- and fly-through" animations. A team assembled by White undertook sales in house. The team's familiarity with the design process enabled it to successfully convey the details of an unfamiliar product.

With a large influx of new residents into Atlanta from northern cities in the 1990s, attached housing—and lofts in particular—has become more widely accepted, and much of the

© 2000, Alan McGee

demand for these products has come from high-end homebuyers. During the mid- and late 1990s, condominiums, mostly in the form of luxury mid- and high-rise condominium complexes, became increasingly acceptable luxury living options. As condominium projects increased in popularity, average sales dollars per square foot rose—from $70, in the early 1990s, to $180, by the time that Buckhead Village Lofts began presales in 1998. By the end of the sales period, the figure had increased to more than $275 per square foot.

The Buckhead Village Lofts project helped to lessen the severity of a grim situation faced by Atlanta developers: the growing shortage of old buildings in the city. The developers' feeling that there was pent-up demand for a luxury loft project in Buckhead from the young, hip, and upscale market was ultimately confirmed, and the success of Buckhead Village Lofts demonstrated that the market would accept —and even prefer—new loft construction to a retrofit.

As a result of White and Loia's successful pioneering of the newly constructed luxury loft product, other developers have undertaken an increasing number of similar projects in the in-town housing market. The trend is expected to last for some time, and will likely reshape the residential landscape of the historically low-density city of Atlanta, adding new options to a housing market that has lacked attached, for-sale residences.

Parking was designed to work with the existing grades, eliminating the need for interior ramps.

Building plan.

Site plan.

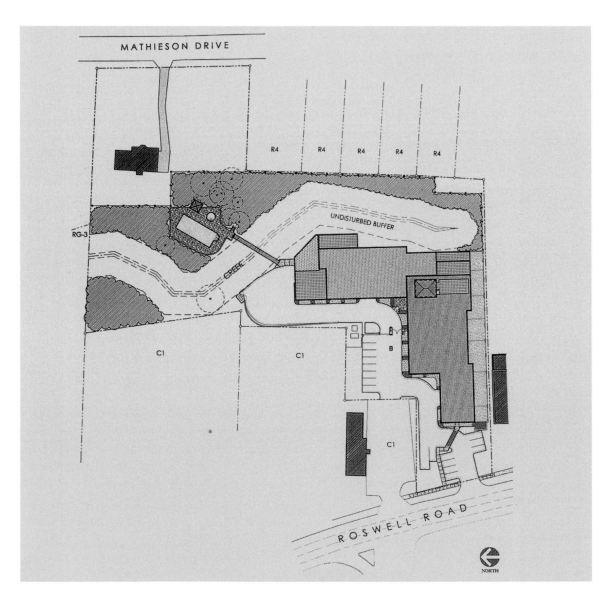

Project Data: Buckhead Village Lofts

Land Use Information

Site area	2.9 acres
Total dwelling units	104
Gross density	36 units per acre
Off-street parking spaces	182

Land Use Plan

Use	Acres	Percentage of Site
Buildings	0.5	16
Roads and paved areas	0.3	8
Common and open spaces	2.1	76
Total	2.9	100

Residential Unit Information

Unit Type	Total Number	Square Feet	Initial Sales Prices
One-bedroom loft	30	1,000	$200,000–$275,000
One- or two-bedroom loft	60	1,200	$250,000–$350,000
Two-bedroom loft	14	1,720	$300,000–$400,000

Development Cost Information

Site acquisition	$2,400,000
Site improvement	1,600,000
Construction	19,800,000
Soft costs	5,550,000
Total development costs	$29,350,000
Average development cost per unit	$281,000
Construction cost per square foot	$152

Development Schedule

Planning started	May 1997
Site purchased	November 1997
Construction started	February 1998
Sales started	March 1998
First closing	March 1999
Sales completed	January 2000

Development Team

Developer
Michael A. Loia and Roddy White
Buckhead Village Lofts, LLC
3325 Roswell Road, Suite 400
Atlanta, Georgia 30305
770-396-3207

Architect
Loia Budde & Associates
5076 Winters Chapel Road
Atlanta, Georgia 30360
770-396-3207

Contractor
Neal & Loia Construction Company
5076 Winters Chapel Road
Atlanta, Georgia 30360
770-379-0636

Project Address

3235 Roswell Road
Atlanta, Georgia 30305

General Information

Michael Loia, president and chief executive officer, Loia Budde & Associates
770-396-3207

Adapted from Samuel Begner, "Buckhead Village Lofts," ULI Development Case Study no. C030016, vol. 30, no. 16 (October–December 2000).

All information in this case study is current as of October 2000.

Paseo Plaza

San Jose, California

The richly detailed facades feature arched entryways, recessed balconies with railings, and traditional front stoops.

Courtesy of Douglas Dun/Backen Arrigoni & Ross

The 210-unit Paseo Plaza condominium project, located in downtown San Jose, represents a hybrid housing form: two-level townhouses at the street level, with stacked condominium apartments above. Developed by SFC Block 4 Residential Partners (a partnership within the Goldrich & Kest Industries, LLC, affiliation of entities) as part of the city's ongoing redevelopment program,

Paseo Plaza was constructed in two phases, which were completed in 1997 and 1998.

Goldrich & Kest Industries, LLC (G&K Industries), of Culver City, California, is a diversified group of real estate development and management companies and partnerships, the first of which was founded by Jona Goldrich as Goldrich & Associates in 1956. G&K Industries develops and acquires multifamily, industrial, for-sale, and congregate care developments and has nationally recognized expertise in government-related financing and operational issues. Its multifamily housing portfolio includes both government-subsidized and conventional properties, primarily in southern California and in the San Francisco Bay and San Jose areas. Its mixed-use properties combine luxury apartments with commercial and/or retail space. An affiliate, G&K Management Company, Inc., manages all G&K Industries's properties. In all, G&K Industries has developed and built more than 350 properties worth an estimated $2 billion.

A former parking lot left over from a 1960s slum clearance project, the Paseo Plaza project site had been designated for redevelopment. According to Tom Aidala, the principal architect and urban designer for the San Jose Redevelopment Agency from 1981 to 1997, the downtown area was "moribund" at the time that Paseo Plaza was conceived. Aidala credits G&K Industries with recognizing the demand for downtown housing that would likely result from the growth in jobs and the development of office space occurring in the city.

Today, Paseo Plaza lies near the San Jose Repertory Theatre and the San Jose Museum of Art, as well as San Jose State University, which borders the project to the east. San Jose offers a number of attractions that draw people downtown, such as the Tech, a museum of innovation; the Children's Discovery Museum;

and the Compaq Arena sports facility. During the past 15 years, in addition to facilitating the development of these civic amenities, the redevelopment agency has improved city streetscapes and parks, installed flood-control projects, created a light-rail transit mall to connect the north and south city employment centers, and enhanced freeway access to make the downtown a more attractive area in which to live and work.

To encourage development of the property, the redevelopment agency provided the developer with a cleared site, paid the cost of constructing underground parking, contributed gap financing, and expedited project approvals and permits (which was possible because the redevelopment agency was the "agency of approval" for designated redevelopment areas).

The design for Paseo Plaza had to be approved at various stages of the process by an urban design review board composed of five to seven people selected by the city's board of supervisors; the board included businesspeople, an architect, and one of the members of the board of supervisors. Paseo Plaza is designed to engage the street rather than to turn defensively inward, as many new urban projects do. Thus, the mid-rise development has a strong public orientation as well as a more private interior core. The townhouses, each with their own street entry, line the Third and Fourth street frontages of the development, while retail storefronts edge the Paseo Mall, a pedestrian walkway that forms the southern boundary of the project. The townhouses are set just five feet back from the sidewalk.

Stacked above the townhouses are single-story condominium units: four stories of flats along Third and Fourth streets, and three levels above the townhouses that line "the mews," an internal pedestrian "street." Along the Paseo, three-story townhouses top the first-floor shops.

Parking is located in a below-grade structure, the top of which forms a podium for the townhouses and for the project's landscaped courtyards. In addition to the multiple street entries to the individual townhouses, a primary building entry, covered by a canopy, is located on the Third Street side. A second, less formal building entry is provided on the opposite (Fourth Street) side.

Both entries open onto the main courtyard, a large open space that is differentiated into three smaller areas: a pool terrace, a lawn terrace, and a central paved terrace. A second courtyard, more intimate in scale, has the feeling of a private garden. Linking the two courtyards is a barrel-vaulted walkway that passes between the residential structures on either side of the mews. A recreation room is also located on the podium level, the roof of which serves as a landscaped forecourt for the townhouses overlooking the Paseo.

At the street level, the design of Paseo Plaza "draws on the inspiration of Boston's Back Bay

First-floor retail space at the south end of the project faces existing first-floor retail, enclosing the public pedestrian area within activity generators.

Courtesy of Douglas Dun/Backen Arrigoni & Ross

The private interior courtyard includes a swimming pool and landscaped areas where residents can congregate.

Courtesy of Douglas Dun/Backen Arrigoni & Ross

The living room of a typical two-bedroom unit.

townhouses and the Georgian terrace housing in England," notes Bruce Ross, principal of Backen Arrigoni & Ross, Inc. (BAR), the project's design architect. The two-story townhouse portion of the facade is sheathed in light-colored stucco, scored to evoke coursed stone. Projecting stoops and planter boxes, as well as the deeply inset townhouse entries, add articulation to the facade. The townhouse entries are raised one half-flight to accommodate the partially subterranean garage and to enhance residents' sense of privacy. Decorative flowerpots and closely spaced street trees further enliven the perspective at the street level.

Above, the condominium flats are clad in an ocher-colored stucco, to contrast with the "stone" of the townhouse facades below. Balconies are recessed five feet from the principal plane of the facade and are grouped together, establishing a rhythm of alternating "in" and "out" planes that breaks up the bulk of the several-hundred-foot-long project. This design approach creates a sense of individual urban structures. The detailing of the building's dark-green metal windows and balcony railings, as well as its cast-concrete sills and trim, ties together the upper and lower sections of the facade into a unified composition.

Along Third and Fourth streets, both the townhouses and flats are double-loaded along hallways, with units looking out over the street and units looking into the courtyards. Townhouses facing the courtyard have private patios. Along the mews, both townhouses and flats are single-loaded. Typically the flats are 48 feet wide and sited directly above pairs of townhouses, each of which is 24 feet wide.

The mews is an intimate space, gated at both ends. The pedestrians-only street spans 40 feet from building face to building face. The actual pedestrian walkway is 15 feet wide, lined with ornamental pear trees and decorative street-lamps. Private townhouse patios, 12.5 feet deep, flank the walkway on either side.

Paseo's townhouses have two or three bed-rooms and range in size from approximately 1,390 to 2,200 square feet. Some of the mod-els have large bay windows, and others have double-height living rooms or bedrooms. The townhouse units sold from the low $200,000s to approximately $500,000.

The flats were targeted to a lower price range. The one- and two-bedroom units, which range in size from approximately 850 to 1,500 square feet, were priced from $165,000 to the low $300,000s. With an eye toward affordability, the two-bedroom flats were designed as "double masters," with two equally sized, mirror-image bedroom/bathroom suites that could be mar-keted to two unrelated singles pooling their resources. The flats have nine-foot ceilings.

The sales program for Paseo Plaza averaged about seven units per month over the full dura-tion, which lasted approximately 30 months. The townhouses, with their entries on the street and their higher prices, were more of a pioneering effort for downtown San Jose; they sold more slowly than the more affordable flats. Sales for all units increased considerably in the final 12 months, however, as the project became established, and resales are realizing gains on the order of 25 percent in just the past year.

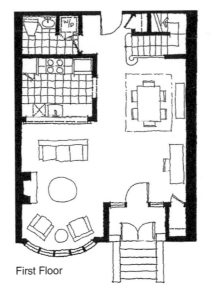

First Floor

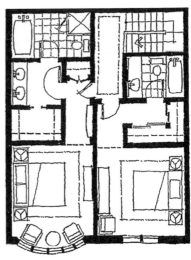

Second Floor

Floor plan, two-bedroom townhouse.

The retail component has been less success-ful to date, and several of the storefronts remain vacant. However, development in the area is continuing—with Phase III of Paseo Plaza, as well as other housing and nonresidential projects—and demand for Paseo retail may eventually catch up to supply.

Bruce Ross, of BAR, credits the redevelop-ment agency for the overall success of Paseo Plaza, noting that the agency was "like a partner in the deal"—programming the site; setting the objective of a pedestrian-friendly, urban environ-ment; and contributing resources, including infrastructure, granite paving, and decorative streetlights. In return, the city has gained an active residential anchor contributing to the rebirth of downtown San Jose.

According to Aidala, Paseo Plaza succeeded because the redevelopment agency made its requirements clear, consistent, and predictable from the outset—and it provided enough assistance when required.

Site plan.

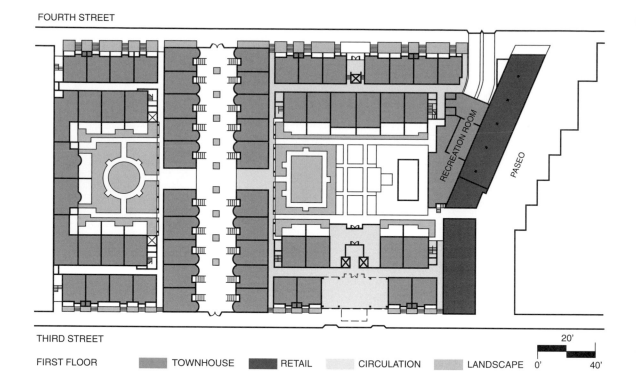

FOURTH STREET

RECREATION ROOM

PASEO

THIRD STREET

FIRST FLOOR

| | TOWNHOUSE | | RETAIL | | CIRCULATION | | LANDSCAPE |

20'

0'   40'

Building cross-
sections.

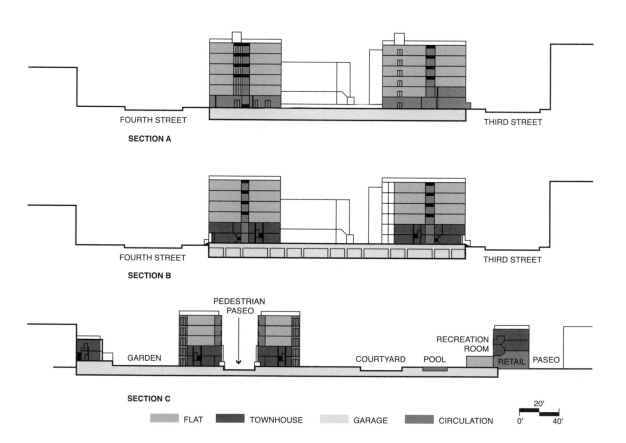

FOURTH STREET

THIRD STREET

SECTION A

FOURTH STREET

THIRD STREET

SECTION B

PEDESTRIAN
PASEO

RECREATION
ROOM

GARDEN

COURTYARD   POOL   RETAIL   PASEO

SECTION C

| | FLAT | | TOWNHOUSE | | GARAGE | | CIRCULATION |

20'

0'   40'

Project Data: Paseo Plaza

Land Use Information

Site area	2.9 acres
Total dwelling units	210
Gross density	73 units per acre
Net density	137
Total parking spaces	369
Parking ratio	1.8 spaces per unit

Land Use Plan[a]

Type of Use	Acres	Percentage of Site
Residential	1.5	53.5
Open space (including recreation and amenities)	1.2	40.2
Retail	0.2	6.3
Total	2.9	100.0

Development Costs

Total[b]	$32,000,000
Per square foot	$125
Per dwelling unit	$152,381

Residential Unit Information

Unit Type	Total Number	Square Feet	Final Sales Prices
One-bedroom/ one-bath flat	45	847– 1,125	$164,900– $209,900
Two-bedroom/two-bath flat or townhouse	97	1,384– 1,483	$220,900– $319,900
Two-bedroom/two-and- one-half-bath townhouse	60	1,316– 1,773	$264,900– $379,900
Three-bedroom/two-and- one-half-bath townhouse	8	1,860– 2,189	$359,900– $499,900

Development Team

Developer
SFC Block 4 Residential Partners
c/o Goldrich & Kest Industries, LLC
One Maritime Plaza
San Francisco, California 94111
415-788-5894

Design Architect
Backen Arrigoni & Ross, Inc.
1660 Bush Street
San Francisco, California 94109
415-441-4771

Executive Architect
Johannes Van Tilburg & Partners
Penthouse, 225 Arizona Avenue
Santa Monica, California 90401
310-394-0273

Landscape Architect
Stephen Wheeler
55 New Montgomery
San Francisco, California 94105
415-974-5995

Project Address

Third and San Fernando Streets
San Jose, California

General Information

Jona Goldrich, principal, Goldrich & Kest Industries, LLC
310-204-2050

Based on Steven Fader, *Density by Design: New Directions in Residential Development* (Washington, D.C.: ULI, 2000).

All information in this case study is current as of December 1999.

Notes

a. Includes approximately 124,000 square feet of below-grade parking.
b. There were no site acquisition costs.

Old Town Square

Chicago, Illinois

Among the first homes to be built in Old Town Square were single-family detached rowhouses, which offer suburban-style space and privacy in a distinctly urban setting.

MCL Companies's Old Town Square development, located just a few blocks from the Cabrini-Green public housing projects, has spurred a renaissance in Chicago's Near North Side. One of the first new housing developments in downtown Chicago to offer residents suburban-style amenities, the community was also developed at a sufficient scale to make a real difference in the character of the neighborhood.

Eighty percent of the housing units in Old Town Square are market rate. The remaining 20 percent are leased by the Chicago Housing Authority (CHA) as "replacement housing" for public housing residents who were displaced by the demolition or renovation of public housing developments.

The first residential portion of the development, Old Town Square, contains 163 newly constructed single-family homes, townhouses, and condominium and rental apartments on just over six acres of land. An additional residential phase nearby, known as Old Town Village, will add 139 units, bringing the total number of dwelling units to about 300. Like Old Town Square, Old Town Village will consist of a mix of single-family homes, townhouses, and condominiums. In addition, the development includes an 84,202-square-foot neighborhood shopping center anchored by a Dominick's grocery store. When completed, Old Town Square, Old Town Village, and the shopping center will, together, cover approximately 15 acres.

Since Dan McLean founded MCL Companies, Inc., in 1976, the firm has become a full-range real estate organization—with development, construction, sales, finance, legal, and leasing and management divisions. Its residential products range from single-family homes and townhouses to low-rise and high-rise condominiums, and from luxuriously appointed homes to public housing replacement units. Its many projects include the Embassy Club, the Residences at Central Station, the Pointe at Lincoln Park, and Cornell Square. In addition, MCL has developed retail products in conjunction with its residential communities, and is involved in redeveloping public housing developments, such as Cabrini-Green, into mixed-income communities.

MCL has concentrated its development efforts in downtown Chicago, but in response to specific opportunities, it now has projects underway in New York City; on Fisher Island, near Miami; and in Denver. River East, a billion-dollar development between Chicago's Michigan Avenue and Navy Pier that will include a hotel, townhouses, high-rise condominiums, retail development, and a 24-screen cinema complex, marks MCL's entry into the mixed-use market.

Low-density townhouses have been MCL's traditional product, but as prices for land in downtown Chicago have risen in recent years, the densities of the firm's projects have also climbed. The key challenge MCL has faced is the need to continue offering its products at competitive market rates despite escalating prices for land, labor, and materials.

Old Town Square is located within Lincoln Park, an umbrella term for several neighborhoods in Chicago's Near North Side, at the intersection of Division Street and Clybourn Avenue. In part because the site is not far from the high-end Gold Coast residential communities of downtown Chicago, the area immediately surrounding the development has been undergoing a transition from a badly deteriorated, crime-ridden slum to a desirable, middle-class —and even upscale—neighborhood. Many other new residential developments are under-

way or planned in the area, and this new development activity is changing the image of the community as a place to live and to invest.

A number of compatible public uses are located close to the Old Town Square site. A public library was built on an adjacent parcel of land that MCL donated to the city during the approvals process, and Franklin Elementary School is nearby. Seward Park, a well-maintained city park with active and passive recreational facilities, lies directly across the street. In addition, numerous restaurants, quaint shops, and the Second City comedy club enliven nearby Wells Street. Other uses in the area immediately surrounding the site include older, high-rise residential developments; some light industrial uses; and older commercial activity, intermixed with some office development.

The land on which the community is built was assembled from several public and private parcels: an old Oscar Mayer processing plant, city-owned land obtained through a request for proposals (RFP) process, land owned by the board of education, and vacated streets.

The selection of this site and the determination and location of the product mix were based more on Dan McLean's longtime experience and expertise than on the results of market research *per se*. In addition, MCL maintained the flexibility to respond to market demand as the development progressed. For example, to provide needed neighborhood commercial stores and services, MCL constructed a community shopping center. Initially, the firm had planned additional commercial development on a site adjacent to the shopping center, but in response to market demand, MCL decided to develop that site for more housing instead.

As part of the approvals process, the city required the developer to obtain a planned development designation for the project, which creates a district in which the city controls development on a unified basis rather than lot by lot. Among other things, approval as a planned development requires community involvement, including the local alderman's approval of the proposed project's use, bulk, building materials, elevations, and tenancy. In response to community concerns about the number of jobs that would be available for neighborhood residents and members of minority groups, MCL agreed to provide a training program for public housing residents who wanted to work on the construction of the project or in the retail stores built on the commercial site. As a result of these programs, residents of Cabrini-Green were hired to work on project construction, and many of the shopping center employees are public housing residents or other members of the existing community.

The inclusion of replacement units for public housing was the result of Chicago's longstanding public policy of "de-concentrating" public housing by incorporating public housing units into mixed-income communities. The most recent redevelopment plan for the Near North Side calls for replacement housing to be included in any new residential development, public or private, above a certain size. So far, two of MCL's developments have included public housing units: Mohawk North, and Old Town Square. The CHA negotiated with MCL

The rear faces of the townhouses, which include the garage entries with patios above, open to a landscaped courtyard.

to determine the specific requirements for each development in the Near North Side to which the mixed-income requirement applies.

The CHA contributed $125,000 per unit to cover the cost of constructing the replacement units. When construction is complete, a third party (a joint venture partnership of MCL Companies, the CHA, and the management company hired by the CHA to manage the public housing replacement units) purchases each replacement unit from MCL, then leases the unit to the CHA for a period of 40 years. After the 40-year lease period, the ownership of the units reverts to the partnership, whose members will share the units' residual value. The management company screens prospective residents before assigning them to specific units.

Old Town Square was built in two phases. The 113 townhouses, condominiums, and single-family homes in Phase I were completed in 1999. Phase II, which consists of 50 condominiums, will be completed in February 2001. Phase III, Old Town Village, is scheduled for completion in July 2003. (The shopping center was built in 1998.)

MCL experienced no unusual construction problems in building Old Town Square, other than some delays associated with the provision of utilities, and there were only minor environmental issues.

No public subsidies were involved in the development of the market-rate units or the commercial property. Developer and investor equity was used to purchase the land, and conventional financing, involving several lenders, funded development.

Old Town Square was designed using neotraditional, or new urbanist, development concepts, with blocks of various housing types integrated into the city's street grid. Architecturally, the development blends into the community. The project's distinctly urban but pedestrian scale and orientation are consistent with its location close to downtown, neighborhood shops and services, and public transportation.

Construction materials and home designs were developed to blend in with the architectural heritage of the community. The classic, four-story brick homes are sited close to the

street and feature front porches, bay windows, and wrought-iron fences. Fifty-six townhouses surround a large, landscaped courtyard where neighbors can gather and interact. Decks, balconies, and patios facing the courtyard enliven the community ambience. Each townhouse has a garage or a parking space, and the largest of the townhouses feature two-car garages. (All single-family homes have two-car garages.) The condominiums and apartments, compatible in their low-rise, brick construction, also offer balconies facing courtyard views. Each condominium includes one surface parking space within a gated parking area.

The public housing replacement units, which are rental apartments, are included within the condominium component of the project. From the exterior, the replacement units are indistinguishable from market-rate units, though the interior finishes are somewhat different. Because of the accessibility requirements of the Americans with Disabilities Act, which apply to public housing units, the CHA replacement units are typically on the first floor.

Because the project is located near a Chicago Transit Authority elevated track (an "El"), it was designed and constructed to minimize the noise and visual intrusiveness of the trains. For example, the solid brick wall of the four-story condominiums was placed against the El, an arrangement that prevents the noise from the trains from carrying to the site. (The sound transfer rating of the brick wall is excellent).

Old Town Square's shopping center consists of 84,202 square feet of commercial and retail space on 5.8 acres at the intersection of Clybourn Avenue and Sedgewick Street. Tenants include a 60,000-square-foot Dominick's grocery store, a Starbucks coffee shop, a Blockbuster video store, a Pearle Vision Express Center, an Army-Navy Recruiting Center, a Citicorp Bank, and AT&T Wireless stores. There are 294 parking places in the shopping center.

The residential development was marketed through print media and a public relations campaign. MCL Companies's marketing staff has worked to create a brand image for the company that associates the company name with "quality new construction" in the minds

of prospective buyers—as well as investors, lenders, public officials, related businesses, and the general public.

Before Old Town Square opened, home sales were underway in a trailer located on the construction site. MCL used large-scale, three-dimensional models to show prospective buyers what the community would look like when it was completed. Buyer response was strong and the units sold quickly. Marketing staff continually generated waiting lists in anticipation of new homes becoming available for sale. The sales pace reflected the market's significant pent-up demand, especially for single-family homes.

Old Town Square's floor plans offered buyers great flexibility in the design of their homes, and the homes proved easy to sell. The 2,270-square-foot Burton model, for example, could be built in any of 12 different layouts, with options that ranged from additional bedrooms and baths to roof decks, decks off the sitting rooms, finished basements, and customized kitchens.

Inside, the homes offered luxury features such as nine-foot ceilings, wood-burning fireplaces, ceramic-tile floors, and soaking tubs. Condominium units included galley kitchens with glass-block windows, living rooms with fireplaces and access to a private balcony, and access to a roof deck. MCL maintains a design center to coordinate interior design decisions for all its projects, with built-in displays where buyers can choose finishes for their homes.

The first homes to be built in Old Town Square were townhouses, which sold in 1995 for approximately $225,000. Reflecting the strength of Chicago's market for infill development, the homes at Old Town Square have

The development includes a much-needed neighborhood shopping center anchored by a grocery store.

Condominium units, some of which are leased by the Chicago Housing Authority, are compatible with the architecture and quality of Old Town Square's larger, market-rate homes.

appreciated significantly, and the homes that were built in the first phase of development resell today for prices upwards of $600,000.

At the time the project was planned, the developer expected that buyers would be young people who would come from within two downtown zip codes. Buyers, were, in fact, mostly young professionals—but, taken as a whole, buyers represented all age groups and diverse geographic origins, including the suburbs and areas beyond greater Chicago. The mix even included some couples with young children, possibly because the neighborhood has good private schools and a "magnet" public school less than two blocks away.

The variety of products available—from one-bedroom condominiums to garage townhouses and single-family homes—and the wide range of purchase prices helped to attract a broad clientele. (And, from the developer's perspective, the diversity of products meant that, at any one time, no single product type dominated the market.) In addition, amenities that were not normally associated with downtown living, such as a private garage, gated parking, and a convenient neighborhood shopping center anchored by a supermarket, helped draw middle-class buyers back to the city.

Though the area has, for some time, had a reputation as unsafe, security was not an issue during sales. Though the project is designed to discourage intruders, there are no security fences or gates to set the development apart from the larger community. Each home has a security system, and the condominium association retains a private security service on an ongoing basis. More important, the development was sufficiently large to create its own neighborhood and sense of community. In addition, "The city has actively promoted the community as a good place to live, and the MCL brand identity gives buyers confidence," explained Karen Schwab, Old Town Square's sales manager. "During the sales process, we invited prospects to walk the neighborhood at different times of day to see how they felt. Most felt very comfortable. If they were not, this was not the right choice for them." Most of the concern was evident during the early stages of the project's development. Some of the more conservative buyers waited to purchase until the neighborhood was substantially built. Those who could foresee the eventual character of the neighborhood—and bought early—benefited from the initially lower prices and the substantial appreciation in value that occurred during the development process.

In fact, the project's location—close to the lake, on the edge of very expensive residential areas, and near restaurants, theaters, shops, and cultural amenities—proved to be an advantage rather than an impediment to sales. And the many new developments planned for the area held the promise that home values in the area would appreciate significantly over the coming years.

Kevin Augustyn, vice president of MCL, noted that as the city's renaissance has progressed over time, Chicago's residential market has grown more competitive, land prices have soared, and buyers have become more demanding. However, because of Chicago's development history, it is easier to "sell the city" today. "You have to love your downtown," he cautioned. "If you don't truly believe it, you will have a hard time."

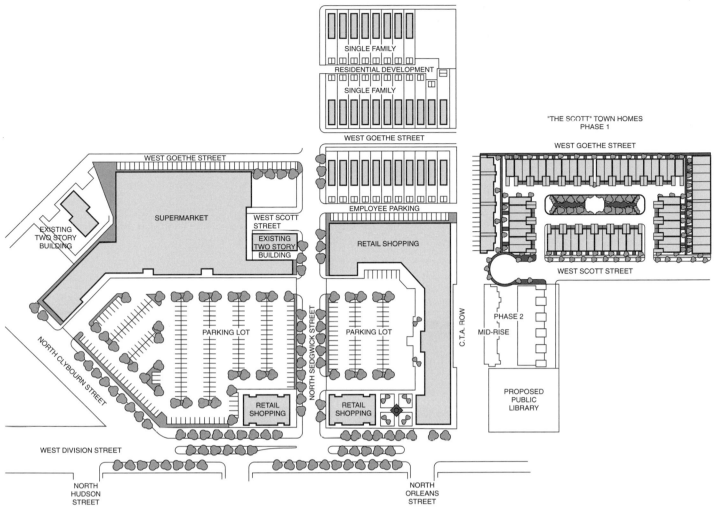

Site plan.

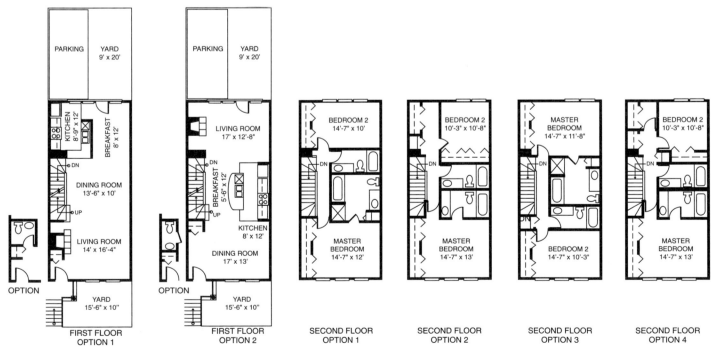

Townhouse floor plans.

Project Data: Old Town Square

Land Use Information
(including Old Town Village)

Total site area	15 acres
Residential use	9.2 acres
Commercial use	5.8 acres
Total dwelling units	300 (approximate)
Gross density	32 units per acre
Total retail/commercial space	84,202 square feet
Total residential parking spaces	392
Indoor and garage spaces	277
Outdoor lot spaces	115

Residential Land Use Plan

	Acres
Phase I	
Townhouses and condominiums	2.8
Single-family homes	2.5
Phase II	
Condominiums and mid-rise apartments	0.7
Phase III	
Old Town Village (single-family homes, townhouses, and condominiums)	3.2

Residential Unit Information[a]

Unit Type	Total Number	Sales Prices (Market-Rate Units)
Single-family detached units	38	$327,900–$397,900
Townhouse units	82	$225,900–$370,000
Condominiums and apartments	182	$125,900–$262,900

Development Schedule

Site purchased	June 1995
Planning began	June 1995
Site work began	June 1996
Project completion:	
Old Town Square	February 2001
Old Town Village	July 2003

Phase I: Old Town Square

Number of units	113
Planning started	November 1995
Construction started	June 1996
Construction completed	September 1999
Sales/leasing started	March 1996
Sales/leasing completed	September 1999

Phase II: Old Town Square

Number of units	50
Planning started	June 1996
Construction started	October 1999
Construction completed	February 2001 (expected)
Sales/leasing started	September 1998
Sales/leasing completed	June 1999

Phase III: Old Town Village

Number of units	140 (approximate)
Planning started	July 2000
Construction started	July 2001 (expected)
Construction completed	July 2003 (expected)
Sales/leasing started	April 2001 (expected)
Sales/leasing completed	October 2001 (expected)

Shopping Center

Site purchased	June 1985
Planning began	June 1996
Supermarket leased	April 1997
Site work began	August 1997
Project completed	August 1998
Fully leased	November 2000

Development Team

Developer

MCL Companies
455 East Illinois Street, Suite 565
Chicago, Illinois 60611
312-321-8900

Architects

Townhouses and Condos
PappaGeorge Haymes
814 North Franklin Street, Suite 400
Chicago, Illinois 60622
312-337-3344, ext. 122

Single-Family Homes and Shopping Center
Roy Kruse & Associates
833 West Chicago Avenue, Suite 200
Chicago, Illinois 60622
312-563-1102

Project Address (construction office)

344 West Scott Street
Chicago, Illinois 60610

General Information

Pete Novak, construction superintendent, MCL Companies
312-482-8441

All information in this case study is current as of November 8, 2000.

Note

a. The number of units includes both Old Town Square and Old Town Village. Prices given refer to Old Town Square only; prices for Old Town Village are yet to be determined.

Gramercy on Garfield/ Greenwich on the Park

Cincinnati, Ohio

On the site of what were formerly surface parking lots, the residential buildings fill a hole in the urban fabric.

Gramercy on Garfield and Greenwich on the Park are two mid-rise apartment buildings representing the first two phases of a six-phase master plan for housing in the Garfield Place neighborhood in downtown Cincinnati. Together, the buildings offer 212 housing units, garage parking, a fitness center, a rooftop pool, and on-site accessory retail services. Developed by Towne Properties, of Cincinnati, these two projects were the first successful housing developments produced downtown in more than 50 years. The support of the city, which granted the developer a ground lease for the project sites and contributed substantial funding, was critical to the project's feasibility.

The first phase of the project, the six-story Gramercy on Garfield, was completed in 1992 and features 148 residential units, 15,000 square feet of ground-floor retail uses, and a 429-stall parking garage with two floors above grade and two floors below. The roof of the garage forms

an outdoor courtyard for the building, and the garage provides structural support for the rest of the building.

Phase II of the project, the four-story Greenwich on the Park, was first occupied in February 1996 and has 64 residential units and 43 garage parking spaces. Twenty percent of the units at the Greenwich (13 of 64) are affordable for households earning 50 percent of the area median income. The Greenwich also includes an 1,800-square-foot ground-floor restaurant.

Since these two projects were completed, the developer has built the third and fourth phases, both of which are adaptive use projects. As of March 2001, negotiations were underway for an agreement to build the fifth phase.

Founded in 1961 in Cincinnati, Towne Properties created a renaissance in the working-class German-Irish hilltop neighborhood known as Mt. Adams by redeveloping properties to take advantage of the view opportunities (the neighborhood overlooks downtown and the river, which is just a quarter-mile away). The firm then branched out into suburban garden-apartment development and to markets in Dayton and in Lexington, Kentucky. Over a 20-year period, the firm also created a 1,100-acre master-planned community, Landen, which included single-family detached homes, townhouses, condominiums, and zero-lot-line homes. In the early 1980s, Towne Properties became involved in retail development, most notably working with Western Development to transform a strip shopping center in the northeast part of the city into Kenwood Towne Center, a highly successful regional shopping mall. Under the leadership of partner Arn Bortz, former councilman and former mayor of Cincinnati, Towne Properties began doing more urban infill projects in the 1980s.

The Gramercy and Greenwich projects were the first two phases of a six-phase master plan that the city had prepared for the Garfield Place neighborhood. To implement the plan, the city solicited developer interest, and selected first one developer (in 1983), then another (in 1986). Each of the first two developers had attempted to respond to the city's misguided mandate—which demanded the construction of high-rise, high-rent apartments—but each finally gave up. Again soliciting interest from developers across the country, the city selected Towne Properties in 1990—as Bortz jokes, "probably out of exhaustion and desperation" —awarding the firm with development rights for the Garfield master plan.

Using a combination of negotiated purchases and eminent domain, the city had acquired the sites, as well as others in the area, over a number of years. Initially, the city clung to its original vision of high-rise, luxury housing— but Bortz persuaded city officials that the market would not support such a use. "We had been developing housing in Cincinnati for 29 years, and knew what the market wanted." The Garfield site was located along a small urban park, but it was not a location that would justify a luxury high rise. "Rents in Cincinnati are low; to build a high rise, the developer must ask for rents that no one would want to pay." Bortz believed that the sites should be developed with lower-density, mixed-income housing with accessory retail space. In fact, the two phases were built at a significantly lower density than the zoning permitted.

The Gramercy and the Greenwich have a prominent location framing the western end of Piatt Park, the oldest park in Cincinnati. Created in 1817, the park currently lies in the middle of Garfield Place. The location is impor-tant because it is at the northern edge of the central business district, where newer, high-density office buildings and retail stores give way to older, smaller buildings with a greater variety of uses. The sites are within walking distance of downtown jobs and of the attractions of the city—its restaurants and shopping, the Paul Brown Stadium, Cinergy Field (where the Reds play), the Music Hall, and the three theaters of the new Aronoff Center for the Performing Arts.

At the time development began, both sites were used as surface parking lots. An old hotel, which included about ten rooms used by a local homeless coalition for single-room occupancy (SRO) housing, occupied a small portion of the Phase II site. Though the city found better living space for the SRO residents in other parts of the city, advocates for the homeless initially objected to the demolition of the hotel. In addition, Towne Properties had to remove rubble from previous structures. Site development was otherwise uneventful.

Brick, stone, tiles, and other high-quality materials were used. Details such as the corner towers and bay windows recall the architecture of the older buildings in the neighborhood.

A central courtyard with a swimming pool offers residents a quiet setting away from the activity of the street.

Towne Properties knew what it wanted to create and gave clear direction to the project architects. To minimize problems during construction, the firm worked with a construction manager—Turner Construction—that was accustomed to working in urban settings. Bortz feels that his firm had a smaller pool of subcontractors from which to choose than it would have had for a suburban project, largely because some of the subcontractors were reluctant to pay prevailing wage rates or to deal with the city's minority, small-business, equal opportunity, and record-keeping requirements. In addition, some were daunted by the prospect of delivering and securing materials at a downtown site.

The first two phases were financed separately. Financing for Phase I, the Gramercy, consisted of a conventional construction loan from Fifth Third Bank, a local lender, and a community development block grant (CDBG) loan from the city. Public financing arrangements were in place when Towne Properties was selected, and the resources had already been set aside.

The conventional financing piece was more difficult. Because there were few other successful downtown housing developments to compare the project to, Bortz had to spend months persuading the local lender that there would indeed be demand for such housing if it was well done and competitively priced. Towne Properties has already paid off the conventional loan with a permanent loan from Fannie Mae. What really made the project work, however, was that the city granted Towne Properties a 65-year ground lease, thereby eliminating site

acquisition costs. In return, the city receives a percentage of the project's net cash flow each year.

The city operates the Gramercy parking garage, which it paid for under a separate contract, with Towne Properties as the subcontractor. Residents of the Gramercy and of all other downtown housing receive discounted parking at the Gramercy garage. The Greenwich parking garage is reserved exclusively for residents.

The financing for the Greenwich, Phase II of the project, was more complex. In 1993, the state of Ohio amended its constitution to permit cities to sell general-obligation bonds to fund market-rate housing. As a result, the development agreement included more than $3 million in tax-exempt general-obligation bonds for the project. A ground lease from the city was used to avoid the prohibitive cost of site acquisition. In addition, the city loaned CDBG funds for general project expenses associated with blight removal, made a below-market-interest-rate loan, and granted funds to cover site preparation expenses. Towne Properties also contributed its own equity to the project.

Under the terms of the development agreements for these sites, the city receives a percentage of the net cash flow generated each year. Moreover, the city will also receive a percentage of the proceeds if and when the projects are sold or refinanced. In the case of the Gramercy, for example, the city would receive 25 percent of the profits from a sale. The tax-exempt bond issue for the Greenwich development stipulated that the project include affordable housing; thus, 20 percent of the units must be affordable to households earning 50 percent of the area median income. These units must remain affordable for 20 years—the life of the bonds. Rents from the retail space in both the Gramercy and the Greenwich contribute to the projects' cash flow.

Both the Gramercy and the Greenwich were designed to respect the traditional character of the surrounding neighborhood. Both buildings make use of brick, stone, tiles, and other decorative materials, and the facades recall those of the older structures in the area. The buildings also feature contemporary, metal-clad tower elements that define the corners of the blocks, and the scale and massing of the structures complement Piatt Park and create an urban street edge. Though security was not a critical issue among prospective tenants, Towne Properties uses electronic card readers to limit access to common areas in the projects.

Because the developer expected the market for the first phase of the project to consist of young, recently formed households, or older, empty-nester households looking for a smaller place to live, 129 of the 148 Gramercy units were studios and one-bedroom units. But, according to Bortz, "We found that the market wanted more room and was willing to pay for it." As a result, 60 percent of the Greenwich apartments are two-bedroom units.

The Gramercy units have a comfortable, contemporary feel. They are average in size for the market, and include appliances, walk-in closets, and eight-foot, four-inch ceilings. All units have their own furnaces and water heaters, and many units have balconies. Building amenities include a fitness center, a clubroom, and a pleasantly landscaped outdoor courtyard and pool on the roof of the parking garage. An interesting feature of the Gramercy is the row of two-story townhouses, their stoops facing Piatt Park. The Greenwich features amenities similar to those at the Gramercy, and the interior design at the Greenwich, with its careful use of wood and tile, alludes to the Arts and Crafts Style. The rear elevation of the building helps form a midblock mews with additional landscaping and traditional paving stones.

The retail uses in this project include restaurants, a dry cleaner, and a market, which help enliven the project at the street level. The market for the retailers includes, in addition to project residents, the many people who work in nearby offices.

For both buildings, lease-up proceeded rapidly—three months for Phase I and four months for Phase II. Both phases remain at 98 percent occupancy and are meeting pro forma expectations. Rents have risen modestly, but the developments now command the highest per-square-foot rent levels in the region.

The tenants, with a median age of 38, range from two retired Catholic priests to new hires at nearby Procter & Gamble headquarters. Many are single women. About 75 percent work downtown, between 15 and 20 percent commute to the suburbs, and between 5 and 10 percent are retired. Only two or three children reside in the 351 units developed in the first four phases of the Garfield master plan.

Towne Properties manages these properties, as it does all the projects that it develops—and, to promote a sense of community, it manages all the phases of this project as a single neighborhood. There is one shared amenity: residents of Phase II can use the swimming pool in Phase I. In order to enhance retention, the firm conducts yearly resident surveys and organizes occasional parties and other social events; to encourage residents of all phases of the project to socialize, these are held at a single location.

Conventional marketing tools, such as direct mail and open houses, were used to advertise the projects; both phases also benefited greatly from positive coverage in the local media. In

The well-defined corner tower draws attention to the project and reinforces its urban style and scale.

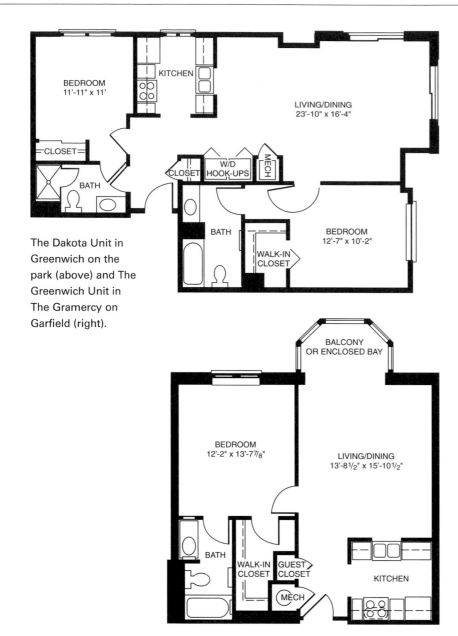

The Dakota Unit in Greenwich on the park (above) and The Greenwich Unit in The Gramercy on Garfield (right).

addition, residents are offered bonuses for referring new tenants.

A number of factors contributed to this project's success. Despite the city's commitment to the idea of developing high-density, luxury residential units, it was the alternative model identified by Towne Properties that proved successful—a clear demonstration of the importance, for the developer, of staying in touch with the demands of the market. Along the same lines, the developer had to be willing to change the product over time to conform to changing market conditions and customer needs; such flexibility is particularly important in multiphase projects.

Another key to the success of this project was the working partnership between the developer and the city. In particular, the city's ownership and provision of the development sites made the deal work, because it would have been prohibitively expensive for the developer to buy the land. "In Cincinnati," explains Bortz, "the economics are challenging. Even a friendly lender who accepts your projections will not write a loan that will cover all you need. There's a 'feasibility gap' because rents are so low and land costs so high." Working from a city master plan that included six sites was important to the developer, because, Bortz says, "It gives us an opportunity to reap the benefits that will result from the higher levels of risk we have to take in the first phases." Thus, his advice to cities seeking to encourage urban infill housing is to put more than one site into the package.

According to the developer, the inclusion of neighborhood and convenience retail uses—especially restaurants—was very important to the success of the project because retail helps create a lively street scene and transparency from the street.

Finally, this project shows that when analyzing the feasibility of downtown housing projects, developers need to ensure that they understand the local market and the fundamental economics of the development they propose. Previous downtown housing developments in Cincinnati had failed not because of an inherent resistance to downtown living, but because they were the wrong type of product for the market.

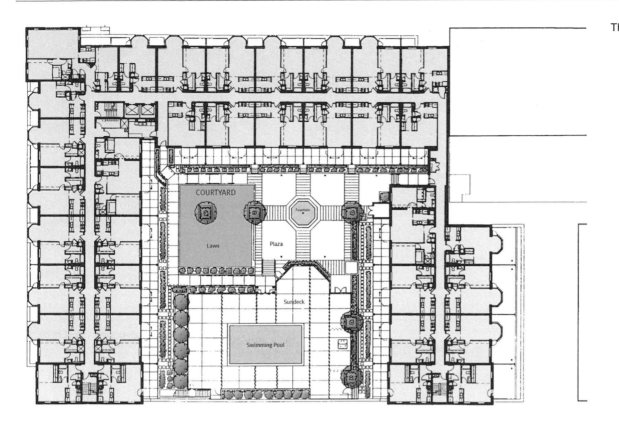

Third-floor plan.

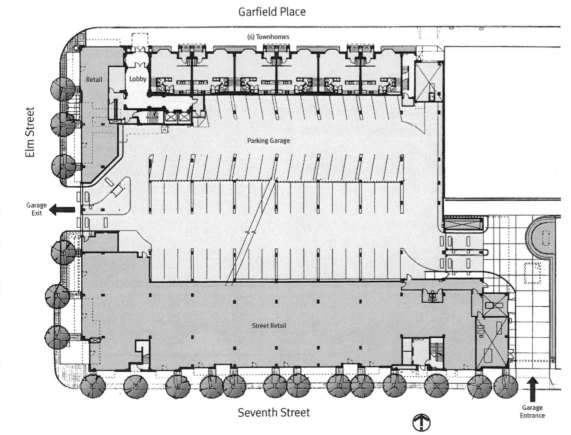

First-floor plan.

Project Data: Gramercy on Garfield/Greenwich on the Park

Land Use Information

Phase I: Gramercy on Garfield

Site area	1.1 acres
Total dwelling units	148
Gross density	135 units per acre
Total parking spaces (public garage below apartments)	429

Phase II: Greenwich on the Park

Site area	0.7 acres
Total dwelling units	64
Gross density	96 units per acre
Total parking spaces	43

Development Cost Information

Item	Total	Cost per Dwelling Unit
Phase I: Gramercy on Garfield		
Site acquisition	N.A.[a]	N.A.
Site improvement	N.A.[b]	N.A.
Construction	$8,230,000	$55,608
Soft costs	1,820,000	12,297
Total	$10,050,000	$67,905

Construction cost per square foot: $59

Item	Total	Cost per Dwelling Unit
Phase II: Greenwich on the Park		
Site acquisition	N.A.[a]	N.A.
Site improvement	$65,000	$1,016
Construction	5,927,000	92,609
Soft costs	832,000	13,000
Total	$6,824,000	$106,625

Construction cost per square foot (including one-level parking garage and 1,800 square feet of retail space): $61

Residential Unit Information

Unit Type	Total Number	Square Feet	Initial Monthly Rents
Phase I: Gramercy on Garfield			
Studio	16	554	$450–$485
Studio	18	592	$450–$505
One-bedroom	95	698–748	$560–$825
Two-bedroom	8	1,167	$695–$715
Two-bedroom	5	1,277–1,407	$750–$795
Two-bedroom townhouse	6	1,468	$895
Phase II: Greenwich on the Park			
Studio	19	550	$375–$545
One-bedroom	8	625	$625–$695
Two-bedroom	37	1,044–1,204	$775–$830

Development Schedule

	Phase I	Phase II
Site leased	May 1990	October 1994
Planning started	January 1990	September 1993
Construction started	June 1992	December 1994
First occupancy	October 1992	February 1996
Leasing completed	December 1992	May 1996

Project Award

In 1994, the Gramercy won an award for best new construction in the National Apartment Association's magazine *Units*.

Development Team

Developer
Towne Properties
1055 St. Paul Place
Cincinnati, Ohio 45202
513-381-8696

Design Architect
Gruzen Samton
304 Park Avenue South
New York, New York 10010
212-477-0900

Executive Architect
PDT Architects
8044 Montgomery Road
Cincinnati, Ohio 45236
513-891-4605

Contractor
Turner Construction
250 West Court Street
Cincinnati, Ohio 45202
513-721-4224

Project Addresses

Gramercy on Garfield
135 Garfield Place
Cincinnati, Ohio 45202

Greenwich on the Park
120 Garfield Place
Cincinnati, Ohio 45202

General Information

Arn Bortz, partner, Towne Properties
513-345-8696

Updated in March 2001 from Oliver Jerschow, "Gramercy on Garfield/Greenwich on the Park," ULI Development Case Study no. C029026, vol. 29, no. 16 (October-December 1999).

All information in this case study is current as of March 2001.

Notes

a. Not applicable: ground lease from city.
b. Not applicable: improvement cost paid in construction of parking garage.

The Huntington
St. Petersburg, Florida

The Huntington is surrounded by a landscaped decorative fence punctuated by brick pilasters.

The Huntington is a 27-unit luxury townhouse development in downtown St. Petersburg. Located amid the city's cultural and commercial attractions and just a few blocks from the shores of Tampa Bay, the project was one of the first new residential developments to be established in downtown St. Petersburg in 30 years. Project planning was characterized by public/private cooperation, and the project's market success has paved the way for a renewal of interest in housing development downtown.

The developer, Hyde Park Builders, Inc. (HPB), of Tampa, Florida, specializes in custom homebuilding and urban infill development in established urban neighborhoods, typically at sites that require the demolition of blighted properties. As executive vice president and co-owner Scott Shimberg explains, "We look for sites that are adjacent to downtowns, but in neighborhoods where you can walk your dog." A full-service real estate development organization, HPB does all its own purchasing, rezoning

work, design, construction management, and sales (both in house and through affiliated companies). Though HPB's projects have ranged in size from eight to 57 units, most are in the 25- to 30-unit range.

St. Petersburg, Florida's fourth-largest city, has long been known as a tourist and retirement haven. In recent years, the development of the Tampa Bay waterfront and its environs as a lively cultural, retail, sports, and entertainment district has created a resurgence of economic activity in the city. Among the many downtown attractions are the St. Petersburg Pier, with its many shops and restaurants; Vinoy Park, Straub Park, and Jannus Landings, the locations of year-round concerts and outdoor activities; the St. Petersburg Municipal Marina; the Museum of Fine Arts; Bayfront Center (the city's convention hall); the new BayWalk retail cluster; and Al Lang Stadium, the spring-training field for the St. Louis Cardinals. Nearby, the Devil Rays draw a regional crowd to major-league baseball games at Tropicana Field.

The 71,750-square-foot Huntington site is located at the northern periphery of St. Petersburg's central business district, at 4th Avenue North and 2nd Street North. It is just three blocks west of Beach Drive, the scenic waterfront corridor that travels the length of downtown, and just steps from the city's finest shops, restaurants, and nightlife. Situated in a transitional, mixed-use neighborhood that lies between downtown and the Old Northeast residential community of St. Petersburg, the site is near small older apartment buildings, single-family homes, churches, hotels, and a home for retired priests.

HPB learned of the site from the owner himself. When the site was purchased, it contained the Huntington Hotel—which, at the time it was built, in the late 1890s, was one of the city's largest hotels catering to "snowbirds" (seasonal visitors). The building was later used as an antiques mall, then fell into disrepair and was abandoned. Derwin Smith, the landowner, owed taxes on the property, the hotel building had been condemned, and fines were accumulating. Though eager to sell, Smith, a native of St. Petersburg, considered the future use of the property to be his legacy to the city and wanted to ensure that it would be developed by a reputable firm whose work he respected. He sought out HPB after seeing similar projects that the firm had developed elsewhere in the region.

Site development required the demolition of the five-story hotel and accessory buildings, including the removal of vagrants who had taken up residence in the building and the expenditure of more than $30,000 for asbestos abatement. As part of the sales agreement, the seller removed the hotel's windows and the hardwood floors from the ballroom and resold them. HPB kept the room keys and gave them to the Huntington's buyers as souvenirs.

An old historic house occupies one corner of the block on which the Huntington was built. Because the developer felt it would not be economically efficient to purchase this house, it is not part of the project site. However, during construction, HPB rented the house for use as the project sales office. (Today, it is used for professional offices.)

Although the site was zoned "CBD-2," which allowed residential use and would have permitted a mid-rise building, HPB chose to develop a low-density neighborhood that would be consistent with both the surroundings and the company's assessment of the market. Because no zoning change was needed, community participation was not an issue.

The city was supportive and participated in the development in a variety of ways. During the planning process, HPB met with the mayor and the St. Petersburg Downtown Partnership to solicit their support. Shimberg recounts, "Early on, Kevin Dunne, in the mayor's office, organized a meeting of the heads of all city departments with jurisdiction over the project

Homes offer luxury features such as polished hardwood floors, French doors, and fireplaces.

so we could discuss their requirements, hear their concerns, and resolve problems and conflicts together." As a result, he adds, "When we submitted our plans, there were no surprises, and they were approved quickly." By working closely with the city in planning the project, HPB cut the usual eight months of permitting time to one month.

Because the project site is located within a state enterprise zone, a small portion of the sales tax on goods purchased to build the project was refunded to the builder. The Huntington was subject to a number of fees levied by the city on new developments, but some of these fees were mitigated by credits resulting from the elimination of the site's previous hotel use. For example, the city imposes water and sewer impact fees on new developments. These fees are based on the number of bathrooms in the development, but the developer can subtract the number of bathrooms in the site's previous use. Because the previous use was a hotel, with more bathrooms than the Huntington would create, HPB's sewer and water impact fees for the project were minimized. The higher-density previous use also helped minimize the transportation impact fees charged by the city. (The city also assesses new projects for their impact on the school system, but this assessment applies regardless of a site's previous use.)

The Huntington consists of 27 three-bedroom, two-and-a-half-bath townhouses clustered in buildings of three to five units that are organized around a gated interior courtyard. Twenty-two of the homes include an attached two-car garage; five have one-car garages. Within the landscaped courtyard, a small swimming pool (complete with a brick-covered cabana), barbecue grills, and seating areas invite residents to relax and socialize.

Despite being close to the water, the property is at a high elevation and did not require extensive provisions for drainage. Differences in slope within the site necessitated height variations in the buildings but also created interesting patterns of relief among them.

Because the project is located in a historic neighborhood, the project design had to conform with the city's architectural review guidelines. The company's signature two-story "Hyde Park bungalow" architectural style (so called because it reflects the traditional style of South Tampa's desirable Hyde Park neighborhood) and siding, stucco, and brick building materials blend well with the scale, mass, and character of the surrounding residential area. The project was designed to "look like it's always been there," explains Shimberg, "which means that it fits in." Shed roofs over French doors and metal flashing above windows protect homes from the weather and add architectural character. The streetscape features brick pavers, lush landscaping, and classic streetlights. (After the project was completed, the city made improvements to beautify and reduce the number of traffic lanes on 2nd Street, consistent with its downtown plan. The improvements included the creation of parallel parking spaces, the installation of median dividers, and additional landscaping.)

The attached, single-family homes average 1,700 square feet in size and include nine-foot, two-inch ceilings on the main floor; large windows; French doors; crown moldings; tongue-and-groove oak floors; gas fireplaces; ceiling fans; walk-in closets; and luxurious master baths. Each unit has some private outdoor space.

Though the community is not a high-crime area, security is an issue among prospective residents, many of whom are single women. Access is controlled by an electronic wrought-iron entry gate that leads to an interior courtyard and the homes' garages. An ivy-covered wrought-iron fence links brick pilasters around the portion of the project's perimeter that faces neighborhood streets. A brick alleyway and privacy wall separate the units from the immediately adjacent residential uses and provide soundproofing. Residents and visitors can enter the homes from the street through individual, secured pedestrian gates. Additional security features include individual alarm systems and direct access to the homes from their garages.

The Bank of Tampa provided a $2.3 million conventional construction loan. At the time of purchase, there were no nearby comparables, so the appraisal had to be based on projects that were 20 miles away. The bank decided to make the construction loan largely because of the developer's track record and reputation.

As a pioneer residential development, the Huntington tested the market for intown housing. To give it panache, the project was marketed as part of the desirable Old Northeast St. Petersburg neighborhood, which technically it was not. In addition to on-site signs and word of mouth, HPB marketed the Huntington through a public relations campaign that included planted newspaper stories. For example, HPB encouraged press coverage of the demolition of the Huntington Hotel. Marketing efforts were modest, however; as Craig Ross, president of HPB, notes, "You can't do a marketing blitz on a small project like you can for a large one."

Pricing was competitive—and once a model home was constructed, presales were brisk: the project sold out in less than a year. "We had no nearby projects to show them," explains Shimberg, "and people want to see the product." The challenge, he cautions, is to resist selling too quickly. Instead, he advises, "Feel out the project's upward price mobility."

The buyers were young professionals, especially those relocating from a big city; young

couples; and empty nesters (who made up between 20 and 30 percent of the buyers). The key attraction for many was the location near the waterfront and other cultural, recreational, and retail amenities. Many of the purchasers were referrals and repeat buyers. To ensure a satisfied customer base, HPB not only provides the standard one-year home warranty but does a walk-through with the homeowner after 11 months of occupancy and fixes any outstanding problems.

A gated entry protects the courtyard that provides residents with access to their garages.

COURTYARD

DINING ROOM
8' X 12'
TRAY CEILING

LIVING ROOM
12' X 16'
9² CEILING

KITCHEN

POWDER

COVERED ENTRY

FOYER

2 CAR GARAGE

FIRST FLOOR

MASTER BEDROOM
21' X 18'

MASTER BATH

WALK-IN CLOSET

W/D HOOK-UPS

A/C

BATH 2

WALK-IN CLOSET

WALK-IN CLOSET

BEDROOM 2
12' X 14'

BEDROOM 3
11' X 15'

SECOND FLOOR

Floor plan.

The Huntington offered prospective buyers another, more urban alternative to the established residential areas near the water in the St. Petersburg area, such as Feather Sound, St. Petersburg Beach, and Tierra Verde. Its primary competition downtown was from the apartment companies, such as Post Properties. However, comments Shimberg, "They build a higher-density rental product, which represents a different lifestyle choice."

The homes were sold on a fee-simple basis. An HOA owns and maintains the common areas and amenities.

Ross comments, "With infill, opportunity is a window of time; if you wait too long, the window closes and the opportunity is gone." For example, HPB bought the land for the Huntington at between $10 and $12 per square foot. During construction, a parcel of land across the street was offered for sale at $30 per square

foot. Today, in part as a result of the project's success, land prices in the area have escalated further. The appreciation has benefited the Huntington's purchasers as well. Homes that were sold in the $170,000s were resold two years later in the $250,000s.

Because prospective buyers wanted large units—and especially larger living areas, HPB has increased the size of the homes in its developments over time to 2,000 square feet. In future projects, because so many of the buyers are empty nesters, HPB is considering a multi-story, "elevator-ready" model, in which space used for closets stacked one above the other could one day accommodate installation of an elevator.

Shimberg notes that the density allowed by existing zoning may make it prohibitive to create the type of housing development that would best fit on a site. Zoning designations largely determine land costs, which in turn determine the design and pricing of housing developments. High zoning allowances mean high land costs—and high land costs dictate high densities, high unit prices, or both. High-density (especially high-rise) development is often unacceptable to neighboring communities and inappropriate from a contextual standpoint, and high unit prices exclude large portions of the potential market. Shimberg suggests that local governments review the allowable densities for urban infill sites and consider downzoning, if necessary, to bring land prices down to levels that would allow development of affordable, contextual, infill housing developments.

City support for the project was essential. And, from the city's point of view, according to Ross, "Working with someone local, they know they won't get burned. We can't leave town and go somewhere else—they know where we live." Shimberg also attributes the project's success to the principals' day-to-day involvement. "You need to live and breathe it."

Site plan.

Project Data: The Huntington

Land Use Information

Site area	1.6 acres
Open space	0.5
Total dwelling units	27
Gross density	16 units per acre
Total parking spaces	54

Residential Unit Information

Unit Type	Total Number	Square Feet	Sales Prices
Royal Palm	5	1,710	$164,900–$166,900
Bougainvillea	14	1,759	$169,900–$184,900
Banyan	8	1,600	$162,900–$173,189

Development Cost Information

Site acquisition	$600,000
Total hard and soft development costs	$3,500,000
Average development cost per unit	$130,000

Development Schedule

Site purchased	April 1997
Planning began	January 1997
Site work began	April 1997
Project completion	May 1998
Sales started	December 1997 (first closing)
Sales completed	August 1998 (final closing)

Project Awards

In the multifamily $125,000–$200,000 category, the Huntington received three awards from the Contractors & Builders Association of Pinellas County's Parade of Homes: Best of Show, Best Master Suite, and Best Kitchen.

Development Team

Developer/Builder/Planner/Architect
Hyde Park Builders
611 West Bay Street
Tampa, Florida 33606
813-251-8552

Project Address

226 Fourth Avenue North
St. Petersburg, Florida 33701

General Information

Scott Shimberg, executive vice president and co-owner, Hyde Park Builders
813-251-8552

All information in this case study is current as of February 27, 2001.

Central Station
Memphis, Tennessee

A complicated public/private partnership was needed to transform the historic Central Station building into a mixed-use development that includes 63 new city residences.

The conversion of Central Station, Memphis's historic railroad terminal building, into a residential, retail, and transportation-oriented development demonstrates how a public/private partnership can transform a derelict public building into an attractive and imaginative new development. Developed by the Alexander Company, Inc., of Madison, Wisconsin, as part of the Central

Station Limited Partnership, Central Station includes 63 rental apartments, 28,000 square feet of retail space, an Amtrak station, a bus station, a police substation, and public parking. The city's support—which took the form of providing both the property and $18 million in public subsidies—was key to the project's success.

Founded in 1985 by Randy and Terry Alexander, the Alexander Company specializes in transforming historic buildings—such as factories, schools, warehouses, hotels, mill buildings, and so forth—into housing. The company also constructs new developments, most of which are infill housing. In addition, the firm has completed several mixed-use, master-planned developments that incorporate new construction, historic preservation, and the redevelopment of brownfield sites. Though its primary geographic focus is the central United States, the Alexander Company's projects range as far south as Fort Worth and as far east as Cleveland. Its staff of 25, operating from the home office in Madison, typically responds to invitations from cities that know the firm's capabilities and reputation. Overall, the company has undertaken the development, financing, design, restoration, construction, and management of over 200 new, rehabilitated, and restored historic buildings throughout the country, typically as part of a public/private partnership; these projects include approximately 2,400 units of rental housing, plus some condominiums and townhouses, and 775,000 square feet of office and retail space. Most of the firm's residential projects contain at least some market-rate units.

The city of Memphis is located on the widest spot on the Mississippi River, where people strolling the walkways along the bluffs can view riverboats plying the water. Known as the birthplace of rock and roll, as the home of the blues, and as Elvis Presley's hometown, the city is a major tourist destination. The Beale Street entertainment district, which generates more tourist dollars than any entertainment attraction in the state, boasts the National Civil Rights Museum, the Pyramid arena, Mud Island River Park, the Memphis Cook Convention Center, a performing arts center, AutoZone Park (a new downtown stadium that houses the Memphis Redbirds, a minor-league baseball team), the Main Street Trolley, and beautiful historic structures —some of which, like the Peabody Hotel, have been restored. Peabody Place, consisting of nine square blocks now under construction adjacent to the Peabody Hotel, will total nearly 2 million square feet of mixed-use, renovated historic properties and new construction. According to Jeff Sanford, president of Memphis's Center City Commission, $1.9 billion worth of development projects have recently been completed or are under construction downtown. About 80,000 people work in the city, where the largest employers include the AutoZone and St. Jude's Children's Research Hospital.

According to Sanford, the market for housing in the urban core preceded, rather than resulted from, concentrated efforts to revitalize the downtown. Beginning in the early 1980s, he explains, "the magnetism of the river and the work of a handful of local visionaries, especially developers Henry Turley and Jack Belz, created a market for downtown housing." In addition, the city has made a conscious effort to encourage housing development in the urban core by offering incentives, including the Payment-in-Lieu-of-Taxes (PILOT) program, which freezes *ad valorem* (real estate) taxes at predevelopment rates for a predetermined period; low-interest development loans; and counseling for developers on how to obtain and use federal low-income housing tax credits and historic preservation tax credits. Today, about 8,000 of the metropolitan area's 1.1 million people live in new or renovated market-rate housing in downtown Memphis, including 4,000 on Mud Island alone, and another 1,500 units are under construction. Among the 4,300 existing rental units, occupancy rates average 96 percent.

The Illinois Central Railroad built the 170,000-square-foot Central Station in 1914, both as the major stop on the line south to New Orleans and as the company's regional headquarters. Designed by famed Chicago architect Daniel Burnham, the station is located in the once-residential part of the city known as South of Main. The people and cargo that the trains brought into the city stimulated a demand for hotels, restaurants, bars, retail stores, and other facilities. In the 1950s, however, when train travel began to decline, so did the area around Central Station. As buildings were abandoned, a neighborhood resident hoping to help preserve the area nominated the area— now known as the South Main Historic District —to the National Register of Historic Places.

Central Station fell into disuse, and was abandoned by the Illinois Central Railroad in the 1980s. With the exception of the Amtrak passenger terminal in the rear of the building, which served a very limited schedule of trains, the building was vacant until the renovation began in 1997. By that time, the weather and stress-related deterioration had damaged the building's exterior, and its interior had been ravaged by vandalism and exposure.

Today, in South of Main, small developers are redeveloping one building at a time, often with lofts above street-level retail. With 18 shops and galleries now in operation, the area is an emerging arts district, complete with periodic arts festivals. Uses immediately surrounding Central Station include old and new retail shops, a café, some older industrial buildings, and vacant land. Some of the nearby retail space is vacant and ripe for redevelopment.

Central Station consists of a three-story terminal building; a five-story office tower; a single-story former Railway Express Agency (REA) warehouse, which is connected to the terminal and tower by an underground tunnel; and a former powerhouse, complete with smokestack. The terminal is constructed of concrete

In addition to apartments, the renovated Central Station houses an Amtrak train station, a bus station, retail space, a police substation, and public parking. Shown here are the waiting room of the Amtrak station and the station's Main Hall, which can be rented for private gatherings.

and steel, and its exterior is cast stone with cast-iron trim. The terminal building has a three-story limestone base. The five-story tower—situated on the northeast corner of the terminal base—has a brick veneer, and elaborate, heavily molded terra-cotta cornices highlight the tops of the east and north facades. Both the warehouse and the powerhouse are constructed of red brick and feature large windows.

Central Station was redeveloped by the Central Station Limited Partnership, which includes the Alexander Company as the managing general partner, the South Main Station Corporation as co–general partner, and the National Partnership Investments Corporation (NAPICO) as the limited partner. The South Main Station Corporation, owned by the Memphis Area Transit Authority (MATA) and the Center City Commission, is a single-asset company established to represent the public interest at Central Station. In 1994, to initiate Central Station's redevelopment, MATA purchased the building from the railroad and obtained $14.3 million from the Federal Transit Administration (FTA), $1.8 million from the city of Memphis, $1.8 million from the Tennessee Department of Transportation, and $100,000 from Amtrak to renovate the existing structures and create a multimodal transportation facility that would include an Amtrak station, a trolley stop, and a bus transfer facility. In addition, MATA hired Community Partners, the consulting arm of the National Trust for Historic Preservation, and Memphis Heritage, a local historic preservation organization, to advise on the use of historic preservation tax credits in redeveloping the structure. When the consultants recommended working with a private developer, MATA issued an RFP and selected the Alexander Company.

The Alexander Company decided to undertake the renovation of Central Station because it was a large enough project to warrant the effort, and the public subsidies would make it feasible. The Alexander Company's financial incentive was derived from fees and from minor participation in cash flow rather than from residual value. The firm charged a development fee, its in-house design staff earned a design fee, and its management company earns a property management fee (though the company views management as a means of controlling risk rather than as a profit center).

The Alexander Company was responsible for crafting the financing structure and developing the buildings (the residential and commercial uses) and accepted most of the financial risk, structuring the financing so that MATA would not be required to cover cost overruns or operating deficits. In return, the developer controlled renovation, leasing, and management, and MATA reviewed and approved plans and specifications, construction-contract change orders, construction draws, commercial leases, and annual budgets. MATA was also responsible for the site work, including the development of the bus transfer facility, the construction of a new passenger platform, and the completion of the surface parking lot.

Central Station Limited Partnership leases the site (with the exception of the bus transfer facility) from the city of Memphis and MATA under a 99-year land lease for a fee of $1 per year. The land lease allows the city of Memphis and MATA to demonstrate to the FTA ongoing control of the property, as required by the FTA grant. In addition to leasing the land, Central Station Limited Partnership acquired title to the buildings. MATA lent the partnership approximately $11.5 million for the renovation of the buildings, securing the loans with second and third mortgages, both of which are 30-year, cash-flow loans. The remainder of the $18 million raised by MATA was used to acquire the property from the railroad; obtain environmental and structural studies; and complete the bus transfer facility, the parking lot, and other site work. After seven years, MATA has an option to buy Central Station for the greater of either the fair market value or the amount of the outstanding debt, an arrangement that allows MATA to regain total control of the property once the private investor has captured the historic preservation tax credits.

In addition to the public financing from MATA, the renovation received funding from two private sources. First, the historic preservation tax credits allowed the Alexander Com-

The terrazzo floors and wood-framed transom windows of Central Station's original hallways were preserved.

pany to raise $3 million from a private investor, NAPICO. Second, a local bank provided $2.35 million of traditional, first-mortgage financing that was to be repaid from the net revenues of the apartments.

The Center City Commission granted the partnership a tax freeze under the PILOT program, holding the assessed value of the buildings at their current value for 15 years.

Redevelopment took 18 months, and today Central Station includes 63 one- and two-bedroom market-rate apartments (51 in the main tower and 12 in the REA building), a customer service center for MATA, a trolley stop, a bus transfer center, an Amtrak depot, and the Memphis Police Department's South Bluffs Precinct. Leases have been signed with service-oriented businesses that occupy 8,000 square feet of street-level space in the tower building. MATA leases the 12,822-square-foot Main Hall and Lower Concourse and actively manages them as event space. The powerhouse, restored on the exterior, is "paint ready" for a commercial tenant.

The apartments range in size from 740 to 1,435 square feet, and rents range from $600 to $950 per month. Among the 63 units are more than 30 different floor plans. The tower units are located on and above the second (mezzanine) floor. The developer was able to preserve most of the original corridors, which featured terrazzo floors and large, wood-framed transom windows. The tower building also includes an exercise room, a laundry room with vending machines offering newspapers and snacks, and a rooftop terrace for private outdoor socializing. (Because of venting requirements, washers and dryers could not be installed in each apartment; the Alexander Company issues residents laundry cards each month for free use of the laundry machines.)

The single-story units in the warehouse building are designed as lofts, with industrial-style finishes such as high ceilings, polished concrete floors, exposed ductwork, and unfinished brick walls. Each of the units opens to a private, attached "front porch" space that is enclosed with painted metal railing.

Above the warehouse is a surface parking lot that serves both Central Station residents and rail and bus travelers. Covered parking stalls and interior garage parking are also available for a monthly fee.

Noise from trains was not an issue because there are only two trains a day; moreover, arriving trains travel slowly, and the Main Hall separates living units from the train tracks. In addition, raised tracks at either end of the site allow the trains to enter and exit the site without blowing their whistles.

Security features include key access to the building, deadbolts on individual front doors, and cameras in some of the public areas, which deter vandalism.

Leasing began in October of 2000, and the property was 98 percent leased within four months. "Part of the marketing was done for us," reports Natalie Bock, development project manager for the Alexander Company, "in the form of press coverage of the grand opening festival, which was a $200-per-plate fundraiser for Memphis Heritage held in Central Station's Main Hall." The Alexander Company also marketed the project through traditional print ads in the *Apartment Guide* and Sunday paper. Prospective renters are offered one free month's rent with a 12-month lease (there are no concessions with a six-month lease). The marketing effort did not target a particular group, though renters tend to be young professionals, retired singles, and couples without children.

The city had no real comparables to use in valuing these units. Some high-rise apartments had been built downtown during the 1980s, but they had no historic character and no parking. For financing purposes, the project's rents were estimated at $.75 square foot, which is in the middle range for the city. (The units now generate $.80 per square foot.)

According to Bock, the transaction was difficult from a legal standpoint. For example, the costs that are eligible for historic preservation tax credits must be paid with funds from project equity or *bona fide* third-party debt, rather than grant money, and she had to structure the significant public subsidy so that it met the IRS guidelines for *bona fide* third-party debt. In addition, MATA needed to demonstrate to the FTA that it maintained continuing control; at the same time, in order to meet the IRS guidelines for tax credits, the partnership needed to demonstrate that it had ownership of the building.

At the time of the site visit, some of the retail space, including the powerhouse building, was vacant. "It's hard to lease retail in this type of project," observes Bock. "We never underwrite income from retail space."

The local contractor recommended by MATA had little experience in historic preservation work, which made the process unnecessarily difficult, time-consuming, and costly. In constructing historic preservation projects, Bock recommends negotiating a contract with a local contractor that has experience renovating existing structures and a style that is compatible with that of the developer. A strong working relationship between the contractor and the developer is important.

Bock believes that working with its own experienced, in-house design team helps the Alexander Company manage construction risk and also makes the firm more competitive. As she explains, "Third-party architects charge 6 percent of construction costs, plus change-of-scope fees. Our design staff understands the

The former Railway Express Agency building has been converted to single-story loft-style apartments, each of which has a private terrace.

kinds of projects we do and is accustomed to working with state historic preservation organizations and the federal government. They design buildings we can afford to build and calculate a guaranteed design fee. If we have to redesign many times, we'll do it. We manage the process."

Arranging financing was the most challenging aspect of the project. Bock takes pride in the fact that the Alexander Company met its goal of creating a viable, mixed-use project from a long-vacant building without using any more public funds than were initially made available. However, the tax structure for the historic preservation tax credits proved complicated. In retrospect, to coordinate the project's complex financing early on, Bock "would have gotten a tax accountant and a tax attorney into the same room from the first day." And, she notes, "Finding the $2.3 million first mortgage was excruciating." The banking community was apprehensive about the downtown location and the complexity of the deal structure. National lenders considered the project too small; local banks were daunted by its intricate financing. Eventually, the Bank of Bartlett, which was interested in opening a downtown office and needed Community Reinvestment Act credits, agreed to provide the loan. In retrospect, Bock feels that working more intensely with local lenders to familiarize them with the Alexander Company's track record would have given lenders more confidence in the project.

Floor plans.

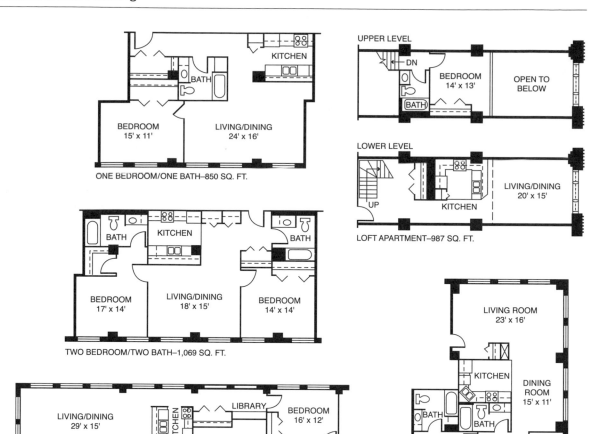

ONE BEDROOM/ONE BATH–850 SQ. FT.

TWO BEDROOM/TWO BATH–1,069 SQ. FT.

TWO BEDROOM/ONE BATH–1,220 SQ. FT..

LOFT APARTMENT–987 SQ. FT.

TWO BEDROOM/TWO BATH–1,218 SQ. FT.

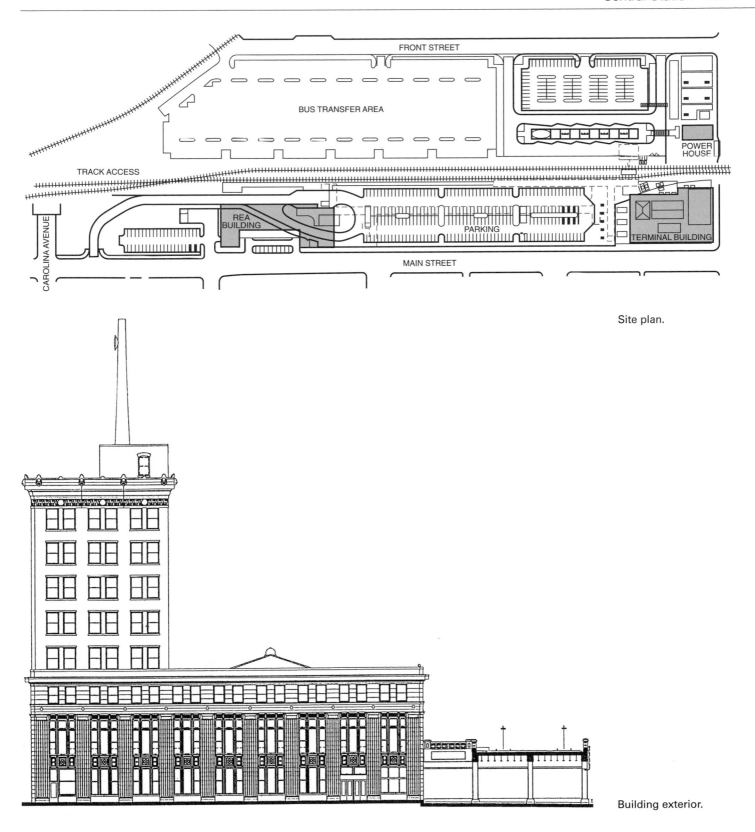

Site plan.

Building exterior.

Project Data: Central Station

Land Use Information

Site area	17 acres[a]
Building area	170,000 square feet
Open space	0.5 acre[b]
Total dwelling units	63
Gross residential density	6 units per acre[c]
Total retail and commercial space	37,000 square feet
Total parking spaces	336
Indoor and garage spaces	43
Covered spaces	23
Outdoor lot spaces	270

Residential Unit Information

Unit Type	Total Number	Square Feet	Average Rents[d]
One bedroom	16	740	$600
One bedroom	11	970	$775
Two bedroom	9	1,060	$825
Two bedroom	15	1,235	$950
Small loft	9	950	$730
Large loft	3	1,435	$950

Financing Information: Development

Funding Sources[e]

Memphis Area Transit Authority (MATA) public subsidy	$18,000,000
Equity	3,000,000
Debt (first mortgage)	2,350,000
Total	$23,350,000

Uses of Funds[f]

Site acquisition	$453,000
Buildings	663,000
MATA site work	5,147,000
Building rehabilitation	14,984,000
Tenant improvements	313,000
Total soft costs	1,790,000
Total hard and soft development costs	$23,350,000

Financing Information: Rehabilitation

Funding Sources

MATA (second mortgage)	$5,517,000
MATA (third mortgage)	6,033,000
Option payment	850,000
First mortgage	2,350,000
Equity	3,000,000
Total	$17,750,000

Uses of Funds

Building acquisition	$663,000
Building rehabilitation	14,984,000
Tenant improvements	313,000
Soft costs	1,790,000
Total	$17,750,000

Annual Operating Cost Information

Total annual operating costs	$400,000

Development Schedule

Site obtained	October 1998
Buildings purchased	October 1998
Planning began	1994
Site work began	1998
Construction started	October 1998
Construction completed	October 1999
Leasing started	September 1999
Leasing completed	April 2000

Project Award

Central Station was designated the Outstanding Planning Project for 2000 by the American Planning Association.

Development Team

Developer

The Alexander Company (as part of the Central Station Limited Partnership)
660 West Washington Avenue, Suite 303
Madison, Wisconsin 53703
608-258-5580

Joint Venture Partner

Memphis Area Transit Authority
1370 Levee Road
Memphis, Tennessee 38108
901-722-7160

Land Planner/Architect

Alexander Urban Resources
660 West Washington Avenue, Suite 303
Madison, Wisconsin 53703
608-258-5580

Project Address

545 South Main Street
Memphis, Tennessee 38103

General Information

Natalie Bock, development project manager,
The Alexander Company
608-258-5599

Dr. Thomas Fox, director of planning and capital projects,
Memphis Area Transit Authority
901-722-7160

All information in this case study is current as of April 4, 2001.

Notes

a. Approximately six acres is excess land held for future development, and an additional one acre is a bus transfer facility.
b. Not including the parking lot, the excess land, and the bus transfer facility.
c. Calculated on the basis of total acreage, less acreage used for the bus transfer facility and land held for future development.
d. Averages are for a unit of a particular size and type, and do not include premiums based on views, location in the building, and so forth.
e. Dollar figures are approximate.
f. Including site improvements.

Firestone Upper West Side

Fort Worth, Texas

Firestone Upper West Side includes 350 newly constructed rental units.

Beeler Guest Owens Architects

Located in what was once a booming automobile sales and services district just a few blocks from the center of downtown Fort Worth, Firestone Upper West Side is one of the city's first new housing developments. The centerpiece of the 350-unit, brownstone-style apartment development is the original 1929 Firestone Building—restored on the outside to its original facade, and rebuilt on the inside as the project's community center.

From its "cow-town" origins, downtown Fort Worth has been transformed, with the city's leadership and support, into a business, cultural, and entertainment destination. Today, a varied array of shops and restaurants line its landscaped brick streets. The center of the entertainment and shopping district, where the city has focused its attention and resources, is Sundance Square, a multiblock area in the city's core. Fort Worth also boasts a cultural district west of downtown that includes the Kimball Art Museum, the Modern Art Museum, and the Amon Carter Museum.

The Phoenix Property Company (PPC) was the first developer to recognize that the city's resurgence made it increasingly attractive as a place to live as well as to visit. PPC was founded in 1994 to develop multifamily housing in urban (and, to a lesser extent, suburban) locations throughout the United States. Its first projects, undertaken in 1996, were Eastbridge, in uptown Dallas, and Knightsbridge, in the Las Colinas section of Dallas. Other projects include Bellaire Ranch, in Fort Worth; Estancia, just outside Austin; Lantana, in Flower Mound, Texas; the Phoenix, in Dallas; Vineyards, in Grapevine, Texas; Commons Park West, in Denver; and the Drexel, in Cincinnati. PPC began its first California project in late 2000. Today, the firm has offices in Dallas and in Newport Beach, California. The company also acquires and develops student housing through its GrandMarc subsidiary, which is based in Atlanta. Through PPC Real Estate Advisors, Inc., the company advises European investors on commercial real estate investment in the United States.

For the Firestone Upper West Side development, principals Blake Pogue and Jason Runnels looked for a site that was within walking distance of the excitement and nightlife of Sundance Square, yet large enough for between

200 and 300 units—or, in Runnels's words, "a development that would create its own environment." In addition, Runnels wanted a site to the west of downtown, both because the western portion of the city has a reputation as a desirable area to live and because of the other key cultural attractions that lie west of the city.

The site is about one-tenth of a mile west of the city center, on three contiguous blocks between First and Tenth streets and between Henderson and Summit streets. Neighborhood-serving stores and services, including a 24-hour Walgreen's, line Henderson Street. The site is within walking distance of two employment centers—downtown and a large medical complex—and it lies between the city core and the cultural district about two miles to the west. On an adjacent parcel west of the site is the Cattle Raisers' Museum. In the 1920s and 1930s, this area—since abandoned—was known as "automobile row" because of its car dealerships and services, and one of its main streets—Seventh Street—is the main entrance to Fort Worth's downtown from the west.

The city of Fort Worth has been proactive in supporting development in the downtown. The city's 1990 plan called for downtown housing —and, according to Runnels, it viewed this project as an opportunity "to fire the growth of a 24-hour city." After preliminary discussions to ascertain the city's interest in supporting the project, PPC hired a broker to assemble the tract. To avoid setting off speculation in land prices, PPC handled purchasing quietly, with different people working with different land-owners. PPC viewed certain parcels as essential; once those were obtained, the project could go forward. As PPC purchased some parcels outright and optioned others, it became heavily in-vested, paying between $100,000 and $200,000 per month just to extend the options.

In all, PPC assembled 15 acres of land from 14 different landowners over a two-year period. Firestone Upper West Side covers just over 11 acres of the site; PPC plans to develop the remaining property at a future date.

Realizing that, despite relatively low land costs, the project would not otherwise be financially feasible, PPC sought tax abatements by documenting how the project would likely stimulate additional development and increase land values in the area. In Fort Worth, the value of land and the value of structures are appraised separately, and separate taxes are levied by the city of Fort Worth, Tarrant County, and the Fort Worth Independent School District. All agreed to allow PPC to pay taxes only on the land value of the project's 11 acres, and to abate taxes on the structures for ten years. PPC agreed to pay full taxes on the remaining property it owned in the area and to initiate another development on the non-tax-abated portion of the land.

At the time of purchase, the site was zoned for light industrial use, but changing the zoning to allow project development posed no problems. The city council; county commissioners; Downtown Fort Worth, Inc.; and groups such as the Bass Family Foundation all supported the project, and community acceptance was not an issue.

PPC retained the area's historic automotive theme in the project's design. Working closely with the Fort Worth Architectural Historical Society, it restored the facade of Firestone Building, which had been an open-air tire company and garage. The building was a combination of neoclassical, Spanish Renaissance, and Italian Renaissance architectural styles, and PPC felt

Beeler Guest Owens Architects

A 1929 service station now houses a leasing office and community amenities.

that its design would appeal to the market of young professionals the firm sought to attract. The finished building (now the community center) displays the original Firestone sign, and PPC has applied to the National Trust for Historic Preservation to designate the building a historic structure. The project's name builds on both the location's historic land uses and on the desirability of the west side of town.

Despite its previous automobile-related uses, the site was essentially "clean" from an environmental standpoint, but site development involved a number of infrastructure issues. The community building sits on a 60-inch sewer line that could not be moved. The city agreed to make any repairs to the sewer line that might be needed in the future. PPC had to relocate utility lines and remove underground fuel storage tanks. The site's slope created expensive grading challenges and dictated the incorporation of retaining walls, but also resulted in a more visually appealing development. PPC had to close some streets during development, but it encountered no opposition since the streets were located within the site. In addition, site planning had to accommodate a "holdout" parcel that contains an automobile-painting service. Essentially, PPC built the community around the existing building, with appropriate visual buffering.

The site consists of three distinct blocks, each of which was designed as a self-contained group of apartments. As a result, the develop-

ment functions almost as if it were three separate communities. The southernmost block, between West Tenth and West Seventh streets, contains four three-story, double-loaded apartment buildings and two buildings of rowhouses, all of which surround a surface parking lot. (The rowhouses have in-line garages for their residents' use.) In addition, this block includes a community center and swimming pool. The block between West Seventh and West Fifth streets holds one building of single-loaded units that form a perimeter around structured parking within. The northernmost block, located between West Fifth and First streets, contains four three-story, double-loaded apartment buildings that front the street, with covered surface parking within.

PPC owns another block between West Seventh and West Fifth streets, across from each of the three project blocks. On this block, PPC plans to renovate an existing two-story building, creating a restaurant on the first floor and four rental lofts on the second floor, and to retrofit a Goodyear tire center into service retail and restaurant uses.

On each block, buildings are sited close to the street, which not only gives the development an "urban face" but also allows the buildings themselves to serve as the secure exterior edge of the project, thereby eliminating the need for extensive fences or gates. Because the buildings are located close to the street, PPC mitigated noise by using heavy, dense, blown-in insulation between the walls, and Sheetrock on the walls that face the street.

Entry doors to each building are secured with fencing and electronic security, and first-floor balconies are enclosed for residents to use as solariums. Residents are issued "clickers" that, when triggered, send out an audible alarm and automatically call a security company, identifying the person and his or her location.

The Victorian architectural style reflects the architectural traditions and details of the homes built in this part of the city in the 1920s and 1930s. The buildings' exteriors are brick masonry and stucco, with steeply pitched roofs. Gaslights, fountains, brick walkways, decorative iron fencing, and landscaping enhance the streetscape. Carrying through the automobile theme, the various types of units offered are named for cars—Fleetwood, Mustang, Eldorado, and so forth. The one- and two-story floor plans range from 641 to 1,614 square feet, with an average of 911. Some of the units include solariums or octagonal "tower rooms" with dramatic views of downtown Fort Worth. Interiors are fitted with luxury features such as marble countertops, nine-foot ceilings with crown molding, pantries, wood-burning fireplaces, and ceiling fans. All apartments have digital high-speed wireless Internet access and cable television.

Project amenities, which were selected on the basis of information obtained in focus groups, include

- A resort-style swimming-pool complex with a spa, water features, outdoor seating areas, shuffleboard, and an outdoor fireplace.
- A 13,000-square-foot community center, which contains a half-court basketball gymnasium with a window wall facing the street; a health club with locker rooms, showers, free weights, aerobics, and cardiovascular exercise equipment; a business center with two conference rooms—one with computers, high-speed Internet access, a printer, a fax machine and a copier; a comfortable lounge with a kitchen, a pool table, and a bar area; and the leasing/management office.
- A small park and pavilion at the corner of West Fifth and Henderson streets. PPC in-

cluded this landscaped green space, where residents can gather outdoors, as a place for special activities such as rotating art shows.

Residents can gain access to the community center 24 hours a day. It was planned to serve not only Firestone Upper West Side but additional PPC residential developments that will be built nearby.

Parking is another project amenity. In Fort Worth, downtown parking costs $150 per

Outdoor recreational facilities include (from top) a spa, an outdoor fireplace, and a swimming pool.

Garage parking, which is available for some of the units, can be accessed from an interior surface parking lot.

month. PPC provides a minimum of one parking space per bedroom either in a secured surface parking lot, gated parking garage, or direct-access garage. Covered parking is available in the surface parking lots. As a rule, surface parking spaces are not assigned, but PPC charges $25 per month for a covered space.

To finance the project, PPC matched its own equity with equity financing from BGB US Real Estate, Inc., an institutional investor, and the two entities own the project jointly. PPC's investors for typical suburban garden apartments have been life insurance companies and pension funds. However, PPC found that these categories of investors were not comfortable, initially, with an urban product, primarily because urban infill housing costs more per unit and is often built in unproved markets where no true comparables exist. As is typical in such cases, no real supporting market data were available, and the value of the projects used as comparables—$90 per foot—was less than the $110 per foot needed to build the project. So, to obtain equity, PPC approached a German bank.

Bank One, Texas, N.A., a conventional lender, provided debt financing. The construction loan from Bank One was for three years, with two one-year options to extend. PPC tries to obtain construction loans with terms that are long enough to enable a project to become financially stabilized before the firm goes to the market for long-term debt. PPC plans to refinance Firestone Upper West Side (with a German bank) on a long-term basis in 2001.

Rents average between $1,200 and $1,300 per month, which is considered high-end for Fort Worth. However, because a number of competitive projects have been built recently in nearby suburbs, within easy commuting distance of downtown, rents are not as high as originally anticipated. The project's other competition is for-sale, single-family housing and other apartments recently built downtown. According to Runnels, Firestone's key competitive advantage is its location. In addition, he cites the variety of the product offerings and the attractive amenity package.

The project is targeted to people without children, including newly married couples, empty nesters, and single young professionals, especially those who work downtown and in the hospital complex. The typical renter is between the late 20s and early 30s in age, with an income between $60,000 and $80,000. As Runnels observes, "These are people who can afford to buy but choose not to."

Project construction began in May of 1997 and was completed in December of 1999. Leasing began in mid-1999. Initially, leasing lagged behind expectations because consumers were not yet familiar with the idea of an urban lifestyle. Housing is generally inexpensive in the region, commuting is easy, and, at the time this project was built, the difference in value between an apartment in the suburbs and one in the city had not yet been established. (Today, people will pay a premium of $125 per month to live downtown.)

The vacancy rate as of January 2001 was 7 percent, which is better than competitive downtown projects but higher than anticipated. Expectations had to be adjusted when a tornado struck Fort Worth in May of 2000, right in the middle of the heavy leasing season, and put five buildings out of service. Tenants had to be moved into other buildings or into hotels for five months, while PPC carried the costs.

Though PPC was insured, the "loss of rent" protection did not apply because at the time of the tornado, the project was not yet 90 percent leased.

Like PPC's other developments, Firestone Upper West Side is managed by Lincoln Property Company. In 2001, the project was included in Downtown Fort Worth, Inc.'s, public improvement district, which will provide added street cleaning, security, and landscape improvements—and, ultimately, will include a trolley connecting the development to the city's cultural district.

According to Runnels, the most successful aspects of the project were "how we kept the historical significance of Seventh Street and 'automobile row' as the front door to downtown, and the partnership with the city that made the project possible."

PPC has learned that these kinds of projects take time and need to be financed with "patient equity." Because PPC invests its own equity, it can buy and hold land, accepting the land acquisition, entitlement, and site-development risk. Although PPC's investment partners do not take the development risk, they do share in the market (lease-up) risk. Runnels points out that if the location is right, the investment in land is not a huge risk for PPC because "we always feel that we have the option of selling the land."

The project has received kudos for its site design, brownstone-style architecture, and the incorporation of the carefully renovated Firestone Building. Runnels explained: "Land costs dictate the type of project you build—expensive land dictates higher density." Favorable land costs, coupled with tax abatements, enabled PPC to design a low-density community with the character of a residential neighborhood. Subsequent projects built by competitors on higher-priced land will have to be designed at higher densities to be profitable.

In retrospect, Runnels would have liked more time upfront to evaluate the market and plan the project. Specifically, he now feels that a slightly higher density would have worked just as well and been more profitable. And, based on market response, he would have built

larger units (which yield higher per-square-foot rents) and a larger proportion of two-bedroom units.

In addressing the lack of market data to support the project, Runnels explained, "You have to accept some risk. If the market was proven, we couldn't have bought the land at a price that would make the project work." Firestone Upper West Side has proved the market and stimulated competition. Since it was built, other developers have undertaken projects in the city, and PPC and others plan future developments as well.

The community center includes a gymnasium; fitness equipment; a large, comfortable lounge; a business center with computers; a kitchen; meeting rooms; and offices.

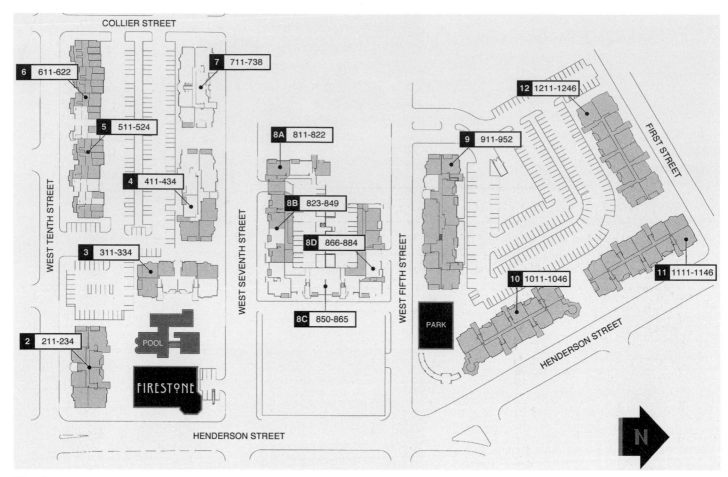

Site plan.

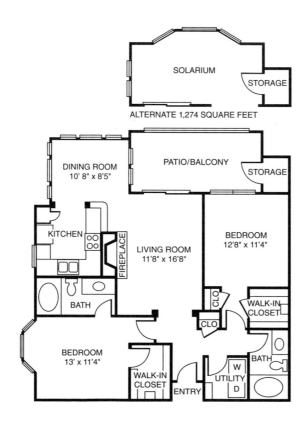

Floor plan, two-bedroom unit.

Project Data: Firestone Upper West Side

Land Use Information

Site area	11 acres
Total dwelling units	350
Gross density	32 units per acre
Community center	13,000 square feet
Total parking spaces	525
Outdoor spaces	388
Garage spaces	26
Covered spaces	111

Land Use Plan

Use	Acres
Buildings	3.2
Parking areas	1.6
Roads and driveways	1.5
Amenities	0.8

Residential Unit Information

Unit Type	Total Number	Square Feet	Monthly Rents
One bedroom/one bath			
Mustang	88	641–779	$785–$870
Malibu	27	651–763	$795–$880
Fleetwood	44	1,119	$1,435
Fairlane	63	812–1,012	$1,445
Bel-Air	13	816–896	$870–$905
Model T	38	924	$1,140
Two bedrooms/two baths			
Thunderbird	8	1,045–1,177	$1,080–$1,100
Continental	50	1,104–1,274	$1,150–$1,250
Eldorado	6	1,252–1,422	$1,290–$1,330
Two-bedroom/two-bath lofts			
Imperial	13	1,581–1,614	$1,630–$1,700

Development Cost Information

Site acquisition	$5,000,000
Site improvement	1,200,000
Construction	20,300,000
Amenities	1,300,000
Total soft costs	7,100,000
Total hard and soft development costs	$34,900,000
Average development cost per unit	$99,714

Annual Operating Cost Information

Total annual operating costs	$1,215,000
Average annual operating costs per unit	$3,471

Development Schedule

Site purchased	February 1996–February 1998
Planning began	February 1996
Site work began	February 1998
Project completion	December 1999

Project Awards

Firestone Upper West Side has received a number of awards: from the National Association of Home Builders, the 2001 Pillars of the Industry Award for the Best Leasing Center; from the Home Builders' Association of Dallas, the 2001 McSam Award for the Best Apartment/Multifamily Community; from *Professional Builder* magazine, the 2000 Best in American Living Silver Award; and from *Commercial Builder* magazine, the 2000 Division III Grand Award for Leasing Station.

Development Team

Developer
Phoenix Property Company
2626 Howell Street, Suite 800
Dallas, Texas 75204
214-880-0350

Land Planner
EnviroDesign
7424 Greenville Avenue, Suite 200
Dallas, Texas 75231
214-987-3010

Architect
Beeler Guest Owens, Architects, L.P.
2211 North Lamar Street, Suite 300
Dallas, Texas 75202
214-740-0080

Project Address

1001 West Seventh Street
Fort Worth, Texas 76102

General Information

Jason Runnels, executive vice president and principal, Phoenix Property Company
214-880-0350

All information in this case study is current as of January 2001.

Noji Gardens
Seattle, Washington

Noji Gardens features innovative combinations of two-story manufactured, modular, and stick-built homes, which provide affordable market-rate and income-restricted housing.

Leslie Holst

Use of an innovative, HUD-code manufactured-home product enabled HomeSight, a nonprofit developer, to produce affordable homeownership opportunities for moderate-income households on an infill site just south of Seattle.[1] The 75-unit development features two-story, two- and four-section zero-lot-line single-family homes, 54 of which are manufactured homes.

HomeSight, a 501(c)(3) nonprofit community development corporation incorporated in 1990, is the largest nonprofit sole-purpose organization for homeownership in Washington State. It pursues its mission—which is to revitalize neighborhoods through affordable homeownership—primarily in Seattle's Central, Southeast, Duwamish, and Delridge communities. During the past ten years, HomeSight has formed partnerships with neighborhood orga-

nizations, foundations, lenders, corporations, and others to construct or rehabilitate more than 200 homes valued at over $22 million. In addition, HomeSight provides homebuyer education and counseling services and loan assistance programs. The organization has won numerous national and local awards for design, land use, and organizational excellence.

Seattle's strong economy; its high land, construction, and regulatory costs; and the resulting high housing prices have created a shortage of close-in, affordable housing. Despite construction efficiencies, it has become increasingly difficult for HomeSight to produce high-quality homes at affordable prices. According to Dorothy Lengyel, HomeSight's executive director, Seattle is becoming very similar to San Francisco, with expensive residential areas and little housing that is affordable to moderate-income households—those earning about $40,000 per year. She reports, "There are not really any developers providing housing for working families."

Manufactured housing presents an affordable alternative to stick-built homes. Lots for manufactured homes can be very small, making possible higher-density developments. The homes are less expensive to construct because they can be produced quickly and efficiently in the controlled environment of a factory, which is protected from weather damage and delays; employs a skilled and consistent workforce; and generates continuous, high-volume production. HomeSight's construction team can "crane," or build, four boxes of manufactured housing—equal to two units—in two hours. Shorter construction time translates to lower financing costs. In addition, the performance-based HUD code allows the use of innovative materials and construction methods. These cost savings mean lower home prices.

HomeSight had been conducting its own research into two-story manufactured housing when a U.S. Department of Housing and Urban Development (HUD) official told the organization about the HUD/Manufactured Housing Institute demonstration project, which was designed to test the potential for cost savings that could be realized by using manufactured homes that look like stick-built homes. HomeSight had already developed subdivisions of 25 to 30 affordable units, and had been looking for a way to take the two concepts—affordability and manufactured housing—and bring them together in an efficient manner. Noji Gardens was HomeSight's first use of manufactured housing.

The use of manufactured homes in this development was influenced by the Snohomish County Housing Authority's successful development of manufactured-home communities, which had demonstrated the potential for savings in construction costs and development time. (Development time can be cut from the five to six months typically required for a stick-built home to as little as two months for a manufactured home.) However, the architecture typical of manufactured homes was not appropriate to the Noji Gardens's neighborhood context, which consisted largely of two-story homes. Furthermore, the state's Growth Management Act required jurisdictions to promote affordable housing at all income levels. Two-story homes are not a requirement of the

The Craftsman-style homes incorporate features such as front porches, horizontal vinyl siding, pop-out windows, variations in rooflines, and traditional roof pitches.

Leslie Holst

Growth Management Act, but as an agency that pioneers small-lot development, Home-Sight sees two-story homes as a necessity in achieving a desirable amount of living space.

After visiting a HUD demonstration project in Pittsburgh, HomeSight officials realized that manufactured housing would enable them to achieve their goals, and began working with an architect to draw up designs that would appeal to their market—and working with the manufacturer to create homes that were consistent with the architects' designs. To learn the procedures for building manufactured housing, HomeSight went through a state-certified training process, toured factories, and learned from the mistakes of other organizations.

Though the industry had already begun to address the possibility of creating two-story manufactured homes, it took three years to develop the manufactured-home products offered at Noji Gardens. Marlette Homes, of Hermiston, Oregon, a division of Schulte Homes Corporation (a subsidiary of Oakwood Homes), worked with HomeSight's deputy director, Tony To; the city of Seattle; the State of Washington's Department of Labor and Industry; and local contractors to create a two-story home that, even initially, cost an estimated 10 to 15 percent less to build than a comparable stick-built home. Cost savings are expected to climb to between 25 and 30 percent once the process has been refined by experience.

The 6.5-acre Noji Gardens site is located at 32nd Avenue South and South Juneau Street in the established neighborhood of Dearborn Park, in the Rainier Valley. Named for the site's previous owner, the Noji family, which had operated a greenhouse on the property from 1918 to 1996, the project is within Seattle's city limits and just four miles southeast of downtown. Schools, playgrounds, community centers, public transportation, and the Columbia City commercial core are all nearby. Noji Gardens is one of the key housing developments included in the 1999 Southeast Neighborhood Revitalization Strategy Area Plan devised by the city and HUD to improve the quality and diversity of HUD-supported housing developments in the area.

Lengyel had initially hoped to build a condominium building (as well as townhouses and single-family homes) to create a more dense, 100-unit development on the site, but the infrastructure requirements and the difficulty of constructing underground parking, given the site's high water table, made that approach infeasible. In addition, residents of the surrounding, mostly low income community were initially concerned about the project's density and the compatibility between the proposed design and existing neighborhood homes. As a result of these issues, the project was redesigned as 75 single-family homes in single-family, duplex, fourplex, and townhouse configurations. The mayor agreed to support the Noji Gardens project, and the community also liked the plan for the site.

The site was divided into 2,400- to 4,000-square-foot lots. In all, there will be 24 two-bedroom townhouses, 40 three-bedroom townhouses, and 11 two-, three-, and four-bedroom single-family detached homes. To develop the site, HomeSight had to create—and pay for—critical infrastructure (streets, curbs, and sidewalks) and to upgrade the utility services, which added $1.7 million to the development expenses. To contain infrastructure costs, HomeSight built private driveways instead of public alleys behind the homes. This approach not only was subject to less rigorous construction requirements, but also gave homeowners control over who uses the road.

In addition, HomeSight had to install a drainage line two blocks past the site to make it available to another 400 units on another site. The city of Seattle is working to develop a "late-comer" policy so that any additional developers that want to use the drainage line will have to reimburse HomeSight for some part of the construction costs for the line.

After reviewing the site plan, the city's engineering department required more curb cuts than HomeSight planned, which necessitated a redesign. The department's slow responses further impeded the permit process, and the resulting delays required HomeSight to mobilize and demobilize workers twice, which was very costly. In all, permitting delays added two years

The community also includes fourplex homes, shown here under construction.

to the project's development and contributed to a 40 percent increase in the homes' prices.

The project's zero-lot-line configurations were the first for manufactured units in the county. Lengyel used Lego blocks to visualize various possible homesite locations and configurations. Although HomeSight had wanted to use manufactured housing to develop the whole project, HUD's window requirements were such that all the fourplexes had to be stick built. In addition, because HUD raised objections to the party walls and zero-lot-line designs, the duplexes are actually six inches apart but share a roof, and homes sited as zero lot line have contiguous siding and attached roofs.

Noji Gardens is being developed in three phases. The manufactured homes in Phase I feature two basic models, each with a number of available variations. Both are two-story, Craftsman-Style homes with front porches, horizontal vinyl siding, and steep roofs. The first model, with a total footprint of 24 feet by 30 feet, four inches, consists of four manufactured modules, two downstairs and two upstairs, which combine to create a 1,400-square-foot, three- or four-bedroom single-family home. In the second model, two sections, each of which is 15 feet, ten inches, by 39 feet, are one above the other, creating a 617-square-foot, two-bedroom, two-and-a-half bath home with a front porch on the first floor. This home can be expanded with a two-story, site-built

structure that includes a garage and bonus room on the first floor and two additional bedrooms upstairs, for a total home size of 1,530 square feet.

The homes are transported to the site by truck. Both models feature hinged roofs, which make it possible to transport the homes to the site with the roof down. Once the home is in place, the roof is lifted to achieve a full 8/12 roof pitch. The first-floor sections are attached to permanent concrete foundations; the second-floor sections are then lifted by crane and connected to the tops of the first floors and to each other. Interior walls largely hide interior seams. All the homes have vinyl siding exteriors, which HomeSight installs on site. Interiors include solid oak cabinets, energy-efficient windows, and name-brand appliances.

The stick-built housing consists primarily of identical fourplexes that are designed to look like townhouses. Some of the manufactured homes are partially stick built: there are single-family homes, for example, that have modular first floors and stick-built, wraparound porches, and some second floors are a mixture of modular and stick-built components.

In 1998, the city of Seattle provided Home-Sight with a 2 percent Section 108 CDBG float loan for interim site acquisition; another CDBG float loan, issued in 2000, was used to refinance the site purchase and to finance the acquisition of the 42 manufactured homes. U.S. Bank, the

National Community Development Initiative (NCDI, which is managed locally by the Puget Sound Local Initiatives Support Corporation), and the Fannie Mae Foundation provided construction loans at below-market interest rates.

Because Noji Gardens falls within a designated revitalization area, all buyers of homes funded with HUD block grants are eligible for special HUD–Federal Housing Administration financing terms that reduce the upfront costs and buyer qualifications. In addition, the development is within the city's tax abatement area, so buyers purchasing a zero-lot-line home in a fourplex or larger structure can defer property taxes on their homes for ten years. Fannie Mae and HUD (through its block grant program and through a special-purpose grant for such assistance) provided downpayment assistance to qualifying families; HomeSight also offers buyer-assistance programs, and provides buyers with homeowner counseling to explain what is involved in homeownership and how to manage budget or credit difficulties.

HomeSight's goal in pricing Noji Gardens was to keep prices low enough so that people in the neighboring area could afford to live there. As required by the conditions of the CDBG loan, 51 percent of the homes are reserved for households with incomes of 80 percent or less of the area median household income ($43,000 a year for a family of three). Up to 49 percent may be sold at market rates.

The "affordable" homes were marketed to people in the HomeSight program; market-rate units were listed with a realtor. There is a 90-day sales turnaround on the market-rate units.

HomeSight did not attempt to presell the large homes built in Phase I. The buyers were either market-rate purchasers or longtime clients who had been with the HomeSight program for years. As of this writing, 35 of the 42 homes in Phase II had been sold.

A number of challenges surfaced in the construction of the manufactured homes. First, Marlette needed to obtain HUD approval for the new product, train its workforce, and adjust its assembly line to produce a new type of home. Second, many subcontractors were unfamiliar with the product and reluctant to bid on the project (a situation that was exacerbated by a shortage of construction labor in the Seattle area). Those that did often made cost estimates that were excessive. By informing and working closely with the contractors, To was able to help them bring their bids in line. Finally, because the manufactured homes are an innovative product, getting the construction and assembly process underway and making it efficient was also a learning process for all concerned.

The manufactured-housing industry is not yet geared to work with traditional developers, and Lengyel found it frustrating—and often

Garages may be incorporated into homes or provided in separate structures; all are accessed from rear alleys.

Leslie Holst

Leslie Holst

time-consuming—to work with the manufacturer. For developers to recognize manufactured housing as a potential housing product, manufacturers need to understand development economics and the importance of meeting deadlines.

Another source of frustration—and significant delays—was the requirement that every design change, no matter how small (for example, moving a window less than a foot), be submitted to HUD headquarters in Washington, D.C. The approvals process would have been much simpler if it had been coordinated between HUD and the city. Furthermore, in Lengyel's opinion, HUD needs a better system for approving changes in the plan. In addition to being unpredictable, the current approach makes phased development difficult. In retrospect, she also feels that the process could have gone more smoothly if HomeSight had worked more closely with HUD to obtain agreement on the design of the proposed development before construction began.

As a result of this experience, HomeSight is currently working on another housing project, in Snohomish County, in which the majority of the 34 units will be manufactured housing. Lengyel believes that manufactured homes offer good value for the money—they are constructed better than stick-built homes that can be built for the same cost. Because manufactured homes are built with plywood and steel framing, they can sustain earthquake damage and 65-mile-per-hour winds.

The risk involved in this type of development, according to Lengyel, is "largely a function of the character of the people implementing the innovation." Specifically, Lengyel suggests that policy makers need to share both positive and negative information and "be shrewd enough to identify nonprofits that can deliver the goods."

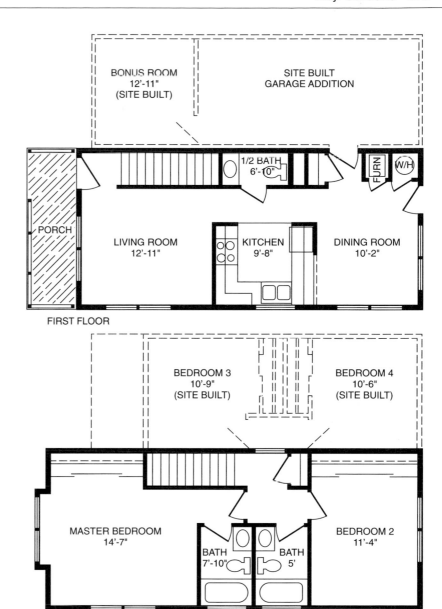

Floor plan.

Note

1. The term *HUD-code* refers to the U.S. Department of Housing and Urban Development's Manufactured Housing Construction and Safety Standards Act. Manufactured homes must comply with this code, a requirement that differentiates them not only from stick-built homes but also from "mobile homes" (built before the HUD code was enacted) or modular, panelized, or precut homes.

Project Data: Noji Gardens

Land Use Information

Site area	6.5 acres
Open space	2 acres
Total dwelling units	75
Gross density	12 units per acre
Total parking spaces	75
Indoor and garage spaces	51
Outdoor lot spaces	24

Land Use Plan

Use	Acres
Buildings	1.1
Parking areas	0.3
Roads and driveways	1.5

Residential Unit Information

Unit Type	Total Number	Square Feet	Sales Prices
Single-family homes			
Four bedrooms	6	1,530–1,450	$221,000–$240,000
Three bedrooms	4	1,400	$215,000–$218,000
Two bedrooms	1	1,000	$175,000
Townhouses			
Two bedrooms	24	1,000	$155,000–$162,000
Three bedrooms	40	1,350	$170,000–$200,000

Development Cost Information

Site value	$2,000,000
Site improvement	1,700,000
Construction	8,565,000
Total soft costs	800,000
Total hard and soft development costs	$11,065,000
Average development cost per unit	$174,000

Financing Information

Source	Type of Financing	Amount
CDBG float loan	Acquisition and materials	$3,400,000
LISC-NCDI[a]	Construction	2,520,000
Bank loan	Construction	5,000,000
Fannie Mae Foundation	Predevelopment	500,000
LISC-NCDI	Predevelopment	100,000
HomeSight equity	Predevelopment	$1,545,000

Development Schedule

Site purchased	July 1999
Planning began	September 1998
Site work began	August 1999
Project completion	June 2002 (expected)

Phase I

Number of units	8
Planning started	September 1998
Construction started	August 1999
Construction completed	April 2000
Sales started	August 1999
Sales completed	June 2000

Phase II

Number of units	42
Planning started	September 1998
Construction started	March 1999
Construction completed	August 2001
Sales started	September 2000
Sales completed	September 2001 (expected)

Phase III

Number of units	25
Planning started	September 1998
Construction started	June 2001
Construction completed	June 2002 (expected)
Sales started	September 2001 (expected)
Sales completed	August 2002 (expected)

Development Team

Developer/Land Planner
HomeSight
5117 Rainier Avenue South
Seattle, Washington 98118
206-723-4355

Architect
John McLaren
2727 Fairview Avenue
Seattle, Washington 98102
206-325-9890

Project Address

32nd Avenue South and South Juneau Streets
Seattle, Washington

General Information

Tony To, deputy director, HomeSight
206-760-4041

All information in this case study is current as of July 20, 2001.

Note

a. Local Initiatives Support Corporation–National Community Development Initiative.

150 St. Mary's
Raleigh, North Carolina

All-brick construction and architectural details, such as corbeling and arched windows, convey the desired image of quality and solidity.

A 48-unit, for-sale townhouse development, 150 St. Mary's is located in a transitional area of Raleigh, North Carolina, between the downtown core and North Carolina State University. The 2.1-acre site is one of several properties that York Properties, Inc., a family of companies, has developed or is considering developing in the immediate area as part of a strategy to rebuild that part of the city by means of infill development.

The York family has been in the real estate development business in Raleigh since 1910.

Today, under the leadership of Smedes York, former mayor of Raleigh and former president of ULI, it operates a number of separate but related real estate companies in the city, including York Properties, Inc., a property maintenance, brokerage, and property management company; York Ventures, a division of York Properties that does predevelopment work and consulting; York Simpson Underwood, a residential brokerage company; and McDonald York, Inc., a general contractor specializing in preconstruction services and the construction of diverse types of real estate developments. Separate companies are formed to develop each project or group of related projects, and the other York companies participate on a fee basis. St. Mary's Associates, LLC, which is owned by Smedes York and Settle Dockery, who is also projects director of York Ventures, was organized to develop the 150 St. Mary's project.

Before initiating the 150 St. Mary's project, the York companies had developed other projects in the general vicinity (including the Cameron Village shopping center, where many of the companies' offices are located), and it recognized the area's market potential. At the time the site for 150 St. Mary's was purchased, the only redevelopment that had been undertaken by others was the renovation of a single low-rise building, located diagonally across from one corner of the project site, which the county had transformed into a social services facility. York Ventures recently completed an office condominium development near 150 St. Mary's.

Dockery feels that "what's around a site is more important than its physical characteristics. The overall location—whether or not people can walk to a park or a restaurant—is what gives it value." The 150 St. Mary's site was chosen because of its location one block off Hillsborough Street, a major connector, and just seven blocks from downtown Raleigh (to the east) and 12 blocks from NC State (to the west). In addition, the site is just one block from St. Mary's School (a private academy that was formerly St. Mary's College), three blocks from a YMCA, and within walking distance of restaurants on Hillsborough Street and a planned intermodal transportation hub that will connect Raleigh to the Research Triangle area. The site is also near railroad tracks, which effectively separate it from uses—including a state prison—on the other side.

The area immediately surrounding the site contains a mix of moderate-density, low-rise, commercial, residential, institutional, and public buildings. Most are in good structural condition, but some have deteriorated or become obsolete. Single-family homes now used as offices occupy most of the remainder of the block that constitutes the project site. Also on that block, on a parcel adjacent to the 150 St. Mary's project, is the Joel Lane House, a restored historic property.[1] Because it is near to, rather than within, the downtown core, and because current densities are moderate rather than high, the area feels more like an urban neighborhood than a city *per se*. And because it is close to, but not on, a busy street, the site enjoys good vehicular access but is not affected by street noise and traffic.

For a number of years, York Properties had tried to acquire the site from a friend who owned it. Finally, in 1998, it was purchased for $4.50 per square foot. Because the successful development of 150 St. Mary's proved the existence of a market for residential development, a similar parcel of land in that general location would sell for $10 to $12 per square foot today.

At the time of purchase, the property was occupied by a lumber company and zoned industrial. Although industrial zoning in Raleigh is very flexible, allowing zero-lot-line development and no setbacks, it does not allow residential use. However, within the Downtown Housing Overlay District, which is designed to encourage residential development, there are no setback requirements and no limits on density for areas governed by underlying industrial zoning. Successfully persuading the city and neighborhood stakeholders to extend the overlay district to the site enabled the developer to create a residential development with a density of 23 units per acre on 18-foot-wide lots. The extension was easy to obtain because both the city and the stakeholders, who were mostly businesspeople, supported the project as a means of improving the area.

To render the site usable for residential development, it was necessary to remove storage structures and concrete paving put in by the lumber company. In addition, during site development, the developer discovered an area of fill that had to be excavated, adding $20,000 to the project's cost. The slope and dimensions were odd, and, Dockery explains, "We had to do a lot of front-end planning and manipulate the site plan to get the desired density." Retaining

The development's landscaped brick privacy walls create an attractive yet secure face for surrounding streets.

walls were built to help manage changes in grade. Because there was no stormwater drainage system in an adjacent block, riprap channels had to be installed after the project was developed, to divert the stormwater runoff that flowed from that block into the development's drainage system.

The 150 St. Mary's project was designed to create an urban streetscape—and, at the same time, through building orientation, limited access, and fencing, to ensure privacy. The 48 two-story brick homes face interior private streets that can be accessed through the project's three entrances. The homes that line the public streets on the perimeter of the project are not set back from the surrounding streets, so the architecture is readily visible and the project looks more like an urban than a suburban neighborhood. Eighty-two unassigned parking spaces are provided, all in front of the homes on the project's internal streets. A brick wall buffers the homes from external streets, and walls separate each private patio from the next. Perhaps because of the security inherent in the project's design, prospective buyers posed few questions about it, even though the property is near a prison, railroad tracks (which attract transients), and a county social services office that serves people who have a variety of problems.

The homes are grouped into eight buildings, each of which includes three to eight units. The use of three different muted colors of brick creates texture and depth, and the buildings feature details such as corbeling on the front facades. Rooflines and facade setbacks are varied to define individual homes. Brick sidewalks, walls, and pilasters, and wrought-iron railings accentuate the impression of formality, substance, and tradition conveyed by the homes' organization, building materials, and architectural style. Common space is minimal, though each home has a private yard, and the project's solidity is softened with landscaping.

York feels that the keys to the success of this project's design are (1) its brick construction, front and back, which gives the homes "a look of permanence," (2) the high density and absence of amenities, which is financially favorable for the developer but also keeps prices and HOA dues low for the buyers, and (3) the decision to include surface parking rather than garages, which enabled the developer to price the homes within range of the target market of young professionals—who, in this part of the country, do not typically demand garage parking.

The developer maintained flexibility in the construction of each home. Buyers could choose among three floor plans and seven elevations.

The 48 townhouse units of 150 St. Mary's are organized around interior courtyards, where residents can park in front of their homes.

Foundations and elevations were designed to accommodate either of two first-floor plans. Construction could proceed to a certain point, at which time the buyer could decide on a floor plan; the home would then be completed for that choice.

The interiors of the two-story 1,100-square-foot townhouses include open floor plans with two bedrooms, generous expanses of windows, kitchens with eating spaces and pantries, and a selection of standard and optional finishes. "We spent our money on the outside," explains Dockery. "All the luxury finishes on the inside, such as fireplaces and hardwood floors, were optional." This approach made the base prices of the homes more affordable and enabled buyers to spend their money on the items that were most important to them.

The developer encountered no problems financing the project. Dockery and York provided the project equity, and Centura Bank provided conventional construction financing. Because this was a townhouse development, the financial risk was manageable: the project was relatively simple to construct, and the construction schedule could easily be interrupted and restarted if necessary. "Townhouse construction is easily staged to match sales, funding, and construction scheduling to minimize financial exposure and maximize flexibility in sales and marketing," explains Dockery. "We had sufficient presales before starting each building of townhouses."

The project was built all at one time. Marketing was primarily through on-site signage, word of mouth, and meetings with brokers active in the area. The marketing strategy was to sell the location and the maintenance, cost, and security advantages of a townhouse product—a type of home that is not generally available in this area. Homes were presold (on a refundable deposit basis) from plans before construction started. The first building closed in December of 1998 and the last unit closed in the spring of 1999. Thirty-seven of the 48 buyers were single, and most were between 28 and 35 years of age. "Younger buyers," observes Dockery, "tend to be less demanding."

The development is managed by an HOA, and dues are $70 per month. The all-brick con-

Variations in stairways, rooflines, brick color, and setbacks create visual interest. Note the all-brick stairways and sidewalks.

struction and absence of common amenities to maintain make the low monthly fee possible.

According to Dockery, the most exciting thing about the project has been its financial success. The units sold quickly, and resales have demonstrated strong appreciation. At the time the first group was sold in 1999, the average home price was around $150,000; for those on the market today, the asking price is in the $195,000 range. Looking back, Dockery believes that York would have made more money if it had sold the homes more slowly and raised prices to higher levels, "though there's something to be said for getting them sold."

York expects to develop additional properties in the surrounding area. St. Mary's Associates, LLC, owns a building across the street from 150 St. Mary's that it is currently redeveloping into five for-sale units. Two other properties within a block of the project site are planned. One has been purchased and is under construction, and the other is under contract, with closing pending resolution of environmental issues. By developing several projects in the same area, York intends to build on the earlier projects' success and, at the same time, have a lasting positive impact on the community.

Note

1. Joel Lane owned the property, which is known as the place where the decision was made, in 1792, to establish Raleigh as the capital of North Carolina.

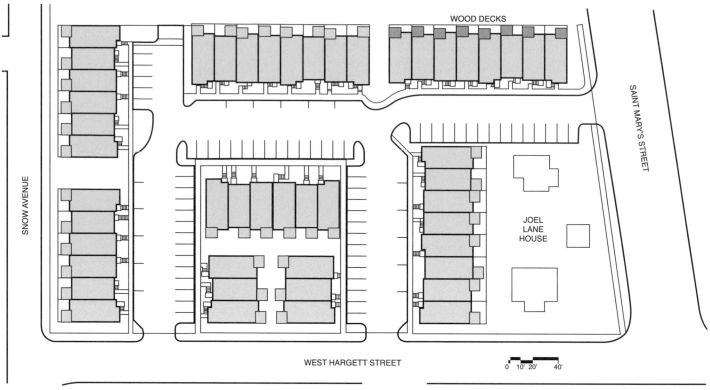

WOOD DECKS

SAINT MARYS STREET

SNOW AVENUE

JOEL
LANE
HOUSE

WEST HARGETT STREET

0 10' 20'   40'

Site plan.

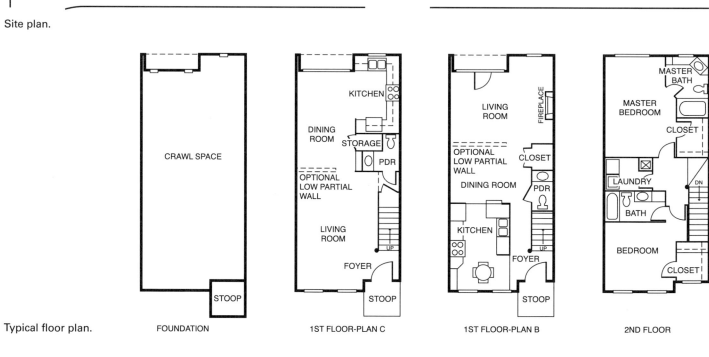

CRAWL SPACE

STOOP

FOUNDATION

KITCHEN

DINING
ROOM

STORAGE
PDR

OPTIONAL
LOW PARTIAL
WALL

LIVING
ROOM

UP

FOYER

STOOP

1ST FLOOR-PLAN C

LIVING
ROOM

FIREPLACE

OPTIONAL
LOW PARTIAL
WALL

CLOSET

DINING ROOM

PDR

KITCHEN

UP

FOYER

STOOP

1ST FLOOR-PLAN B

MASTER
BATH

MASTER
BEDROOM

CLOSET

LAUNDRY
DN

BATH

BEDROOM

CLOSET

2ND FLOOR

Typical floor plan.

Project Data: 150 St. Mary's

Land Use Information

Site area	2.1 acres
Total dwelling units	48
Gross density	23 units per acre
Total parking spaces (outdoor)	82

Residential Unit Information

Unit Type	Total Number	Square Feet	Initial Sales Prices
A	5	1,170	$130,000–$138,000
B	25	1,400	$140,000–$155,000
C	18	1,400	$138,000–$155,000

Development Cost Information

Site acquisition	$420,000
Site development	600,000
Construction	4,000,000
Soft costs	170,000
Interest	100,000
Sales commissions	360,000
Development fees	170,000
Total project cost	$5,820,000

Revenues

Total project revenues	$7,200,000

Development Schedule

Site purchased	May 1998
Planning began	October 1997
Site work began	May 1998
Construction started	August 1998
Sales started	May 1998
Sales completed	April 1999
Project completion	May 1999

Project Award

150 St. Mary's received the Sir Walter Raleigh Award for Community Appearance from the City of Raleigh.

Development Team

Developer
St. Mary's Associates, LLC
1900 Cameron Street
Raleigh, North Carolina 27605
919-821-1350

Land Planner
York Ventures
1900 Cameron Street
Raleigh, North Carolina 27605
919-821-1350

Architect
J. Davis Architects
414 West Jones Street
Raleigh, North Carolina 27603
919-833-6413

Civil Engineer
John Edwards
333 Wade Avenue
Raleigh, North Carolina 27605
919-828-4428

Contractor
McDonald-York
801 Oberlin Road
Raleigh, North Carolina 27605
919-832-3770

Project Address

150 St. Mary's Street
Raleigh, North Carolina 27601

General Information

Settle Dockery, projects director, York Ventures
919-821-1350

All information in this case study is current as of January 25, 2001.

Post Uptown Square
Denver, Colorado

© 2000, Steve Hinds

© 2000, Steve Hinds

Brickwork, color, elevation details, and dramatic corner treatments create visual interest and variety, which are particularly important in a large urban residential project.

Combining adaptive use and new construction, Post Uptown Square has created demand for market-rate rental housing and stimulated other new investment in the previously transitional Uptown neighborhood just four blocks from the center of downtown Denver, Colorado. The 974-unit development, located on a site formerly occupied by St. Luke's Hospital, also includes retail uses on the first floor, structured parking, a health club, gathering spaces, a full calendar of social activities, and other amenities.[1]

Post Properties, Inc., headquartered in Atlanta, Georgia, is one of the country's largest developers and managers of multifamily apartments, with developments in Atlanta, Georgia;

Austin, Dallas, and Houston, Texas; Charlotte, North Carolina; Denver, Colorado; Nashville, Tennessee; Phoenix, Arizona; Orlando and Tampa, Florida; and the Washington, D.C., area. Overall, the company owns more than 35,000 apartment homes in over 100 communities; an additional 5,000 units are under development. Since its founding in 1971, Post's primary focus was on resort-style suburban apartments, but during the past decade it has concentrated on creating high-density, mixed-use, urban infill communities. Its 1997 merger with Columbus Realty Trust, a successful mixed-use residential developer based in Dallas, created the Post Properties Western Region operations and reinforced Post's commitment to intown housing. Post Uptown Square is being developed out of the company's Dallas office.

Located at the foot of the Rocky Mountains, Denver is one of the nation's fastest-growing cities. The location, the climate, and the technology-oriented economic base draw well-educated young people to the city. Downtown Denver boasts attractions such as the state capitol; the U.S. Mint; the Larimer Square historic district, with its selection of fine restaurants; and Coors Field baseball stadium. Other attractions include the Paramount Theater, the Denver Museum of Nature and Science, the Denver Performing Arts Complex, the Colorado Convention Center, the Denver Art Museum, the Museum of Contemporary Art, and shopping and dining on the Sixteenth Street Mall and at the Denver Pavilions.

The city has proactively encouraged downtown infill housing development in a number of ways: creating a downtown housing office to give developers information on available properties and market conditions; changing the zoning ordinance to encourage housing development and protect historic buildings; establishing design standards for infill housing; and providing financial assistance to housing developments deemed desirable; such assistance has involved allocations of private-activity bonds and the creation of a multimillion-dollar revolving loan fund for housing.

Though Denver has a vibrant downtown housing market, until Post Uptown Square was built, most new, market-rate housing was built in the LoDo and Golden Triangle areas of the city. The Uptown neighborhood, located just east of downtown, is characterized by a mix of land uses, but is predominately residential. Post Uptown Square is located at the corner of 19th Avenue and Pennsylvania Street, close to the shopping, dining, and entertainment establishments along 17th Avenue. The area

surrounding the site includes some fine older homes; many small, single-family homes owned by people of moderate means; some high-rise rental apartment buildings; and some retail uses, including a neighborhood strip shopping center. A Section 8 (HUD-subsidized) development (which will soon be redeveloped) is just across the street. Located between downtown and the city's medical district, the site is convenient to two major employment centers, and light-rail transportation is within walking distance.

Post chose this site because it wanted to build enough units to enhance the neighborhood and thereby transform the market—and here, it had the opportunity to obtain 10.5 acres from a single owner. In addition, Post wanted to create a mixed-use project. (According to Cindy Harris, vice president–development with Post Properties in Dallas, it takes a population of approximately 1,000 to 1,500 to justify ground-floor retail uses.)

At the time of purchase, the site was the abandoned campus of St. Luke's Hospital, and the vacant buildings had become a neighborhood eyesore. According to Jennifer Moulton, director of community planning and development for the city and county of Denver, the site's owner, Columbia Health One, offered the property to the city for free after trying to sell it for some time without success. The mayor's office declined the offer but agreed to help market the property for redevelopment. The Denver Urban Renewal Authority (DURA) began the process of obtaining neighborhood input in preparation for soliciting development proposals. At the same time, Columbus Realty Trust (now Post Properties) contacted DURA in search of a development site in the area. Because its development approach and the community's vision were similar, DURA made the match. "We were lucky," Moulton explains. "The right developer showed up."

Because the site is within a designated urban renewal area, DURA was willing to invest public money if the development met the goal of providing market-rate housing. Post and DURA worked together to create a mixed-use land plan. DURA contributed $8 million in public infrastructure improvements, including new water and sewer lines for the development (though Post paid the fees to access them), and streetscape improvements (such as trees, brick sidewalks, pedestrian lights, and benches). DURA also funded some of the upfront planning and design costs. To facilitate the development, the city created a new zoning designation, "RX-4," for urban, mixed-use zoning.

Post made presentations to about 20 neighborhood groups in the Uptown area during the schematic drawing stage. The groups advised Post on architectural style, density, streetscapes, parking, and other issues. As a result of the community's input, Post decided to renovate rather than demolish the landmark hospital administration building, a 1941 art-deco structure. In addition, the community spurred the developer to include more brickwork in the buildings. "People want—and will pay for—something authentic," Harris notes, and both of these changes "added value to the development."

A number of environmental problems arose during site development, including the discovery of toxic wastes and leaking underground oil tanks on site, and lead-based paint and asbestos in the hospital building. It was also necessary to demolish nine of the ten hospital buildings. As part of the sales agreement, the hospital covered the costs of environmental cleanup and building demolition.

Post Uptown Square is being developed in phases. Phase I, with a total of 449 units, consists of the transformation of the six-story St. Luke's Hospital administration building into 70 loft apartments; the construction of three new buildings of standard apartment units on three separate blocks; and the construction of 25,000 square feet of ground-floor retail space. Phase I also includes courtyards; a ground-floor, 3,300-square-foot fitness center that residents may use at no additional fee; and a rooftop garden and terrace with a fireplace and outdoor shower atop the renovated hospital building. The new residential buildings are four-story, wood-frame construction, and the residential units are directly above the retail space at the street's edge, creating an urban facade. The residential/retail buildings surround an interior parking structure, and courtyards where residents can socialize.

Phase I was completed in May 2001. Preleasing began in September 1999; as of March 2002, the property was 82 percent leased. Market response has been tremendous, and rents have been higher than anticipated. (Post expected to get $1.15 per square foot; the project has actually yielded $1.44.) No retail uses are yet in place. As Harris observes, "Retailers

The gritty industrial style of the project's loft apartments, in the old hospital building, appeals to the young, hip, target market.

like to know that people are here before committing to a specific location."

Phase II will consist of 247 apartments in two new, four-story buildings; an outdoor swimming pool; and 10,000 square feet of incubator office space, which the developer envisions being divided into spaces of 600 to 900 square feet for use by tenants such as music teachers, artists, and mortgage bankers. Land is available for a third phase, which would accommodate 200 to 250 units. In addition, the development will include some 30 to 40 furnished "corporate" apartments for short-term lease that will provide maid service, concierge service, telephone, and utilities. Post sold a portion of the site to another developer for the construction of 42 loft-style flats and two-story condominium units. Post estimates that the entire development will be completed in three to four years.

Each building in the Uptown Square development will include a private interior courtyard with tables and chairs; gas grills; a water feature, such as a fountain; landscaping; and an outdoor fire feature, typically a fireplace. Many courtyards will feature public art created by local artists. Common amenities, such as the fitness center, party rooms, and laundry rooms, are located adjacent to the courtyards or facing a public street.

Post has found that, in general, a four-story building height works well in a neighborhood setting because it creates enough density for street life and retail use and is compatible with the existing street width. To reflect and sustain the urban fabric, the company creates variety in the building elevations by, for example, including brickwork; lots of windows; and details such as pop-outs, pilasters, and changes in materials and in the color of the brick. Harris explains, "We design and build for the pedestrian." To that end, the buildings are visually porous: first-floor windows to retail space add interest, and passersby can glimpse the courtyards through wrought-iron entry gates.

The use of similar building materials ties together the various phases of development. "We want them to look like they fit together, but we don't want them to look alike," explains Harris. Post uses different architects for different phases, so that while all the buildings fit the neighborhood context and have the same setbacks and streetscape rhythm, each has its own character.

Phase I includes one- and two-bedroom loft-style apartments in the renovated hospital building, townhouse-style apartment homes, and flats. The apartment units are organized along double-loaded corridors that give each residence a view of either the courtyard or the street. In keeping with the idea of reconfigured industrial space, the loft apartments have stainless-steel entry doors, cement floors, unfinished walls, exposed pipes and ductwork, and open floor plans. The standard apartments feature large windows; French doors; and high-quality carpeting, tile, and appliances. Most units include washer-dryer hookups and high-tech wiring that can provide high-speed Internet access and accommodate multiple telephone or modem lines. Says Harris: "Our developments are unique in the sense that the exterior environment is treated with the same attention to detail as the interior living space."

The development also includes units with more traditional finishes.

Streetscape improvements provided by the Denver Urban Renewal Authority, such as brick sidewalks, benches, and street trees, underscore the quality of the development and help integrate it into the urban fabric.

Security is provided at the building face rather than through perimeter fencing. To be admitted to a building, visitors must ring a bell; residents have electronic "key fobs," and individual units have a lock and a deadbolt. Public parking for the retail patrons is on the ground floor; access to the residents' parking floors on the upper levels is through a gate.

In accordance with the local zoning ordinance, there is one parking space for each dwelling unit. Parking is provided both on surrounding streets (for guests and retail patrons) and in structured parking decks within the residential block. The mandatory $50 fee for structured parking is included in the monthly rent. Each floor of the parking structure is connected to the residential buildings by walkways, making

it easy for residents to reach their cars or bring in their packages.

Because Post is a public real estate investment trust, it raises capital on a revolving line of credit and uses its credit line to finance all its projects. This financing method gives the company an advantage over small development firms, which often must sign personal guarantees to finance their developments. In addition, Post Uptown Square received financial assistance from city tax increment financing funds, CDBG funds, and HUD Section 108 loan guarantee funds, which were used for infrastructure construction.

Post Uptown Square is located in a city maintenance district that imposes a separate fee on property owners to maintain the streets and streetscapes; the fee is prorated according to the number of linear feet of street frontage in the property.

Compared with suburban products, the leasing and management of Post Uptown Square require more sophistication. Many different unit types are offered (65 in Phase I alone), and the leasing team needs to know them all. Post Uptown Square includes 24-hour, on-site emergency maintenance, and a full program of social events as well as physical amenities. The maintenance staff must deal with controlled access, community spaces, and the complicated fire systems needed to meet city building codes. Because of its urban location, management of the development involves dealing with noise and traffic issues, and creating relationships with city staff as well as with retail tenants and neighbors. As a result, Harris reports, "We staff differently. There is a higher ratio of people to units—1:70, compared to 1:120 for a suburban project—and we look for people who are more skilled in business management."

The legal issues involved in developing a project such as Post Uptown Square are far more complex—and therefore more expensive—than those that arise with suburban projects. Negotiating a public/private partnership is difficult and time-consuming; buying and developing a site with environmental problems, easements, and abandoned alleys is far more complicated; and developing a project that includes retail uses can be tricky. Working through these and other problems results in large and ongoing legal costs.

The most challenging aspect of the development, according to Harris, was that Post came to the Denver market assuming that the development environment would be similar to that in Texas—when in fact it was not. "In particular, the residential building codes here are more like those for a commercial structure, especially regarding structural designs, electrical wiring, and firewall issues." The company had difficulty finding local subcontractors, who found the unfamiliar four-story, wood-frame construction process complicated and had trouble predicting their costs. And Denver's inspection process proved time-consuming. Harris advises developers to work with local people who know how the market, the city, and local subcontractors operate, "or else pay a big idiot tax."

In addition, if it were beginning the project today, Post would design the retail space to be more user-friendly. In particular, it would create larger windows, provide more head-in parking, and build in enough ventilation for restaurant tenants.

Post Uptown Square offers a new and different housing choice in the Uptown area, and Post's investment in the development has proved large enough to make a real difference. According to Harris, "The company has invested $55 million so far and by the project's completion will have invested more than $100 million." Before this development, the Uptown area of Denver was considered blighted and had been in decline. But, as Harris notes, "The first phase alone has spawned an additional $200 million in investment in the area." In addition, residents of nearby existing neighborhoods have begun to reinvest in their homes.

Post finds that developing Post Uptown Square has made it the victim of its own suc-

© 2000, Steve Hinds

cess. "Buy as much land as you can afford while prices are low," Harris advises. "We would like to develop more property in the Uptown area, but land prices have risen so high, we can't afford to build here anymore."

The rooftop garden offers magnificent views of the city and the surrounding mountains.

Note

1. Estimated number of units at buildout.

Site plan.

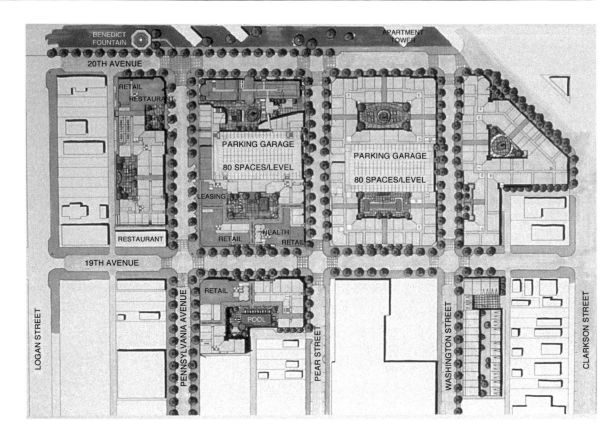

Floor plans.

Phase 1
1 Bedroom/1 Bath
666 square feet*

Phase 1
1 Bedroom Loft/2 Bath
1302 square feet*

Phase 1
Efficiency/1 Bath
517 square feet*

Phase 1
2 Bedroom with Den/2 Bath
1083 square feet*

Phase 1
1 Bedroom with Mezzanine/1 Bath
1013 square feet*

Project Data: Post Uptown Square[a]

Land Use Information

Site area	10.5 acres
Open space	1 acre
Total projected dwelling units, including condominiums	974
Gross residential density	90 units per acre
Total retail and commercial space	37,000 square feet
Total parking spaces	1,233

Land Use Plan

Use	Acres
Buildings	7.0
Parking areas	1.2
Roads/driveways	1.3
Amenities	1.0

Residential Unit Information, Phase I

Unit Type	Total Number	Square Feet	Monthly Rents
E	85	658	$983
E/M	39	799	$1,120
A	117	843	$1,200
A/D	2	947	$1,268
A/TH	23	941	$1,270
A/M	30	1,025	$1,488
B	49	1,153	$1,503
B/M	19	1,282	$1,835
C	2	2,026	$2,760
C/M	1	2,244	$3,200
L	75	850	$1,373
L/M	2	1,673	$2,633

Development Schedule

Site purchased	April 1997
Planning began	January 1997
Site work began	December 1997
Project completion	
Phase I	May 2001
Phase II	April 2002

Development Team

Developer
Post Properties, Inc.
5040 Addison Circle, Suite 300
Addison, Texas 75001
972-851-3200

Land Planner/Architect
RTKL
1717 Pacific Avenue, Suite 100
Dallas, Texas 75201
214-871-8877

Civil Engineer/Landscape Architect
Huitt Zellers
3131 McKinney Avenue, Suite 600
Dallas, Texas 75204
214-871-3311

Project Address

1938 Pennsylvania Street
Denver, Colorado 80203

General Information

Cindy Harris, vice president–development, Post Properties
972-851-3218

All information in this case study is current as of May 2001.

Note

a. Development cost information not available.

Appendices

Appendix A
Issues and Challenges Associated with Market-Rate Urban Infill Housing Development

The issues and challenges associated with infill development will differ with the circumstances of the specific project—for example, the metropolitan area in which the development is located, the characteristics of the particular location and governing jurisdiction, the nature of the local housing market, and the characteristics of the development itself. Thus, not all the challenges listed in this appendix will apply to every project.

Site Readiness and Assembly

- As it is for any real estate development, location is a key issue for infill projects. In some cities, land that is located in areas that have potential market value may not be available at prices that are low enough to make a project economically feasible.
- Project economics or marketing strategy may require that a site be assembled from two or more (perhaps several more) parcels. Working with several different owners to assemble land can increase the risk, costs, time requirements, and complexity of a project. In particular, complicated land assemblies can increase the possibility of speculation and hold-outs.

- Especially for infill projects involving the reuse of a previously developed site, land development and site preparation may cost more than they would in undeveloped locations.
- Development sites formerly used for other purposes may be subject to an array of issues, including contamination, unstable soil conditions, the presence of old foundations or building debris, and the need to protect historic or archaeological resources.
- Title and ownership issues, such as unclear titles, tax liens, and multiple or absentee owners who are difficult to locate, can present problems in acquiring infill sites.
- The physical characteristics of the site, such as topography, shape, slopes, and drainage, may make development of infill sites difficult, especially when the sites are small or in physically constrained locations.

Infrastructure and Amenities

- Infill sites are typically developed within an existing street system, which may or may not adequately serve the intended project. Street and lot patterns in urban areas may be obsolete and unable to accommodate the proposed project design.

- Neighborhood streets, intersections, and streetscapes may need repair, improvement, or both.
- Developers may need to alter the street patterns within a large site to accommodate the project.
- Project design may need to take into account the location of nearby uses such as transit stations and freeways, both to provide access and to protect residents from noise, vibration, and unattractive views.
- Especially in the case of high-density developments, parking requirements may be difficult to meet at reasonable cost.
- Utilities are typically available to urban infill sites but may be inadequate or out of date. Developers must ensure sufficient sewer and water capacity, modern utilities, and good site drainage.
- The responsibility for funding for project-related infrastructure may be unclear or the subject of public/private negotiation.
- If open space or public parks are not available nearby, the developer may need to provide such spaces within the project.

Market and Marketing Issues

- Market evaluation and analysis for infill housing may be difficult, especially in locations where no new residential development has occurred in recent years and where there are no comparables against which to evaluate recent market performance.
- Because infill projects are often unique responses to specific development opportunities, it can be difficult to identify the target market for a proposed development.
- "Pioneering" infill developments designed to create new markets for residential development or to serve as catalysts for the revitalization of a deteriorated or transitional area involve greater risks than projects for which demand has been demonstrated.
- Because development costs are often higher in infill locations than in suburban green-

fields, it can be challenging to produce housing at affordable prices.

- Creating a design concept that appeals to the target market may be more difficult in infill locations because developers are working within an established historical and architectural context and often at high densities. Specific design issues that may be more challenging in built-up areas include scale, texture, identity, light, noise, views, landscaping, lighting, security, and parking.
- Infill projects are developed within an existing neighborhood context that will affect a project's marketability. Key considerations include the physical, economic, and social conditions of the surrounding neighborhood; the nature and condition of nearby land uses; the presence of "problem properties"; the adequacy of neighborhood-serving shops and services; the location of parks and other community amenities; the quality of public services; the location and quality of local schools; real and perceived safety and security; and the neighborhood's historical reputation or image.
- A developer who is considering phasing project development will need to evaluate the tradeoffs between (1) creating a critical mass to engender consumer confidence and (2) undertaking the higher risks involved in bringing a large number of housing units to market at one time.

Community Acceptance

- As with any development, community acceptance will be essential to navigating the development process, but neighboring residents are likely to be suspicious of any change in their surroundings. This is especially true in the case of infill projects, because the sites are physically close to their neighbors.
- Existing communities in urban areas may consist of longtime residents who are well-organized and politically entrenched.
- In some cases, existing residents may fear gentrification and displacement.

- Neighboring residents may object to specific aspects of an infill development, including density and scale; and the quality, compatibility, and overall image of the project design.
- Current residents may fear that additional development within their community will result in overcrowding, traffic congestion, or excessive street parking.
- Members of the community may desire to retain existing vacant properties as green space rather than see them developed for any use.
- Attitudes toward a proposed infill project will be influenced by the neighborhood's development history and experience. If residents have had bad experiences in the past, they may not trust developers or the government to protect their interests.
- Residents may be concerned about the preservation of historic buildings or other historic resources.
- The possibility of disruption during construction may be an issue. Specifically, community residents may be concerned about trash removal, sanitation, noise, dust, street repair, construction traffic and parking, and conservation of trees.

Legal and Regulatory Issues

- In general, government regulation of urban infill development tends to be more extensive and costly than the regulation that applies to newly developing areas.
- Rezoning is often required. Urban infill parcels may be zoned for uses that are no longer economically feasible, or for nonresidential uses that the new development is designed to replace.
- City codes and standards are often more restrictive and inflexible than those in suburban areas. Moreover, building codes designed for new construction may be unrealistic for rehabilitation or adaptive use projects.
- A large number of environmental laws have the potential to affect urban infill development. In particular, the federal Comprehensive Environmental Response, Compensation, and Liability Act, which requires cleanup of contaminated sites, can determine the redevelopment potential of vacant city land.
- The reuse of older buildings may require the remediation or removal of asbestos or lead-based paint.
- The development approval (entitlement) process in urban areas is often complex and characterized by a lack of coordination among regulating agencies. The myriad requirements can take a significant amount of time, impose additional costs, and constrain innovation—and the outcome is not always predictable.
- Rehabilitation projects involving historic preservation or developments located within historic districts must comply with the standards for rehabilitation set by the U.S. secretary of the interior. Compliance requires additional reviews, which translate into a requirement for more time, expertise, and money.
- The reuse of an urban infill parcel may require the demolition of existing structures, which triggers additional regulations.
- All development is subject to local laws governing labor practices, but in urban areas labor laws tend to be more numerous and to include worthwhile but potentially costly socially motivated requirements, such as those governing hiring and bidding practices.
- Developments involving rental properties with existing residents will be subject to laws governing tenants' rights.
- The local tax structure may discourage the redevelopment of infill parcels.

Other Public Sector Issues

- The nature and extent of the challenges involved in infill development are determined in large part by the presence or absence of political leadership, political will, vision, and a supportive policy context, all of which vary from city to city (and within the same city over time).

- Many cities lack the resources to facilitate infill development. For example, some do not have or make available current data on land use patterns, property ownership, zoning activity, and so forth. Others lack the financial incentives, programs, resources, or imagination to create effective partnerships or incentives for desirable infill developments. Some city staff do not have the experience or expertise that would be needed to properly evaluate or assist projects.
- Public investment in infrastructure, economic development, or both is often required to make an older urban area attractive to potential residents.
- From a local government's perspective, encouraging an urban infill development may require political as well as financial costs and risks.
- In some urban areas, where the relationship between the public sector and the private development community has historically been uneasy, trust may be an issue.

Financing

- Because the costs associated with urban infill developments tend to be higher than for comparable projects in undeveloped areas, financing requirements may also be greater.
- Project costs may make it difficult to produce affordable housing in infill locations. The cost of developing an infill parcel may, in fact, exceed the market value of the completed project. When this is true for a proposed project with societal value, the developer may need to seek gap financing from public and/or socially motivated private entities.
- Urban infill developments can be financially riskier than other types of development, especially when they involve pioneering markets or product types.
- Though financial returns can be generous, more time is typically required to achieve those returns.
- Accurate appraisals can be difficult where few comparable developments have been built or when a project represents a response to a unique development opportunity—situations that are fairly common for urban infill developments.
- Because they are often unique, urban infill developments may need financing partners who are flexible and willing to innovate.
- The private financial sector may lack familiarity and experience with urban infill projects and the issues involved in their development.
- Many infill developments, especially those designed for residents with a mix of incomes, involve the coordination of multiple funding sources, each of which will typically have its own timetable, restrictions, and requirements.
- Often, and especially in deteriorated or transitional areas, the development of urban infill housing will require a public/private partnership, which can raise a number of location- and project-specific issues regarding responsibilities, risks, and coordination.

Appendix B
People Who Were Interviewed for or Quoted in This Book

Thomas Aidala, former principal architect and urban designer, San Jose Redevelopment Agency, San Jose, California.

Kevin Augustyn, vice president, MCL Companies, Inc., Chicago, Illinois.

Hank Baker, vice president for marketing, Forest City Stapleton, Inc., Denver, Colorado.

Harold Barnette, president, Heak Associates, Inc., Atlanta, Georgia.

Joseph Barry, president, Applied Development Company, Hoboken, New Jersey.

Matthew Birnbaum, vice president for development, AvalonBay Communities, Inc., Alexandria, Virginia.

Natalie Bock, development manager, the Alexander Company, Madison, Wisconsin.

Arn Bortz, partner, Towne Properties, Cincinnati, Ohio.

Jack Buxell, chief executive officer, J. Buxell Architecture, Ltd., Minneapolis, Minnesota.

Donald Carter, managing principal, Urban Design Associates, Pittsburgh, Pennsylvania.

Thomas Carter, general partner, Carter Reese & Associates, San Diego, California.

David Chase, principal, Thrush Development, Chicago, Illinois.

Norman Coleman, Mayor, St. Paul, Minnesota.

Douglas Crocker, president and chief executive officer, Equity Residential Properties Trust, Chicago, Illinois.

Tracy Cross, Tracy Cross & Associates, Inc., Schaumburg, Illinois.

Michael Curzan, chief executive officer, UniDev LLC, Bethesda, Maryland.

Bruce Dammann, architect, San Diego, California.

Settle Dockery, vice president, York Properties, Inc., Raleigh, North Carolina.

Hattie Dorsey, president and chief executive officer, Atlanta Neighborhood Development Partnership, Atlanta, Georgia.

LeRoy (Terry) Eakin III, chairman, Eakin/Youngentob Associates, Inc., Arlington, Virginia.

Steven Fader, principal, Steven Fader Architect, Los Angeles, California.

William Frey, demographer and research scientist, Population Studies Center, University of Michigan, Ann Arbor, Michigan.

Rochelle Grubb, chairman, Grubb Properties, Charlotte, North Carolina.

Mossik Hacobian, executive director, Urban Edge Housing Corporation, Boston, Massachusetts.

Cynthia Harris, vice president–development, Post Properties, Inc., Dallas, Texas.

Robert Harris, executive partner, Holland & Knight, LLP, Bethesda, Maryland.

Monty Hoffman, president, P. N. Hoffman Construction Development, Bethesda, Maryland.

Lawrence O. Houstoun Jr., principal, the Atlantic Group, Cranbury, New Jersey.

William H. Hudnut III, senior resident fellow for public policy and ULI/Joseph C. Canizaro Chair for Public Policy, ULI, Washington, D.C.

Daniel Hunt, partner, HuntGregory, Minneapolis, Minnesota.

Reese Jarrett, general partner, Carter Reese & Associates, San Diego, California.

William A. Johnson, mayor, Rochester, New York.

Marty Jones, president, Corcoran Jennison Companies, Dorchester, Massachusetts.

Michael Jones, executive director, Greater St. Louis Regional Empowerment Zones, St. Louis, Missouri.

Pres Kabacoff, president, Historic Preservation, Inc., New Orleans, Louisiana.

James Kane, development manager, Charles E. Smith Companies, Arlington, Virginia.

Frederick Kober, president, the Christopher Companies, McLean, Virginia.

Robert Koch, president, Fugleberg Koch Architects, Winter Park, Florida.

William Kreager, managing partner, Mithun Partners, Seattle, Washington.

Michael Lander, president, the Lander Group, Minneapolis, Minnesota.

John Leith-Tetrault, director, Community Partners of the National Trust for Historic Preservation, Washington, D.C.

Dorothy Lengyel, executive director, HomeSight, Seattle, Washington.

Bruce Levin, senior vice president, CIG International LLC, Washington, D.C.

David Listokin, professor, Center for Urban Policy Research, Rutgers University, New Brunswick, New Jersey.

Gregg T. Logan, managing director, Robert Charles Lesser & Company, Atlanta, Georgia.

Michael A. Loia, president and chief executive officer, Loia Budde & Associates, Atlanta, Georgia.

Arthur E. Lomenick, president, Workplace Urban Solutions, Dallas, Texas.

William Lucy, professor of urban and regional planning, School of Architecture, University of Virginia, Charlottesville, Virginia.

David Mayhood, president, the Mayhood Company, McLean, Virginia.

Maureen McAvey, senior resident fellow for urban development, ULI, Washington, D.C.

Dan McLean, president, MCL Companies, Chicago, Illinois.

Richard Michaux, chairman, AvalonBay Communities, Inc., Alexandria, Virginia.

Anne Vernez Moudon, professor of architecture, landscape architecture, urban design, and planning, College of Architecture and Urban Planning, University of Washington, Seattle, Washington.

Jennifer Moulton, director of community planning and development, city and county of Denver, Denver, Colorado.

Al Neely, group senior vice president, Charles E. Smith Residential Realty, Inc., Arlington, Virginia.

John O. Norquist, mayor, Milwaukee, Wisconsin.

Douglas Porter, president, Growth Management Institute, Chevy Chase, Maryland.

Lee Quill, principal, Cunningham + Quill Architects, Washington, D.C.

Laura Cole Reblitz, development consultant, McLean, Virginia.

Bruce Ross, principal emeritus, Backen Arrigoni & Ross, Inc., San Francisco, California.

Craig Ross, president, Hyde Park Builders, Inc., Tampa, Florida.

Jason Runnels, executive vice president and principal, Phoenix Property Company, Dallas, Texas.

Jeffrey Sanford, president, Memphis Center City Commission, Memphis, Tennessee.

Adrienne Schmitz, director of residential community development, ULI, Washington, D.C.

Karen Schwab, sales manager, MCL Companies, Chicago, Illinois.

Scott Shimberg, executive vice president and co-owner, Hyde Park Builders, Tampa, Florida.

Robert Silverman, chairman and chief executive officer, the Winter Group of Companies, Atlanta, Georgia.

Margaret Sowell, president, Real Estate Strategies, Inc., Wayne, Pennsylvania.

Debra Stein, president, GCA Group, San Francisco, California.

Edwin A. Stromberg, program manager, U.S. Department of Housing and Urban Development, Washington, D.C.

Ron Terwilliger, national managing partner, Trammell Crow Residential, Atlanta, Georgia.

Henry Turley, president, the Henry Turley Company, Memphis, Tennessee.

Alexander von Hoffman, research fellow, Harvard University, Cambridge, Massachusetts.

Smedes York, president, York Properties, Inc., Raleigh, North Carolina.

Robert Youngentob, president, Eakin/Youngentob Associates, Inc., Arlington, Virginia.